# Glol Conscious Entrepreneurs

## 49 Entrepreneurs Changing The World

**Marie Diamond**

***Star From The Secret***

To Elisabeth
Planting the seed of the future Treescape
love and best wishes



www.MarieDiamond.com



Tom x

**Global Conscious Entrepreneurs**

Published in the USA

By Marie Diamond Publishing
www.MarieDiamond.com



www.MarieDiamond.com

ISBN: 979-8-9878335-3-7

SOCIAL MEDIA
Follow Me on Facebook: @MarieDiamondFans
Follow Me on Instagram: @Mariediamond8
Check Out My YouTube Channel: @MarieDiamondChannel

For Spanish-Speaking Students:
Go to www.MarieDiamondEspanol.com

# Table Of Contents


**Foreword** 1

**Chapters**

**1** Creating Success and Abundance by working in A Conscious Office by Marie Diamond 4

**2** Publish Books That Transform The World & Create A Magnetic Brand by Lily Patrascu 11

**3** Free Yourself: Find Your Purpose. My Self Journey To Self Actualization by Haleh Aleman 18

**4** Finding my Soul's Calling by Elvira Balderas 24

**5** Living The Law by Pandora Bolt 30

**6** Becoming a World-Class Speaker by Harriet Bratt 35

**7** Reaching Rock Bottom To Find My Path by Tina Burke 41

**8** Build Your Self-Worth To Grow Your Net Worth by Lisa Cavender 46

**9** Rising to Your Soul Blueprint by Anaelle Coulon 52

**10** Who Do You Think You Are? by Nina Deissler 58

**11** The Power of Forgiveness: Free Yourself to Find Yourself by Channin Dionne 64

**12** Origin Of A Sound Therapist by SueZee Finley 69

**13** Lie Not?! by Myrna Flick 75

**14** The Sustainable Foodie by Nicole Frith 81

**15** I Am The Baseline by Liah O. Goldenberg 87

**16** Looking For The Light: Finding The Light Can Lead To True Healing by Sarah Preston Hesler 93

**17** Conversations With Teeth by Dr. Kathrin Huzelmann 99

| | | |
|---|---|---|
| **18** | Designs On Success: Just Get Up And Keep Going by Angela Jones | 105 |
| **19** | Nurture Your Mind & Find Your Path To Happiness And Contentment by Charmaine Lang | 111 |
| **20** | Life Is A Story Of Love And Appreciation by Altantulga (Tulga) Mandakh-Ayush | 117 |
| **21** | Believe And It Will Happen by Maria Matias | 122 |
| **22** | The Comeback Trail by Maximilian Messler | 127 |
| **23** | A Wounded Healer's Path To Wholeness by Jocelyn Michel | 133 |
| **24** | Heal Your Home with Feng Shui & Diamond Dowsing Techniques by Deborah Miller | 138 |
| **25** | A Letting Go Miracle by Anne Moore | 144 |
| **26** | Strategies To Build A Purposeful And Profitable Business starts With "Passion" by Wendy Nguyen | 149 |
| **27** | The Essence And Energy Of Food by Olelo pa'a Ogawa | 155 |
| **28** | Miracles Happen When You Follow Your Heart by Denisa Riha Palečková | 160 |
| **29** | Creating Results That Stick! by Tara Pilling | 166 |
| **30** | "Universe, Be Really, Really Good To Me!" by Shannon Powell | 172 |
| **31** | Lean Into The Whisper by Jessica Quimby | 177 |
| **32** | A Pathway To Inner Peace by Kathleen Rafter | 182 |
| **33** | A Path To Healing Chronic Diseases Using Food As Medicine by Kyung Rhee | 188 |
| **34** | Life Is Short, Might As Well Travel First Class! By Anne Rigaud-Walker | 194 |
| **35** | "Fake It Till You Make It" - The Art Of Possibility by Sandra Roth | 200 |
| **36** | Unbecome Everything The World Has Made You And Fully Embody The Miracle You Are by Katarina Runa | 206 |

**37** Menopause To Marathons By Theresa Russell 212

**38** Paying It Forward With "Speakers Are Leaders" by Harry Sardinas 217

**39** Lessons Learned: Reflection On The Experiences That Shaped Me by Yvonne Schimmel 224

**40** "Let This Life Be For Freedom" - Mooji by Snehal Shah 229

**41** A Feng Shui Awakening by Holly Andra Small 235

**42** Problems Usually Solve Themselves If You Don't Disturb Them by Rabea Katharina Stenger 240

**43** Charted by Christopher Stilson 245

**44** Treeconomy: Why Trees Are Important For Your Health, Your Wealth, And Your Well-being by Tom Thompson 250

**45** My Journey Of Becoming A Multi-Talented And Multi-Passionate Global Entrepreneur And Coach by Lu Wang 256

**46** How To Find Your Strength In Your Own Journey by Patricia Whyte 263

**47** A Transformation To Radiant Beauty by Michelle Williams 269

**48** The Law by Pearl Williams 275

**49** Visiting Hours In Heaven by Renata Maria Wirtz 280

**Conclusion** 284

**Dedication** 285

**About The Author** 286

**Recommended Products and Services** 287

## Foreword

In life, there are times when you're lucky enough to be given an opportunity that forever changes the trajectory of your path. For me, that opportunity came in 2005. I was asked to be a contributor, along with a range of globally-recognized authors and speakers, on a unique new project. That project was to become *The Secret*, a ground-breaking film and follow-up book that went on to become a worldwide chart-topper and change the lives of more than 500 million people across the globe.

The moment that film was released, I was catapulted onto a global platform! I went from an unknown speaker and author to a worldwide sought-after Conscious entrepreneur. With my name being linked to the other acclaimed authors featured, such as Jack Canfield, Dr. John Gray, and Bob Proctor, I was quickly realizing the immense effect of the power of association. It allowed a fresh, new audience to discover me and gain awareness of my work and Conscious journey. Without my being part of this incredible collaboration, who knows how long it would have taken me to build my business to its current level?

Just a few months ago, I felt a strong calling to pass on this opportunity to those at the start of their own Conscious journeys. It's my time to pay it forward to the young entrepreneurs who are just finding their way; who have had their awakening of who they are and what they want to bring to the world, but just need a little nudge to the next level.

I've always believed that entrepreneurs have, perhaps without even realizing it, unlocked the very secrets of the Universe. Anyone familiar with the Law of Attraction knows that the Universe can only grant you your desires if you yourself know what they are. It's not enough to want to be rich or successful, you have to be prepared to show the Universe the blueprint behind your dreams. With their mission statements, five-year plans, and countless hours spent deconstructing the *What, Where, How* and *Why* of their business proposals, it is the entrepreneur who stands tall and tells the Universe what exactly it is that they want and when they want it. On the surface, it may seem like just a business plan but it's also manifestation in its purest form.

There were times when it was believed that business and spirituality were not compatible with each other. It seemed as though business and entrepreneurship were more aligned with the "left brain" and a person's Conscious journey (with its associations in meditation, healing, and self-help) were more aligned with the "right brain". In the last 20 years however, many businesses are waking up to the simple idea of "Why not both?". Why shouldn't entrepreneurs be able to bring themselves and those around them to a new level of consciousness? Indeed, I have built my business empire on the premise that you can't have one without the other; you need to be able to manifest success and abundance, but you also need to search deeper in yourself for your soul's true purpose. Each time I reached a new level of consciousness in relation to my personal journey and how I can, with love and compassion, support those around me, I found that success and abundance flowed all the more easily towards me.

The stories that my co-authors share throughout this book are guaranteed to move you. Some are inspiring tales of overcoming obstacles for the sake of making their dream come true. Some are brimming with nuggets of wisdom; the kind that only comes with the perseverance of getting up and dusting yourself off each time you fall down. Some are challenging stories, shared from the heart, that are only now being shared with the world for the first time. Either way, I'm so very proud of all of my co-authors for their courage to uplift, inspire, and motivate us with their words. I can confidently say that reading through the pages of this beautiful book will teach you that your business, through personal transformation, can expand and grow to reach new levels of abundance.

It is my wish that you read all the chapters of this book, from start to end, as part of your journey to become a Global Conscious Entrepreneur. Then, keep it in your office close to you and dip into it anytime you need it. Whether you want a daily inspiration boost or an answer to a business dilemma, simply offer your intention to the Universe and open it up to a chapter at random. You'll find a solution quicker than you think! I hope that you share this book with your team and those around you to expand the impact that this book will have.

The knowledge and wisdom shared by the co-authors is just a taste of what they have to offer. Reach out to them on their website and social media platforms and honor them as the valuable resources they are. My thanks go out to each one of them for their vulnerability and insight. You can see all the authors speak during the Global Conscious Entrepreneur Summit where they will each be interviewed by me. Head to www.MarieDiamond.com to find out more. Similarly, if you wish to be part of an upcoming compilation book in the series, you'll be able to find the relevant information on the website.

My special thanks also go out to Lily Patrascu and her amazing team for going on this journey with me to create this book. Without her and her amazing support, marketing skills, and publishing knowledge, I would not have been able to make this dream come true!

With Love,
Dame Marie Diamond
www.MarieDiamond.com

Creator of the Global Conscious Entrepreneurs Series
Feng Shui and Energy Master
International Best-Selling Author
Global Transformational Speaker and Business Mentor

# Creating Success and Abundance by working In a Conscious Office

## By Marie Diamond

What first comes to mind when you hear the term "conscious office"? It might make you think of relaxing color palettes, soothing water features, and desks adorned with expensive crystals and golden money frogs. For me, I created a conscious office by using Feng Shui. "Isn't Feng Shui just interior decorating though? What does any of that have to do with being a successful entrepreneur?". Well, what if I told you that your environment has a direct, immensely significant effect on your success and abundance?

Feng Shui is an Ancient Chinese energy system all about maintaining a positive flow of energy, or "chi", in your home and workspace. By putting the right items in the right places and by activating your Personal Directions, you can manipulate this flow of energy in order to manifest your goals. Simply put, Feng Shui transforms your office into a three-dimensional vision board.

Speaking of manifestation, Feng Shui is the often overlooked last pillar of the Law of Attraction. I was referred to as "the secret behind *The Secret*" because I made people aware of just how important a part their environment plays in effective manifestation. In the Law of Attraction, there is the belief that each person's fortune is the sum of three different, but equally important, kinds of luck – Heaven Luck, Human Luck, and Earth Luck. Heaven Luck refers to the life circumstances you were born into – your family, culture, your physical abilities, and so on. These tend to be fixed conditions that can't easily be changed. Some view this as the path that God has chosen for you, or you may refer to it as your destiny or karma.

Human Luck refers to your attitude, behavior, and the choices you make every day that affect your life. Traditionally in the self-help industry, this is the part of the Law of Attraction that is spoken about the most. How often have you been told that by changing the way you look at things, you can completely transform your life and your business? Now, it goes without saying that a positive outlook is a must-have for the entrepreneur – it's what keeps you going each time you're faced with a challenge. If you're reading this book right now, I believe that you have already mastered these first two pillars of the Law of Attraction. You've had to develop the right mindset to work towards your goals, overcome obstacles, and develop an unshakable trust in yourself and your skillset. You've also figured out that manifestation requires action – you can't just sit and wait for the Universe to hand you your dream project. You have to be committed to take action, each and every day, to get that little bit closer to making your business vision a reality. All these things will take you far in your career, but what about that last step?

Earth Luck refers to the Feng Shui principle of changing your environment to improve the good "chi" in your workspace. If your workspace is filled with clutter, dust, and broken objects, do you think you'll be able to do your best work there? If your office is uninviting, how can you expect potential clients to want to visit you? By utilizing the principles of Feng Shui in your workspace, you'll improve your Earth Luck and find that your business attracts success quicker and more effortlessly than ever before.

The first task on your Feng Shui to-do list is something referred to as space-clearing. This involves sorting through your workspace to see what you need to keep and what items you don't want or need anymore. This is an important step for two reasons. The first is that it's easier to work in an organized environment. Mess can be a source of stress, so eliminating it is just one thing you can do to increase your business productivity. Secondly, Feng Shui teaches us that energy must be able to flow freely throughout a room. Unnecessary clutter disrupts this flow and can result in the energy becoming stale and lifeless. After all, chaos in your environment equals chaos in the mind.

Go through all your drawers, filing cabinets, and bookcases. Figure out what needs to be kept, what needs to be thrown away, and what needs to be organized into a proper filing system. Be critical – everything in your office should represent order, productiveness, and success.

Once you've finished, place the items that you've decided to keep back in their correct place. Neatly return items to cupboards, drawers, and cabinets in such a way that you would be able to easily locate something should you need to.

Next up on your Feng Shui to-do list is to make sure you're sitting in the Power Position. A concept used frequently in the business world, the Power Position is exactly what it sounds like – it's the way you position yourself so that you're the most powerful in the room. You want to tell the Universe that you look at yourself as the King or Queen of your workspace!

As a quick exercise, think carefully about any photo you've seen of someone powerful sitting in a room. Maybe it's the President of the United States sitting in the Oval Office or a CEO sitting in on a business meeting. Think about where in the room they're positioned, what kind of chair they're sitting on, and the location of everyone around them. What does this convey to us about their power and status?

The first rule of Power Position is to have your desk positioned so that you have the door in your line of vision. You don't have to be directly sat across from it, but you should be able to comfortably see it without having to twist your body or turn your head when you're sitting at your desk. If there's absolutely no way you can move your desk to face the door, try hanging a small mirror across the door instead. Then, position your desk so that you can see the mirror so that you'll still be able to see the people coming in and out of the room. In Feng Shui, this is important because you want to make sure you're in the path of the incoming flow of energy, and you want to make yourself easily accessible to any good fortune that comes knocking.

Secondly, position your desk so that there's a solid wall behind you and you don't have your back to the room. From a business viewpoint, how can you feel engaged if you're facing away from all the action and things are happening, quite literally, behind your back? Thirdly, you want to ensure there is at least 3-10 ft of space between you and the door. If you often have meetings in your office, make sure there's enough space to place a chair in front of your desk. Think about a typical office seating chart – the receptionist or secretary tends to be sitting closest to the door and the most important people (for example the CEOs or executive managers) are seated furthest away from the hustle and bustle of incoming visitors.

Lastly, make sure your chair is supportive enough for you. Pick one with a solid, high back with neck support and armrests. You want to feel like you're sitting on a throne! If you tend to have off-site meetings, in restaurants or coffee shops, you can still apply the rules of Power Position. Pick a seat that's facing towards the exit and don't be afraid to ask for a new chair if you find yourself sitting on one that's broken or wobbly.

The third item on your to-do list is to activate your Success Direction. Each person has a Personal Energy Number which is a number from one to nine and is based on your date of birth and the gender you were assigned with at birth. Each Energy Number has four Personal Directions where the energy in your office is the most powerful for you. There's a Personal Direction for attracting success, good health, good relationships, and personal growth. Simply head to the free Marie Diamond app and enter in your details. Search "Marie Diamond" at the App Store for iPhones and at the Google Play store for Androids. You'll also be able to use the Diamond Compass to locate each of your four Personal Directions in your workspace.

To activate your Success Direction in your office, the most important step is to make sure your desk is facing your Success Direction (or one of your other Personal Directions in case this isn't possible). To check this, sit behind your desk with the Diamond Compass in the direction you're facing. If this direction matches one of your four Personal Directions (whilst also still following the Power Position rules), amazing! If not, use the compass to work out which direction you should move your desk to.

If there's a trash can placed in your Success Direction, move it away to a different area (one that isn't one of your other Personal Directions). As you can imagine, having trash in your Success Direction doesn't send out the best message to the Universe. Perhaps you've been wondering why you're having such a hard time achieving your goals – it's because you're literally throwing your success away in the trash!

The key goal in activating your Success Direction is to create a space that reminds the Universe who you are and what it is you do. Display any diplomas or certificates you've earnt in gold frames to celebrate the success you've already had. Hang up a pinboard or place a small table in your Success Direction and display on it your company logo, company flyers, and photos of the products your business deals with (this can be anything from the handmade items you sell on your online store to the cover artwork of the books you write). It may seem obvious, but you'd be surprised at how many entrepreneurs lack a basic sense of product knowledge. If you find that there are some items that aren't selling well, or if you're looking to launch a new product, make sure they're displayed so that the Universe doesn't forget about them.

To activate your Relationship Direction, hang up a similar pinboard or place a small table in your Relationship Direction. Pin here things that represent your target audience. If the majority of your clients are from a particular country, display that country's flag. If they're mostly from a particular age, gender, or income bracket, display something that represents that. Show the Universe that you respect and value your customers enough to know everything about them. Place a photo of you with your team or work colleagues too in order to maintain a positive working relationship with them.

There are so many more ways to activate your office for abundance, this is really just the tip of the iceberg. To continue on your Feng Shui journey and see just how quickly and easily you can manifest great success to your business, download the free Marie Diamond app for daily tips, messages, and meditations. Similarly, check out my global best-selling Amazon books: *The Diamond Energy Principles*, *The Diamond Energy Journal*, and *The Energy Number Book*. These books will teach you the basics of Diamond Feng Shui and how to use it to manifest the life, and career, of your dreams.

Visit me on: www.MarieDiamond.com
Follow me on: www.linkedin.com/in/mariediamond
Follow me on: www.instagram.com/mariediamond8
Follow me on: www.youtube.com/c/MarieDiamondChannel

Get your free access to the "Marie Diamond" Application, where you will receive daily energy messages, access to Marie's famous "Tubes of Light" meditation, and monthly healing meditations. You will also receive a free Energy Number report and access to the Diamond Compass which will locate the four Personal Directions you'll need to activate for success, health, relationships, and wisdom. You will be guided by videos and can start creating your Conscious Office.

For Apple phones, head to:
www.apps.apple.com/us/app/marie-diamond/id971250423

For Android phones, head to:
www.play.google.com/store/apps/details?
id=com.mariediamond.magicalliving&pli=1

## Marie Diamond

Marie Diamond is a globally renowned Transformational Leader and star of the worldwide movie phenomenon *The Secret.* She uses her extraordinary knowledge of quantum physics, the Law of Attraction, and Feng Shui to help people transform their lives. Her vision is to enlighten more than 500 million people during her lifetime.

Her clients include A-list celebrities in film and music (such as Steven Spielberg, Big Sean, Jason Bateman and Jodie Foster) and top-selling authors and speakers (such as Rhonda Byrne, Jack Canfield, John Gray, the late Bob Proctor, Marianne Williamson and Vishen Lakhiani). She has also advised leaders from Fortune 500 companies, sports athletes, governments, and royal families. Marie Diamond combines her intuitive gifts, the growing science of energy flow, ancient wisdom, and modern tools to enlighten homes, businesses, and people. She is known for her passion to help create enlightened leaders around the world.

She is a founding member of the Transformational Leadership Council, created by Jack Canfield, and President of the Association of Transformational Leaders in Europe.

She has more than one million online and in-person students in more than 190 countries. You can connect with her for personal mentoring, consultations, seminars, online courses, e-books, and home study courses at www.MarieDiamond.com.

Her Spanish students can join her at www.MarieDiamondespanol.com.

Her teachings are published in online programs such as Mindvalley, Learning Strategies and YouUnity. For her charity work, she is a knighted Dame.

Currently, she lives between the south of France, London, and the USA with her family and her dogs.

**Contact Marie Diamond:**

- www.mariediamond.com
- office@mariediamond.com
- @mariediamond888
- www.facebook.com/mariediamondfans
- @Mariediamond8
- www.youtube.com/@MarieDiamondChannel
- www.linkedin.com/in/mariediamond

For Spanish-Speaking Students:

- www.MarieDiamondEspanol.com

Marie Diamond App:

- www.mariediamond.com/app

# Publish Books That Transform The World & Create A Magnetic Brand

## By Lily Patrascu

### Born To Win

Eighteen years ago, I first came to London from Romania to work as an au pair, taking with me just two suitcases filled with hopes and dreams and €100 in my pocket. Deep down, I knew I was a champion; I was born to win, even if it didn't always feel that way. Despite sometimes having low confidence and feeling like a failure, I was feeling hopeful and optimistic for whatever the future had in store for me. I decided, right there and then, that this was my time to finally prove myself.

### Be The Best At What You Do

Everywhere I went, I was aiming for excellence. I was seeking to constantly optimize my activities and services offered to the families I was working for. It was important to me to be seen as a helpful, productive worker and to make them happy. As I moved from family to family, I gradually rebranded myself as the "Supernanny". I rewrote my CV and filled out job applications so beautifully that even I was astounded at what a badass nanny I was! I was getting pitched to extraordinarily successful families such as the founder of lastminute.com, by agencies, and got interviewed by famous families such as Tamara Mellon (founder of the Jimmy Choo footwear brand), TV presenter Anneka Rice, and some other high profile entrepreneurs living off Bond Street in London.

I quickly came to appreciate my dynamic copywriting skills and found that being well-presented, showing initiative, being productive, and having an allround pleasant attitude were all secret weapons when it came to finding the right opportunities in life.

***Lesson: Make customers fall in love with you***

### The Joy Challenge

Despite extensive traveling, dancing, and the enjoyment that came with being of service to the families I worked for, I soon began to feel like something was missing. I had just turned twenty-nine and I was filled with regret. I had no boyfriend, no property, and no proper job. It felt like I was somehow being left behind. I was running out of time; if I died tomorrow, there'd be no legacy or anything to be remembered by.

I decided that to find something better, I'd have to make the most of what I had. I started replacing boredom with the pursuit of even higher excellence. By reframing my daily activities, I found so much joy in the so-called tedious activities. I enjoyed arriving thirty minutes early to work and found multiple ways to leverage my house chores and school pick-ups by listening to the world's best audiobooks. I got enormous joy in waiting around at the tennis club for the children's classes to end and reading books on my Kindle. I hired a cleaner for my own house and every time I got home, I'd feel my spirits lifted from the tidiness and gratitude for living a truly exquisite lifestyle.

I raised my energy by creating my own happiness calendar. Every hour after work was filled with activities that I knew would raise my vibration: salsa dancing, swimming, getting my nails done, long walks in nature, buying red dresses, and catching up with good friends over a latte. I learnt to be grateful for, and appreciate, every moment. I may not have been rich but I was filled with abundance, love, and a sense of freedom. I soon began to feel magnetic and attractive. I had unknowingly created a **Magnetic Brand** for myself; it was all being reflected from the inside out.

***Lesson: Joy makes you magnetic.***

### Create A Legacy By Publishing Your Book

You never know what the universe holds in store for you; I certainly had no idea what publishing a book would do for me! I'd only wanted to feel like I had done something important but it led to me becoming a magnet for unbelievable opportunities. The book, *Meet The Nanny*, attracted hundreds of entrepreneurs to me, keen to know how I'd published my book on my own and how I'd made it so beautiful, too! I started to get invites to free marketing and entrepreneur events, invites for lunch, job offers, and even a boyfriend!

### George Clooney Reinvented

Whilst attending marketing events, I met a lovely guy. I'd been on the lookout for my knight in shining armor and the book had brought him to me. He was no George Clooney but Harry Sardinas, or my "Clowney" was a delightful, teddy bear-looking gentleman with chubby cheeks and a 24/7 comedic streak. We soon started dating and I truly felt his generosity, kindness, and caring spirit. I was a funny, introverted person and he had a level of confidence that could match the force of an atomic explosion. We made a perfect pair together too, almost like the blind and the deaf; me with my lack of confidence and him with his imperfect English. It seemed I had a full-time job correcting Harry's English!

**A "Picasso" In The Making**

Harry soon realized I was going to be a great asset for his business so he hired me to manage his English school, property business, and to ghostwrite and publish his books. Intuitively, I started optimizing the image and brand of the property rentals and realized I had a knack for turning ordinary things into extraordinary things. I was able to increase his property revenues and do the copywriting and branding for all his books, websites, flyers, and adverts. I was my own version of Picasso; creating extraordinary things everywhere, and just like Picasso, I was creating from the heart and the results were better than I could have imagined. I was on a high; turning my creations to reality.

**If You Don't Brand Yourself, Others Brand You**

I had seen the impact that brand optimization had made for Harry's business. Every new book I published worked to better the lives of thousands of potential clients and enhanced our memorable **magnetic brand**. I started out with putting together Harry's ideas for his book *Climbing Big Ben*. This book earned Harry invites to speak at events and enhanced requests for collaborations, web designs, and done-with-you events in organizing and marketing. Harry also started to get recognized on the street as "the man in purple" so I insisted on him wearing his brand colors everywhere, at all times. Then, I published *Learn English Fast* which helped our tenants learn English quickly so they could get a job faster. That worked to double the price of the English courses that we were offering and to attract more clients.

**Speakers Are Leaders And The Making Of A Global Brand**

After a while, I had reached a limit. Harry was getting invited to so many events but I was still too afraid to speak about our business in front of thousands of people. I was terrified of public speaking. Harry decided to create a fun public speaking workshop to empower both me and the other leaders that he had met at various entrepreneur events. That was how the "Speakers Are Leaders" global brand was created. It was astonishing how much fun it was and how I, along with thousands of others across the world in five countries, had managed to overcome fear of speaking in just twenty-four hours. Now, this isn't to say that my fear had disappeared, rather that I had learnt to feel the fear and do it anyway. The workshop became a book and a powerful tool for attracting our desired tribe; global, heart-centered entrepreneurs and leaders. It also became a motivational and keynote speaking topic, an online practice club, an interview topic, and the basis of many social media posts and online courses. I was focused on increasing Harry's brand's reputation by overdelivering and as a result, we were getting great reviews. Our attendees were raving fans, leaving thousands of great reviews. The book and workshop led to attracting high-profile entrepreneurs and influencers to us.

***Lesson: People remember how you made them feel***

### Creating Books That Transform The World

I was in awe at the incredible outcomes and opportunities that we were attracting as a result of our books and the global brands that we were building worldwide. It was then I decided that I was going to help others to optimize their businesses as well. I was the branding ninja, the Optimisation Queen, and I had the Midas touch. I created Brand For Speakers (Book Publishing) and, after seeing Marie Diamond speak at our event, my mission became to empower 100 million people to be happier, to go after what it was they wanted, and to share their stories in books that transform the world.

I wanted to create books that made a difference; books that mattered because to some extent, I'd always felt that I didn't. The authors that I worked with went on to achieve a range of things, such as: gaining hundreds of client referrals, speaking opportunities, media features, a brand new chance at life (and a new husband found on a speaking tour!), going from suicidal to being awarded by the USA president for impact created, getting accreditation for courses and products from a UK medical association, turning one book into an upcoming app, and rebranding from housewife to positive parenting coach. Harry even got invited to see Queen Elizabeth II and the Royal Family at the Commonwealth Celebrations in London. Together, Harry and I reached a million people on social media and spoke in front of ten thousand people on worldwide stages.

### Creating A Magnetic Brand

Millions of people publish books each year and the reason why a lot of them don't work to get the right results is because they don't have the right luxury image, the right title, the right message, the right aligned brand, or the right blueprint for the right market. The wrong title and incorrect branding can prevent you from attracting the right opportunities.

## Your Positioning Is Ultra Important

If you position yourself as a cheap coach, you'll get treated poorly and you'll get asked for a discount too, regardless of your results (which is heartbreaking!) It's hard to build trust and credibility without authority. People pay a lot more for things they want if you use the right title. That's why it's important to choose a simple, short, easy-to-understand, outcome-based title that speaks volumes. That's why I recommend that you brand yourself as a high-end luxury entrepreneur. You'll be able to look incredible in every social media post, become magnetic for your ideal target market, and get paid your worth. Ensure to leverage copywriting, extraordinary branding, and a luxury book cover to make your uniqueness stand out. Through branding makeovers, fun photoshoots, wardrobe styling sessions, and social media image makeovers, I can create extraordinary luxury brands and I get incredible fulfillment knowing I, who was once seen as the ugly duckling, is now the helping hand to help clients show their confidence and attract more business.

## People Judge A Book By Its Cover

Whether you like it or not, people will judge your image, your business, your book. That's why I invest so much time in creating spectacular branding for influencer websites, social media, media kits, and speaker reels.

Here are some steps you can take to grow your business with magnetic branding:

- Write a book
- Gift your book to those most likely to do business with you
- Do seminars on the same topic as your book
- Turn your book into multiple pieces of content
- Leverage the book to get invited to speak
- Offer your book as a lead generation
- Organize your own event and do a seminar on your topic for your target market
- Introduce yourself correctly (with a maximum of six words)

## Invest In A Peak Performance Image

To become a **magnetic brand:**

- Wear your brand colors
- Invest in a luxury business card
- Invest in luxury event banners and roll-up banners
- Invest time in creating a polished, professional written offer

- Invest in creating a luxury freebie to attract leads
- Invest in a luxury speaker funnel and/or ecommerce website
- Review how you look in Google
- Manage your reputation

**Build Relationships To Become An Influencer**
Great authority, copywriting, and branding attracts influencers to you. It's all about what you know, who you know, who knows you, and what network or value you can add to influencers. Make yourself valuable for influencers and you will notice your own wealth expanding.

So, whether you've been thinking about publishing a book for one year or ten, I know one thing:

**It's Your Time Now To Publish Books That Transform The World And Create A Magnetic Brand.**

## Lily Patrascu

Lily Patrascu is an ultra creative book publisher for luxury influencers, thought leaders, and CEOs. She is an influencer with 140k+ followers. As a personal branding strategist, author, and copywriter, she supports busy entrepreneurs. She is the founder of "Brand For Speakers" book publishing and the co-founder of "Speakers Are Leaders".

**Lily Patrascu can help you by:**

1. Turning your story, message, knowledge, and experience into books, influencer websites, online courses, and coaching and workshops that transform the world. You'll learn how to become a luxury influencer and global brand, make a worldwide difference, leave a legacy, and become well-known international speaker
2. Teaching you to go from unknown to unforgettable within ninety days with her **Brand For Speakers** system, so you can enhance visibility & credibility - Position yourself as an expert, so you can attract the right clients to you
3. Assisting you to get anything you want through becoming a published author
4. Connecting you with investment opportunities, startups, investors, and joint venture partners from her inner circle
5. Giving you the complete solution to start and grow your speaking business

**Contact Lily Patrascu:**

- Book A Free Strategy Call Here: www.lily.global/free or Email her at hello@lily.global
- www.lily.global
- @lily.global
- www.facebook.com/lilypatrascuofficial
- www.linkedin.com/in/lilypatrascu
- www.youtube.com/@lily.global

Check Lily's case studies:

- www.lily.global/success-stories

# Free Yourself: Find Your Purpose. My Self Journey to Self Actualization

## By Haleh Aleman

Picture an elephant and the image that comes to mind is one of outsized strength. Yet why do so many of them sit placidly in zoos, barely restrained? From a young age, elephant trainers condition baby elephants, tethering them with chains they can't break at that stage of development. The elephants learn that struggling to free themselves causes pain. And even after they become full-sized adults, they don't dare risk testing the chain that in reality can no longer hold them.

For thirty years I was like that elephant. Trapped from a young age in a marriage that was from the outset abusive and controlling, I didn't realize how easily the bounds that held me could be broken. Year after year, I was conditioned by my spouse to believe I was worthless and couldn't live my life without him. I lived in his shadow, a passenger riding in his car, living his life, the life he wanted, dancing to the whims of his imagined slights, jealousies, and indignities, fearful of his outbursts, of triggering him.

How did I build the courage to challenge the chain, to end my entrapment, and embrace a larger life? How did I break away from a past that imprisoned me and limited my achievements to build a present that nurtures and supports me? How would I get my power back? First, I had to free my soul.

Major perspective shifts often happen in a season of hardship. The hardest time of my life was also the most transformational. Early in 2008, I was spiraling in my mind, caught in a cascade of calamities. We were on the verge of bankruptcy in a business that my husband owned when I received the news that my father had unexpectedly died of a heart attack. I was completely crushed by that loss and in a state of mourning.

A few months later my husband went for a routine heart check and was rushed directly to the emergency room with a blood clot. Had he waited just one more day, he would also have died of a heart attack. After these two life-changing events I received word that my brother-in-law had been in a horrible accident and that his life and my sister's would never be the same. The compounding of these events sent me into an emotional state of shock; my life was in crisis. I decided to go on a short getaway to save my sanity. Taking my seat on the plane, I discovered a copy of *The Secret* by Rhoda Byrne in my seat's back pocket. At that moment, I had no idea that my life was about to change forever. I did not know exactly what I was looking for, but I knew I did not want to continue to live in this hardship season of my life. I do believe that once you make a decision and find your resolve then the teacher and people will appear to show you the new way forward. With each heartbreak or setback, you become stronger, and the solutions come, either through a book, a person you meet, or a quote you stumble upon online. If you are present and mindful, the message you need will find its way to you.

This is the story of my life; I had seen the pattern manifest many times. Earlier in my design career, I wanted nothing more than to revive the classical architecture and design that originally shaped the character of the Washington DC region in my hometown, Potomac, Maryland. Once I committed to my vision, the right architect, contractor, craftsmen, and vendors appeared to help me actualize my dream.

So here I was in this dark moment of my life on a plane with *The Secret* in my hands. Life has a strange way of putting you in the right place at the right time. You just have to give yourself over and have faith that you are exactly where you are supposed to be. I have always felt, from a young age, a strong spiritual connection, and it was with me now. As I began reading it was as if God came to me and said: "Haleh, I'm still here, watching over you, don't worry, everything is going to be okay." I devoured each page, absorbing the information wholly and with intention. It was in these pages that I first encountered the transformational teachers to whom today I am forever grateful. I became their student and began to realign myself, creating new habits and shifting my thought patterns through practicing the law of attraction —whatever you focus on, you attract it to your life. Of these teachers, Marie Diamond became a power for helping me break the chain of my past. My study of Diamond Feng Shui transformed not only my home, but also my office, and my work projects.

Meditation, movement, gratitude, and recording and listening to affirmations all helped me reorient my mindset, allowing me to reframe my thoughts and put myself in a new space not only in my personal life but in my professional life as well. I began applying methods of daily movement and meditation with my staff. Each morning we began our day gathered in the conference room to meditate and visualize our day, bless our clients and projects, and write down ten things we were grateful for. I created two boxes: a God's box and a Thank you, God box. All our fears, worries, concerns, and desires went into God's box. Within a few days, our worries and concerns were addressed. We would then take them from that box and put them in our Thank you, God box. The concept was "Don't try to solve your problems, hand them to God and let him take care of them." I learned to create a toolbox that helped me uplift myself and uplift my energy especially when life challenges occurred to take control of my mind. I learned to not react to a situation, but instead, to breathe and keep my focus on the outcome I desired, instead of on the reality I was experiencing. I taught this technique to my staff, with an eye on the importance of keeping us all on the same wavelength.

These practices completely shifted my office, staff, and clients and my business began to blossom. During the worst global economic downturn in years, my company thrived. I refused to listen to the news, or to anyone that did have a similar mindset. As Jim Rohn entrepreneur, author and motivational speaker famously advised, "Keep guard of your mind. All it takes is one poison to kill your day and your dreams."

The mindset shift that had taken place was unimaginable. I was now in possession of all the tools needed to transform all that grief, and all the fear into hope, love, faith, and excitement. My YES for life was back! I went from fearing the day-to-day to only seeing the result I desired. I was no longer focused on the negative energy in my life. I made it intentional to be grateful daily, to speak positively to myself, and to surround myself with transformational teachers, coaches, mentors, and those who could show me how to evolve further in my life. The support I created for myself contributed not only to my improved daily health but shifted my vibration from a lower vibration to a higher frequency vibration.

Changing my mindset and allowing myself to reframe my thoughts put me into a new space in not only my personal life but in my professional life as well. As I became more conscious of the power of my own thoughts and more awakened to the world around me, I found myself exploring not only a new way to think but learning how to create a loving healing home environment for myself that would support all the spiritual work I was doing. And, at the same time, I found myself envisioning a new approach to my work with Haleh Design, Inc, a luxury-focused design practice, one that would mirror all I was learning. I wanted to share the transformation I was experiencing in my own life with my clients. From my personal struggle a mindset grew that provided me with the knowledge to bring healing into the home through strategic placement, custom materials, and the alignment of healing methods personalized for each client's needs.

I began using sustainable materials and furnishings as much as I could, doing business with companies that also wanted to give back to the planet. I studied Diamond Feng Shui and Diamond Dowsing, finding new insights that further evolved my design awareness. I worked with a Feng Shui master on each new project, from the selection of the land to the siting of the house, to an overview of the space planning to make sure the property would be positive for the clients' well-being.

Bringing the personal into my process allows me to serve each of my clients in their own well-being journey and in the creation of their balanced and functional healthy home. As I continue to evaluate my purpose, I have come to know that I am here to teach, inspire, and heal through my work in design. In partnership with Marie Diamond, I recently launched Home Wellness Interior Design (HWID), an exciting new expansion into online design services that I oversee with the aim of supporting designers and consultants to work from home to create modern, sustainable, holistic, and affordable interior design.

HWID has given my vision unimaginable reach and the privilege of connecting not only with audiences everywhere but with other talented and likeminded designers who are interested in integrated interior design services and sustainable furnishings.

Marie Diamond's team of consultants help with Diamond Feng Shui and Diamond Dowsing services, to establish harmony between the client's home and the environment to promote a well-balanced beautiful space. The Diamond Dowsing service detects and addresses the presence of unseen earth energies which can cause disruption. This service promotes an increase in focus, productivity, enhanced moods, restful sleep, romance, enhanced money flow, and improved healing levels.

Everyone deserves to have a healthy home with great style; this is the vision of HWID. We work with like-minded eco-conscious and sustainable companies that provide organic and non-toxic materials and products used in realizing each unique project on an affordable budget. We merge the beautiful with the mindful to create modern, energetically balanced, healthy spaces that transform people's lives. How incredible is that?

Where I find myself and my businesses today is a true dream come true, one I could never have envisioned before I began my personal wellness journey and walked my own path to personal freedom. I'm so gratified to have thriving businesses where I can share all that I've learned and provide clients access to beautifully designed, unique spaces where health, wellness, and a sense of sanctuary can now enhance their own best lives.

## Haleh Aleman

Haleh Aleman, formerly Alemzadeh Niroo, is a renowned luxury interior designer and founder of Haleh Design, Inc & Home Wellness Interior Design, LLC, and Haleh Design Boutique, providing services worldwide. Haleh marries luxury with sustainability to bring overall harmony and healing to her design practice and to the forefront of home design. Grounded in Classicism and supported by diverse healing modalities, her projects bring balance to her clients' lives, making sustainability, life enhancement, and comfort the foundation of home design.

Connected to the finest and most beautiful things in the world, Haleh was born into the world of design. The daughter of a textile executive and innovator who advanced Iran's reputation for high-quality silks and upholstery fabrics, her life has been shaped by her early embrace and consistent devotion to the design discipline. Her sensitivity for the exquisite and timeless was shaped and enhanced by the foundation of a classical education in France, extensive international travel, and formal design study.

An Institute of Classical Architecture & Art member and a silver member of the United States Green Building Council, Haleh delivers timeless work that invites harmonious functionality and calm into the home by creating healthful spaces imbued with cohesive warmth.

Known for her love of people and her desire to bring elegance and beauty to all, Haleh's life tapestry is woven from a confluence of disciplines and approaches shaped by her ongoing passion for creating beautiful, healthy, restorative, and harmonious home environments.

Working with Haleh brings an experience of an uplifting collaborative journey between client and designer in which she inspires and guides a self-discovery journey resulting in a whole home health and wellness environment individualized to the client's needs.

She works with Marie Diamond, Feng Shui Master and master dowser, as well as with clients' personal Feng Shui or Vaastu Shastra masters, demonstrating the collaborative versatility she leverages to best serve her clients by designing spaces that are unique to them and their own health needs.

Passionate about children's healthcare and women's issues, Haleh supports over fifteen charities and nonprofit organizations, including St. Jude's Hospital, Children's Hospital, Susan G. Komen Foundation, and the National Museum of Women in the Arts. Haleh's dream is to bring clean water to the entire world.

**Contact Haleh Aleman:**

- www.facebook.com/HalehDesignInc
- www.linkedin.com/in/halehdesign
- @halehdesigninc

Home Wellness Interior Design Social Media:

- www.facebook.com/HomeWellnessInteriorDesign
- @homewellnessinteriordesign
- www.halehdesign.com
- www.homewellnessinteriordesign.com

# Finding my Soul's Calling

## By Elvira Balderas

Have you ever wanted to move forward, but no matter how hard you have tried, there is a force that pulls you back? Have you ever had enough of feeling anguished, stressed, moody, that not even you can stand yourself?

Hello, I am Elvira Balderas, a spiritual healer, hypnotherapist, coach, and teacher. I love to help people to connect with their true self, their soul and to live an accomplished life. My greatest achievements are having formed a lovely family, having built an excellent relationship with my partner, having my dream job, being a mom, enjoying my children, and currently living in the country where my husband and I had dreamed of living someday. One of my favorite's accomplishments is to listen to my soul, because it is the one who tells me what fills me with joy.

One of my principles is to "Enjoy my life no matter what." But I have not always thought this way. The mind is always creating expectations of how things are going to happen, this becomes our "should be". That in order to enjoy life, "I should be happy all the time".

At the beginning of my spiritual quest, I wanted to avoid undesired experiences. Once my spiritual teacher told me: "Elvira, if you are expecting that being in this spiritual path is going to put you in a bubble that protects you from living undesired moments, you are mistaken". I must confess that I didn't like to hear that, my ego grumbled: "What! Why should I do this? What is the purpose of being out of my comfort zone?"

One of the moments in which I grew the most was when I fell into total depression. Ironically, this was when I was already trained in ontological coaching, in how the mind worked, how to meditate in many ways, to manage emotions, and to find meaning in situations. I had worked on my shadow, my ego and accepted them and even after all of that, I couldn't deal with myself.

I was pregnant and had just returned from an Ashram, in India. Over there, I had learned how the ideal child delivery "should be" so that children are born free of trauma. I got the right gynecologist to help me with my plan and I did a thousand other things in order to accomplish it. I complied with all the requirements set to achieve the perfect birth for the high consciousness being, as it should be. I was in labor for thirty hours; in the end I was screaming: "Get me the epidural!" and in thirty minutes, I had a c-section. My disappointment began when they left me alone in the recovering room. I thought: "So much effort and I didn't even get what I wanted". My "should be" had not been fulfilled.

Depression starts with a single, disappointing thought. The expectation about a particular situation multiplies into many unfulfilled expectations. This emotional burden triggers the negativity in your internal dialogue. Your perception is distorted and you become fatalistic, inflexible, and self-absorbed.

After being depressed for a while, another emotion appears: repressed anger. When it does, the first thought that comes is to find out the culprit; who or what is "causing" this. It could be a situation, a person, or group of people.

I wanted to forget how I felt but my c-section wound was like an anchor that reminded me of my failure moment. It hurt so bad; if I moved, if I nursed, if I coughed, even if I laughed. I could not do much, just stay in bed. Every time it hurt, it was like a horror movie in my mind that played over and over. Catastrophic thinking and bitter feelings overtook me.

And to top it all off, my baby was crying incessantly every afternoon at four. I was tired and I was having a hard time getting out of bed. I thought: "God, this is so hard, I can't do it." We had been accompanied by our relatives for forty days but afterwards we were by ourselves. I began to feel very sad. When my baby cried, I called my husband desperately, telling him that I did not know what to do.

A part of me did not want to ask for help. I used to tell myself: "This isn't a big deal, I can handle it." I am ashamed to confess this, but I thought every day: "What if I take our lives?". At first, I reconsidered it: "No, Elvira, what are you saying?" But the days went by and each time, I thought of different ways to do it.

Sometimes life can be overwhelming, but when you are depressed, it is too much; you want desperately to end that suffering. In depression, life looks black and white, without shades or color. Although I hate to admit it, my logic went like this: "I'm suffering so much and life is getting to be too overwhelming for me. Even if I have tools, I don't want to suffer anymore neither does my baby, so I'll take both our lives."

One day I said: "Enough! I need help!". I managed to text my pediatrician: "I don't know what's wrong with me, but I have this constant thought and I'm very worried about it". Minutes later, my gynecologist called me. That was it; at that precise moment I had found the courage. I told myself in the mirror: "I don't know how Elvira, but you will overcome this without taking any antidepressants."

When I was with the psychiatrist, I wanted to share everything I knew about how the mind works. I was already an ontological coach, I had just arrived from a spiritual retreat in India, and I knew a lot of ways to meditate, but I still did not understand why I was feeling that way. "What did I do wrong? What's wrong with me?" I asked.

He told me: "There is nothing wrong with you." He started explaining how the body takes time, especially the hormones, to go back to how they used to be, before birth and before pregnancy. "If you take antidepressants, the process speeds up," he told me. I told him that this wasn't an option for me. "This is what you will do then; you're going to take four omega-three pills every day, you're going to sunbathe, go for walks, and you're going to put into practice everything you just told me you do. But if after several days you still have the same thoughts, you'll need to take antidepressants." I left the office determined to overcome my depression. That was my first and last time with a psychiatrist.

The universe always sends the right people to walk with you in your process. It turns out that my spiritual teacher had just gone through postpartum depression. We talked and she became my guardian angel. She encouraged me: "You can do it, Elvira! I could, and so can you." Days later, I saw a friend who experienced baby blues and her thoughts revolved around how to take her and her babies' lives too. When I heard that, I felt very liberated as I was not alone in this dark moment of my life.

I built a plan and told my husband about it. From then on, every day, my husband would come home from work at six in the evening. I would leave our baby with him and go out to take as many classes, meditations, and alternative therapies as possible. I can tell you everything I did to overcome the depression or, better yet, I can tell you what it was that got me out of it; spirituality.

In the areas of your life that you don't like or want to improve, there are habits that stop working for you and so you need to do something different. Also, there are soul fragments you need to recover in order to fulfill the emotional emptiness created over time or life after life. The spirituality that I teach helps you to do this and to find meaning in your life. Depression helps to turn inside and question yourself "what is important to you?" Because of emotions, your perception is distorted; things that were important stop being so and what was super important becomes a priority.

The question that helped me the most to overcome this process was "Why did my soul choose to live this?" You can go with the first answer that crosses your mind: "To have more patience", "To learn about forgiveness", "To recognize that you are worthy", "To know that you deserve happiness", "That you are more than enough", but this goes deeper.

Understanding your soul chose this experience you are living, you take responsibility on your behalf. I opened the door to depression due to my high level of self-demand that I had put on myself, the famous "should be" and then believing that some friendly gurus were going to give me my happiness, when I am the one who creates my own happiness. Happiness lives in me and comes from me; this is the gift this experience gave me.

Buddha said that if you want to be enlightened, turn your attention to yourself. Maybe you already knew this but sometimes knowing it is not enough; sometimes you need courage from someone else to make that change, and if I can give you courage, take it! I will lend it to you, until you find yours.

In the end I want to tell you: "I made it, I made it, I made it, and without taking antidepressants". Something that helped me find my courage was putting myself at the service of others. This feels as if something inside me wakes up, the soul's happiness, as if I connect with my soul's purpose.

Thanks to depression, I am writing this chapter. I opened myself up to a lot of knowledge, therapies, trials and errors; I opened to listen to intangible concepts, such as a soul's call, and now I help others to listen to it too. I love to see how a client comes to me and how they transform.

They recover their soul's fragments and they recover their internal light with a smile that lights up the room. I want to leave you with a powerful message that I wish I have heard when I was going through this process: there is nothing wrong with you, you did nothing wrong to attract this into your life and, although it feels never-ending, even if you feel like you cannot handle it, you can and you will overcome it.

You are stronger than you think; the courage you need right now to get up and overcome it, is within you, you just have to find it. Even though you do not see a way out right now, I know you are going to get out of this. I believe in you.

Today I teach people to live a fulfilling life, regardless of the circumstances, to listen to the call of their soul, to unlock different areas of their lives, such as their mind, emotions, relationships, success, finances, sexual energy, self-love, spirituality, to decode your dreams, but above all, sow awareness.

I also teach moms to teach their children about feelings. I love what I do and I do all this through the "Academia del Alma 22" (Soul's Academy 22), my spiritual school, as well as through intensive programs, and online therapies.

## Elvira Balderas

Elvira is a specialist in helping people to connect with their true self, their soul and to live an accomplished life.

She is a spiritual healer, hypnotherapist, coach, and teacher. She has helped more than a hundred people, especially women and mothers.

She has been lecturing and teaching classes for over ten years to over 1,000 people.

Elvira studied at one of the most prestigious Universities in Mexico, Tecnológico de Monterrey. She also has a master degree in Innovation Products & Design and taught classes at this University.

She is certified in ontological and team coaching, she studied techniques and therapies such as Emotional Integration, Spiritual Response Therapy, past-life research, subconscious reprogramming, soul fragment recovery, Opening & Clearing the Power of your Family Tree, Dream Decoding and Mindvalley Certified Hypnotherapist with Paul McKenna, among others.

She created the AMARSE methodology, a process that helps people to clarify their fulfillment, help them to work deeper in the areas they want and to sustain those changes. She has 99k followers on Facebook.

Elvira is from Mexico and currently lives in Spain; she was awarded Best Communication Speaker in Monterrey, Mexico. She was featured in Businessweek magazine and is an author of the book *Diseño de Interfaces para Niños* (Interface Design for Kids).

**Contact Elvira Balderas:**

- www.facebook.com/elvbalderas
- @elvbalderas_en
- www.tiktok.com/@elvbalderas
- www.elvbalderas.com

# Living The Law

## By Pandora Bolt

I grew up in Santa Barbara, California, in one of the most affluent neighborhoods in America. But we lived in a cabin with an outhouse and no running water or electricity. It was an exciting and adventurous upbringing, albeit an odd one with the juxtaposition of high affluence and the reality of where our family was living.

When my mother was four, she went to Morocco. While there, she saw children living in cardboard boxes. So affected was she by the sight that from that day on, she vowed to live a life of poverty. Though she grew up in the most wealthy country in the world, the USA, she gave it all up to make poverty her identity. And thus the law of her life—and the lives of her children—was influenced by the Law she set out for herself.

We all make the laws of our life into the reality we are living. What laws are you living by? What laws/patterns are you running on that you are not even aware of?

Often your emotions are so strong you will stick to the law of life you have created rather than the law of life you want to create. Therefore, you must change the laws of your life, as well as your mindset, to recalibrate yourself towards truth, not pain, suffering, and/or lack.

The only way to start this is to give yourself a new law. Change your law and change your life. This is the same as manifesting. You manifest by claiming the "I Am." Yet you must also believe the "I Am." You can say "I Am" until you are blue in the face, but only until you truly believe in the law, the law will manifest. How do you believe in the law? You must use techniques, products, ideas, and practice until you find what will trigger yourself to believe your "I Am."

One size does not fit all. That is why there are thousands of books on the same topics. Your Being is innately honest, so if you are telling yourself a law that you don't truly believe, that law will be rejected. This is why you must ask: Why do I believe? What do I believe? And, how can I change that belief?

The blueprint for success is spiritual success. It is a success in which you are able to live your life by the values and principles that are important to you. A successful life is different from a successful career, where you may succeed at work but fail at home, or vice versa. Successful people have certain qualities and characteristics that make up their character, which together create an integrated whole.

There are many ways to achieve success in life. Some people focus on money, others on education, others on social status or power. I am going to tell you about the blueprint for success that I have found works best for me. This is a blueprint for success in all areas of your life: business, relationships, and spiritual development.

A spiritual success means being happy and satisfied with who you are, where you are, and what you do, even though it may not be what society expects from you or what your friends think would make them happy. Having spiritual success does not mean that everything goes well all the time; it means that when things go wrong for you, instead of giving up or losing hope, you try harder so that things will turn out right in the end.

Though I grew up with a poverty consciousness, I worked my way up to attending one of the most prestigious ballet schools in the world, the National Ballet School of Canada, on a full scholarship. After my dance career, however, I began running on the old familiar patterns of poverty, and I found myself with a degree and three jobs, working more than forty hours each week. I did not want to work to live, but instead live to work! So, I set a goal for myself—to become a world traveler. One year after setting the goal, I received an offer to be an instructor in China and took it.

When I took that job, my life changed forever: I started with a $7,000 a year job and worked my way up to a teaching salary, and eventually earned a DBA (doctorate) in business and strategy. I went from eating $10–$20 meals to thirty cent street food, from rent to no rent. This meant I was free to travel the world.

I visited well over thirty-five countries, and have checked off an entire bucket list: Paris, the Leaning Tower of Pisa, seeing the running of the bulls in Pamplona, Shaolin Temple, the Great Wall of China (over fifteen times), Patagonia, sailing the River Nile, staying in Agatha Christie's suite in Egypt, Dubai, Malaysia, Stonehenge, Hogmanay in Edinburgh, Easter Island, and more. You can flip your life around; it is available to ALL of us. Life is simple; set your goal. It can be one item or it can be a big and audacious goal (your BHAG)! We just need to have the courage to make the first move.

You all have the divine right to be happy, healthy, wealthy, and wise. What feelings are you dedicating your life to? What patterns are you running? Look at your life and what you have created to this point—are you happy with it? Are you running a family member's pattern? Or are you creating the unique blueprint of your life?

Find your unique blueprint. As I traveled the world and lived my dream, I also mentored thousands of students on finding their own purposes. Your direction and motivation may change, yet your conscious effort towards that unraveling must not end.

The blueprint for success is a map that shows how you can make your dreams a reality. It consists of seven steps:

1/ Make a plan.
2/ Prepare yourself to succeed.
3/ Be consistent and persistent with your vision and strategy.
4/ Listen to feedback from others and adjust your plan accordingly.
5/ Stay focused on your goals, no matter what happens around you or how many distractions there are in life that try to keep you from achieving them.
6/ Set yourself up for success by surrounding yourself with people who are supportive of your efforts and offer advice and guidance when needed. Don't get dragged down by anyone else's negativity or lack of motivation to help you achieve your goals and dreams!
7/ Remain positive at all times, even if things seem dire at times, because all things will work out just fine! The goal is to get to the point in your life where you can say you have accomplished everything you have wanted to do.

Why? So that you can set new goals and accomplish more! At this stage, it usually involves influencing even more people on higher levels. I am an expert in connecting people with products that can change their lives —I have tried hundreds of products and I know what works. I highlight programs and products that have worked for thousands of people to refill their bucket lists, become aware that their buckets are never empty, and embark on their journeys to spiritual and physical riches!

The first thing that you need to start doing is to start living with intention. You need to live by your values and principles so that you can act from those principles in your everyday lives. When you live with intention you will find that everything starts falling into place much easier than if you were just going along with the flow of life.

The second thing that we need to do is create a vision board where we display your goals and ambitions for the future. This is especially important if you have goals such as being rich, powerful or famous, because this will help you stay focused on what really matters in life.

The third thing that you need to do is create a mission statement which tells everyone why this person exists in this world and what they want from life. You may even want to write out your own personal mission statement so that everyone around you knows exactly where you stand.

At bespiritual.com, we want to fill your soul with joy and happiness, and often joy comes from setting goals and attaining them. Certain products can help us accelerate that process, and we have vetted the best of the best, from high-end tools to supplements, books, and self-care items, within the biohacking community. We want to help you be the best version of yourself physically, mentally, and spiritually. You deserve it!

You deserve to feel good and look your best, and you deserve to have all the money in the world to spend on things that make you happy. You deserve to be surrounded by people who are supportive of your goals in life and who work hard to help you achieve them. You want to be those people for you—and we promise it will be worth it!

The answer is simple: You don't have to figure it all out on your own! We've got the information you need, and we will teach you how to create healthy ways of being that lead to happiness, wealth, wisdom, and more.

Join us at bespiritual.com for ideas, products, and books, and at bestfundme.com for a crowdfunding platform to fund your dream or project.

## Pandora Bolt

An expert in leadership development, Pandora Bolt has mentored thousands of university students in pursuit of their personal and business goals through leadership courses in both China and the USA. She has also published leadership works for Palgrave Macmillan, and spoken at conferences in Malaysia, Sri Lanka, Dubai, Macedonia, Norway, and at the Oxford Women's Leadership Symposium, England, UK.

Bolt's own leadership strategy combines vision, values, strategies, goals, managing change, and letting go of ego. She is passionate about the subject of leadership and has helped thousands of leaders discover their unique blueprint in life.

Bolt has transitioned her business, "be spirituality," into finding products to share with others that support their transformation process. Let her team help you find your perfect tools to help you heal and prosper on your journey to discovering your life's purpose.

**Contact Pandora Bolt:**

- www.bespiritual.com
- www.linkedin.com/in/pandora-bolt-74347619
- @7rupert

# Becoming a World-Class Speaker

## By Harriet Bratt

I felt sick. In a split second, I had gone from feeling happy and content to total shock and disbelief. Sitting in one of my favorite places, literally experiencing what once was a dream, suddenly the dots connected and I knew that it was time to leave.

I should rewind. I'm sure many of you reading this have desires. You have something, or many things, that are important to you in life. Great health, a fun and loving marriage, career progression, running a business, a charity, writing a book; it's a HUGE list that is different for everyone!

My vision was becoming an inspirational speaker, traveling the world and impacting over 100 million people to Step into their Power and Speak with Confidence. I'll be the first to admit that I was a whirlwind of enthusiasm, Hurricane Harriet, but I didn't have a single clue. I didn't know this world at all, not many people near where I lived knew it either. I had no idea how I was going to do it, only that it was possible. I watched hundreds of hours of video on YouTube with multiple speakers, attended webinars and online events, but I couldn't just pick up the phone or email anyone to learn the exact steps to build a business and create a huge impact as a speaker... YET.

Yet, in March 2017, carrying this vision, I attended my second personal development event. It was three days. "Mindset, Mechanics, Mastery". Three days of inspirational and thought-provoking content. Three days of strategy to progress, new connections to be made with those that had similar visions, and being given what felt like EVERYTHING I needed at the time. Talk about a kid on Christmas morning and the excitement. Try 1,000 kids eating bags of sweets, opening everything they asked for on Christmas morning, plus a unicorn, or two. I was on SUCH an emotional high!

The surge of motivation was only building and I was getting more and more hooked by everything that was happening in the room. The main speaker started to sell and I was at the edge of my seat, eagerly hoping I could be a part of it. Even daring to dream that I would one day be speaking with him from the stage. He was selling a twelve-month mentorship including various events, public speaker training, masterminds and coaching. The price was usually £50,000, "But for today only - £10,000." There was an interview process but if the team decided you're suitable, "you're in." Every single piece of me was lit up and I was the first in line at the back of the room. With tears rolling down my cheeks, I said to a team member and now good friend, "I finally know where I belong."

I raced outside and sat on a cold stone wall, watching the London traffic slowly chug past. I, still on cloud nine, phoned my husband, James and shared the good news at a million miles an hour, loudly proclaiming I was going to prepare for the interview! I seemed to pass with flying colors and after about ten minutes, I shook hands to confirm my space in the mentorship.

Now I had to find the £10k fee. I ran out of the room filled with even more excitement (if that was even possible!), high-fiving everyone I passed by and heading back outside to call James again. "I'm In! This is it! Everything we spoke about, everything I'm dreaming of - this is the beginning," I screamed down the phone. As always, James supported me, gave me love, and said we would talk more when I was back. The adventure had begun.

With what seems now like rocket-speed, I quickly became one of the most committed and determined mentees. Driving over seven hours each way to attend events, showing up for every coaching call, asking questions, taking action, investing in further packages, and pretty much doing everything "I was told to."

Have you ever had a year or even a month where everything changes? Within the twelve-month mentorship, my life completely flipped. I attended some of the best public speaking events of my life, became part of the events crew, and was invited to become a team member for this global personal development company. It was surreal and vastly different from the previous care home manager role I had.

Joining the team meant moving away from James and our awesome dogs temporarily and whilst this was tough, it also meant I got to immerse myself in becoming a world class speaker. We chose this short term sacrifice for the sake of a long term lifestyle together.

Fuelled by desire, I moved 380 miles away from the home we had just bought, my little family and everything I knew to go back into shared living and follow my passion. For a long time, I put my heart and soul into everything, 1 million percent. Hungry to learn and eager to progress, the walls in my room became full of flip chart notes and I would stay up practicing each day until 3AM. I was doing the inner work plus learning everything I could about speaking.

Learning internally, externally, anywhere I could to master this skill. This paid off as out of thousands of people, I was the one who became the main speaker at the signature event (the same event I signed up at–cue vision board tick off!) and became the leader trainer for the exclusive public speaking events.

Whilst my confidence was growing and I was starting to gain more clarity, I was still in "Go!" mode, riding the wave of everything that was happening. In about eighteen months, we had over twenty-five events with most being three or five days. Nine internationals–in America, India, Taiwan, etc, and the rest being in London and the UK. Thousands of people to inspire, share knowledge with and support.

I know this might not be your dream, or the route to it, but can you imagine getting to live out your dream job every day?! The events, the people, the travel, the impact, the fun–it was all magical and seemed to be everything I wanted, except that I wasn't happy. In fact, whilst my mindset was good and I was practicing gratitude every day, I hadn't "felt right" for a long time. I could no longer ignore how I felt or pretend things would change. So there we sat. In a sunny LA conference room with just over one hundred people intently listening and watching us on stage.

My previous mentor and I were about a meter apart on stage, sitting on typical hotel-event seats for the final Q&A. One of the participants who was a mentee in the community asked us a question. She was growing a team and wanted to know more about leadership. I had the mic and so responded first and spoke about "leading by example", having a shared vision, valuing each role and more inspirational leadership support.

As I passed the mic across, everything suddenly went in slow motion. I sat and listened to my mentor, business partner, and friend, our team leader, leaning forward in his seat and sharing that his teams are completely dispensable, that they must serve his agenda or they can go.

I will never forget the exact quote: "When they no longer serve a purpose, they are gone," as he reached out with his right arm and flicked thin air. I physically shifted in my seat. It wasn't my most professional moment, yet my personal realization took over. I turned away from him, crossing my legs and arms as if to instantly repel this moment. On stage, in a split second, as I couldn't help but recoil at this short speech, a slideshow of Polaroid moments, lies, hidden agendas, ego, and narcissism from the last two years played in my mind. I recalled the many times this style of manipulation had occurred, to so many people including myself. I realized that people can be doing similar things, even teaching similar content, yet have very different intentions and very different approaches in doing so.

Feeling sick was now being overpowered by a calm, grounded enthusiasm for the next chapter. Hand-in-hand with James, I left the event and walked back to our Airbnb as I declared: "I would fulfill the remaining commitments but no more." We discussed the vulnerable, people-pleasing girl who had sat wide-eyed at the event back in 2017 and her journey to the Spiritual Warrior Woman I now was.

As enthusiastically yet not so emotionally as I had originally declared myself "in", here, strolling down the streets of LA, gazing at each palm tree we passed against the night sky, I calmly, proudly, and with new insights declared myself "out". This was a lesson in trusting myself, listening to the source, and always speaking "my truth in my way" that will always stay with me.

Two months later, I was self-employed and building my own speaker business. As I write this chapter, I continue to travel the world for events, speaking engagements, collaborations, and train hundreds of speakers to Speak up and Shine, both online and in-person. This time however, I am fulfilled, happy, and aligned with how I speak, lead and work whilst enjoying the continuous expansion.

In my upcoming book *Becoming a World Class Speaker,* I will have so much more to share and offer you from this rollercoaster of experience but through it all, the best lessons I can impart for you are as follows:

1/ **Master Your Self Talk**
Stop people-pleasing and be your own best friend. Learn to speak to yourself in a way that supports and serves you every day, and LISTEN to what the universe is communicating to you.

2/ **Step Into Your Power**
You have a Warrior Within. Consciously choose and follow through with decisions that support you and make you feel aligned. It's always our

choice. If you feel you made the wrong decision–what can you learn from it? If it feels right - take action!

3/ **Mentors Are Important**
All of them. Yes, after this experience I make sure to choose my mentors very differently now. I know everything was my choice and WOW, there were tough times. Yet, all of it led me to where I am today. #grateful

4/ **Speak Up**
Whether it's on stage, at work, in meetings, with friends, or in a group, speak up. It's okay if it feels a little, or alot, scary, most people feel this way at the beginning. You have value to offer and a story that can help or inspire many others. Go for it.

5/ **Speak From Your Heart**
Yeeees, there are many ways that you can become a more effective and inspirational speaker, but those that truly create the most impact are deeply authentic, vulnerable and speak from their heart.

## Harriet Bratt

International speaker, trainer and firewalk expert Harriet helps driven entrepreneurs, leaders, and coaches step fully into their power and communicate their message confidently, in a deeply impactful way from live and virtual stages.

Harriet has spoken to thousands of people around the world and facilitated training hundreds of speakers including her own signature event–Speaker Mastery. Speaking with and learning from some of the greatest speakers and entrepreneurs in the industry (such as Les Brown, Lisa Johnson, and Marie Diamond), Harriet is committed to continuous personal expansion herself, and by learning from the top speakers. Through practicing and experience, Harriet is also world class and able to impact any audience.

Through her own journey, Harriet saw she was able to break down every step and provide a solid and proven method to help anyone feel confident speaking up.

Harriet created Speak Up and Shine, a method which has helped hundreds of entrepreneurs become confident speakers and centers her programmes, interviews, live events, speaker membership and her upcoming book *Becoming a World Class Speaker* around these principles.

Harriet also shares her expertise on many online platforms and podcasts. such as *Selling with Love*, and also features on Amazon and Apple TV. Described as a powerhouse for humanity, the president of the Global Speaking Association Martin Laschkolnig says that Harriet is one of the best speakers he has ever seen.

Les Brown shared: "Harriet; you are Coby, you are the Le Bron of storytelling, for anyone listening–this is how you do it" If you would like to book a powerful speaker for your events, or learn how to become a powerful speaker yourself, connect with Harriet now.

**Contact Harriet Bratt:**

www.harrietbratt.com

www.facebook.com/harrietbrattspeaker

@harrietbrattspeaker

# Reaching Rock Bottom To Find My Path

## By Tina Burke

Growing up in a challenging environment, I had to learn to be resourceful and resilient from a young age. At seventeen, I found myself in a difficult situation, living on my own in a poor neighborhood and relying on a receptionist job to make ends meet. To supplement my income, I turned to my entrepreneurial spirit, offering typing services to university students, and teaching fitness classes. Despite these challenges, I never gave up on my education. I took advantage of the opportunity to attend accounting classes, eventually earning my diploma through part-time evening classes over the course of nine years. With my newly acquired qualifications, I was able to secure a job as an accountant and worked in that field for seven years. It was during this time that I discovered my passion for helping others find jobs in accounting and transitioned into a career in recruiting. As my career progressed, I was able to achieve financial stability and purchase my own home.

Unfortunately, I made the mistake of moving too quickly in my marriage, and did not recognize the signs of abuse in the relationship until it was too late. Despite the difficulties I faced, I never let go of my determination and drive to succeed, but the end of the marriage left me feeling desolate and overwhelmed by a deep depression. However, my children were my greatest source of strength and inspiration, providing me with the motivation to keep going and not give up even in the darkest of times. Through my journey, I have learned the importance of resilience, perseverance, and self-motivation, and I am now dedicated to sharing my experiences and insights to help others overcome their own obstacles and achieve their career goals.

Thankfully, I had the means to create my own business and was able to provide for my children while also being able to be present in their lives, taking them to school, sports, plays, and other activities. Even though it was challenging and difficult, I knew that it was necessary to create a safe and nurturing environment for them. We also rescued a pet, which brought joy and laughter into our lives and helped to brighten our spirits. To aid in my healing process, I turned to practices such as yoga and Transcendental Meditation. These practices allowed me to regain a sense of inner peace and I began to feel good again. Unfortunately, I later met someone who was again not the right fit for me; it was an even darker period than my last relationship.

When I reflect on my past, I can understand why I kept picking the wrong men over and over. I had to dive into my childhood, my past lives, and release and heal before I could move forward again and enter into another relationship. I am filled with gratitude for the difficult times I faced, as I know now how important it was to truly reach rock bottom in order to heal. Each experience ultimately proved to be a blessing in disguise as it forced me to confront the abuse I had endured and begin the healing process. The healing moment for me—or my "aha!" moment —was a very dark day when I was crying on the kitchen floor, with broken glass all around me. My eight-year-old son walked in and just hugged me and told me it would be OK. That hug and that encouraging voice gave me all my strength I needed to pick myself up and move forward. I needed a plan.

From that moment on, I never stopped growing and learning. I studied under spiritual leaders such as Michael Beckwith and Marie Diamond, and people started to take notice of the positive changes in me. My once hard exterior began to soften and the once cold businesswoman began to warm up. They asked me how I had been able to transform myself and if I could help guide them on their own journey of healing. I gladly shared my advice and experiences, and that is how my passion for helping others began. After experiencing the profound effects of energy healing firsthand, I was inspired to delve deeper into the practice. I attended classes and seminars on various techniques, such as dowsing, Feng Shui, and energy healing to gain a broader understanding of how to help my clients restore balance and well-being in their lives. One of the most remarkable cases I was able to support through energy healing was a close friend of mine. She had undergone a wrist operation a few months prior and was experiencing swelling and a lump in the area. She was convinced that she would need another surgical procedure. I offered to see if I could help through energy healing.

To her amazement, after just a couple of sessions, her soreness had disappeared, and the lump had vanished entirely. Not only were her family and friends surprised by the improvement, but her doctor was also astounded. To maintain the healing effect, I provided her with special healing water to spray on the area and to drink. Her family, friends, and doctor all believed that it was the energy healing that had cured her. To this day, they remain in disbelief at the remarkable healing that took place. After seeing the positive impact of energy healing in my own life and in the lives of those around me, I felt compelled to share my knowledge and skills with others. I began to offer my support and healing services to friends of my son and daughter who were going through difficult times. One such instance was when my son's friend was struggling with emotional stress; my son brought him to me and asked for my help. I engaged in conversation with him, asked him questions, and provided energy healing techniques. I also gave him a crystal to take with him and some healing water. He returned for a few more sessions and as a result his emotional and mental state greatly improved. He is now thriving in university, and it is a great satisfaction for me to know that I was able to play a part in his healing and success. I have been asked to help with cures, activations, and directions with a couple of my clients. I have been helping gently and suggesting different directions their desk should face, or placing rods as cures in their offices.

After years of supporting close friends and family through surgeries and mental health struggles, I felt a strong desire to give back to my community in a way that blended my expertise as a recruiter with my spiritual knowledge. I decided to offer free spiritual guidance and tips to those who are often marginalized, such as single mothers, and anyone else in need of assistance in finding a job. To better equip myself to do this, I began writing a book that would provide practical guidance on everything from building resumes, dressing for success, and incorporating mindfulness and visualization techniques in job interviews. Additionally, I provided healing crystals and specially prepared healing water to those who sought further support.

My efforts have been met with tremendous success and have left my family, friends, and even doubters in awe of the positive impact that I have been able to make in the lives of those around me. I learned how to clear entities and help others in their homes to release anyone that felt "stuck" in this dimension. It proves successful when anyone feels there may be ghosts, or hears strange noises, experiences "off" occurrences, or perhaps just doesn't feel right. After the clearing, I sage and cleanse the home or office. I continue to work on myself, and with the guidance and help of my spiritual teacher, Marie Diamond, I am able to continue my healing journey. Eventually, I found love and my world transformed. I took my time to meet a man who would treat me with kindness and respect, without any abuse.

It was as though the universe had brought me exactly what I needed. He was loving and kind, and his presence in my life allowed me to heal even more. The walls that had surrounded me for so long began to crumble, and my shield was gone. I started to feel alive again. We share many wonderful experiences together, such as hiking, laughing, volunteering, sharing household chores, and so much more. I now have inquiries on how I was able to find the love of my life. I am starting to help others with some tips on how to "manifest" your ideal partner.

I start with checking energy within the body, then energy in the home, and then look at Feng Shui at different levels. It is very important to speak in the positive, and keep meditating every day. This should be done whether you want to find a dream job or the love of your life, to feel as healthy as you can or to create peace and harmony in your life.

It's remarkable to me that my journey has taken me from finding the right employee for a job to helping others to find their perfect partner in life. The logo I designed in 2000, with its circular shape and its motion of going in and out, is a true representation of this journey, from careers to interpersonal relationships. This concept plays an essential role in my professional life, and now I see how it is relatable in my spiritual life.

I have come a long way from that dark place in the past, and it is all thanks to the transformative power of Love.

## Tina Burke

Tina Burke is a highly experienced accounting recruiter and owner of Burke Recruiting Inc. in Vancouver, BC. With over twenty-five years of experience in the field, she has helped thousands of accountants and hundreds of companies find their perfect fit.

Tina, who identifies as a Métis woman, has been recognized for her success and community involvement, winning the Business in Vancouver Forty Under 40 award and dedicating her time to volunteer work, including feeding the homeless on East Hastings Street.

She has also been guided in her personal growth by her spiritual teacher, Marie Diamond, and is now combining her accounting education and human resources skills with her spiritual knowledge to write a book on how to find a job using spiritual tips to boost your career. Through this book and her dream of creating a charity to help single mothers with their job search, Tina hopes to empower others and lower poverty rates in her community.

Tina Burke's upcoming book, *Spiritual Job Search: Find Your Dream Job and Achieve Your Career Goals*, is a comprehensive guide for job seekers on how to use spiritual principles to enhance their job search process. The book will provide readers with valuable insights and practical tools to improve their resumes, interviewing skills, and knowledge, to help with in-person job interviews and help them stay positive and motivated during their job search. It will also guide readers on how to identify and pursue their dream job, regardless of the circumstances.

In addition to the book, Tina's ultimate goal is to create a charity that will support single mothers in their job search by providing them with access to resources such as career counseling, spiritual guidance, and mentorship from employers.

By creating video resources and other forms of support, Tina hopes to empower single mothers and help lower poverty rates in her beloved city. With the help of a team of dedicated spiritual advisors, career counselors, and employers, she aims to help others gain the confidence and skills they need to land their dream job.

**Contact Tina Burke:**

www.linkedin.com/in/tinaburke4444

@Tinaburke

www.facebook.com/tina.burke4444

# Build Your Self-Worth To Grow Your Net Worth

## By Lisa Cavender

As I stood on the courthouse steps, I asked myself, "How–Did–I–Get–Here?" The afternoon sun was blinding and hot, but I stood there for a moment trying to process what had just happened, in fact what had just happened over the past several years. The judge had said, "Well, in these kinds of cases, unfortunately there has to be a winner and there has to be a loser, and you, Ms. Cavender, are the loser here today." I took a deep breath, composed myself and didn't react.

A loser? The words hung there like they were looking for a place to land. I had never lost at anything. I knew I was not the loser, we all were. No one wins in divorce. I stood there frozen for a few moments because I knew enough not to let the words in, not to let them land inside of me, otherwise they would fester and eat away at my soul.

I excelled at most things that I set my mind to, I dedicated myself to my work and family with all my energy, but yet, it wasn't enough. Our marriage didn't survive and, just like that, I lost the business I had spent twenty years building, half the time with my kids, most of my friends, and my livelihood, all because I said "yes" when I wanted to say "no," all because I had unconscious beliefs in the way, which prevented me from seeing my own value and feeling empowered to speak my truth. That realization lit a fire inside me. I set out on a quest to get back inside myself for the reasons I had those beliefs and what I could do to change them. I knew that I needed a radical change, but where to begin? I took some time to think about where I should go from there.

***"In the face of massive change, stay calm, keep it simple, and get back to the basics." by Lisa Cavender***

I was determined to move forward, start over, and rebuild my life from the ground up, yet at the same time, I could hear the whispers of doubt creeping in. "I'm fifty now; can I really do this?" I wondered. "I'm exhausted and completely spent emotionally and spiritually, and I don't know if I have anything left in the tank to drive on." "Focus on what you can control," I reminded myself. I could control my thoughts, my actions, and my energy. When my feelings of fear, despair, and worry kicked in, I told myself that I am strong, I have energetic tools and support, and that I can do anything I set my mind to. My training in energy work, healing, and psychotherapy techniques became the building blocks for my new foundation. I knew that the basics of mind/body integration would need to be revisited and enhanced to release the fears and beliefs of the past.

I started living more in alignment with my values, and scheduled time for the activities and work that I was passionate about pursuing. I surrounded myself with mentors and online communities that were positive and uplifting. I began coaching and mentoring again. I love to see people feeling confident and fulfilled. I rediscovered the joy of empowering people to be courageous and go for their goals and dreams. It inspired me to develop a new program called the **Passion, Purpose and a Plan Masterclass**™, to help people tap into their passions and purpose and make a plan to live them out. My spiral of momentum was going upward.

However, as I coached and mentored more and more clients and businesses, I came to realize that very smart and capable people were regularly getting in their own way; holding themselves back or sabotaging their success and relationships. I saw how people were stressed and struggling, or having poor business success despite doing "all the right things." I saw how fear was causing people to lash out and hurt the ones they loved and admired. I truly want a more peaceful and abundant world for them, and for all of us. I was determined to find a deeper solution because it was clear that mindset and willpower alone was not working for people. With my big "why?" and vision firmly in place, I did the rewarding work of helping people get back inside themselves to get to the root of the matter, reframe, and heal it from the inside out. It was so simple, yet extremely powerful, and I was thrilled that my clients were overcoming their obstacles more quickly and easily than ever before!

And then, over the course of the next few years during the COVID-19 pandemic, I was faced with more obstacles and more challenges, just like many of you. The borders closed in Turks and Caicos, and I was separated from my kids. My mom and a close friend passed away in 2020, and my father about a year later. I KNEW it was an opportunity to go deeper, to dig deeper, to look for the rainbow in the storm. After my mom passed, my energetic gifts and sensitivities heightened. I began hearing from clients' loved ones from across the veil during Zoom calls, I could sense and feel my mom around at various times and I was receiving more and more downloads of inner knowing and guidance.

Often, I woke in the morning to hear a song in my head only to search the song and lyrics on the internet and be astounded to realize that it was a message from my spirit guides or passed-over loved ones. This increased intuition began to bring me back into flow and alleviated a lot of struggle. Intuition is like a muscle; it must be exercised to stay strong. I added several exercises to my daily routine to hone and improve my connection. When my father passed away, the responsibility, the grief, and the isolation of the pandemic finally took a toll on me. I entered the dark night of the soul. What was so puzzling to me was the intensity of the emotion. I was close to my parents, but not super-close. We had not always seen eye to eye on things. So why did this feel so hard to move on from? So, inward again I went, to find the answers.

With the support of mentors like Marie Diamond, I cleared my energy layer by layer. And with each layer that cleared, I felt more calm, clear, courageous and confident about myself and my business. We really do have everything we need to thrive inside of us. As a result of this in-depth work, I developed the **Inner Dimensions Blueprint™**. It is an essential roadmap on the journey back inside yourself for your own answers, to release what is holding you back and increase your self-worth. There are three tracks to this blueprint; the first one is called AWARE, the next is called AWAKE, and lastly, there is ASCEND.

As clients travel the road through the blueprint their awareness expands, they free themselves of the limitations of the past, and they gradually build more and more self-esteem. An essential element of the Inner Dimensions Blueprint™ is an amazing process I had developed before COVID called the **Personal Freedom Code™,** which takes you from feeling stressed and triggered to being calm, clear, and centered.

The journey I took to develop The Inner Dimensions Blueprint™ was the answer to my quest. I found that the key to removing limiting beliefs and obstacles to success lies in the body and in all layers of our energy field, not just in our mindset. We inadvertently absorb energies from our parents, caregivers, teachers, and friends. We take on their energies of judgment, shame, and criticism, and it gets lodged in the body, the mind, and in the energy field. Mindset alone is not enough to release these deeply ingrained belief patterns, and what doesn't get healed keeps repeating. Now is the time to get off that wheel of repeating cycles and patterns, and set yourself free! Whether or not your tower of beliefs has only a few cracks in the foundation or it came crashing down due to a major life or business crisis, rest assured that transformation and growth is easier than you may think! It takes some courage and willingness to try a new approach, to be sure, but with this newfound sense of self-worth, you are unstoppable. And that unstoppable you will take new actions which create better results, and the better results create increased net worth. I see first-hand how clients all around the world are having amazing results. Like Ted, who was a successful media host and was looking to move forward with a new business, but just couldn't bring himself to take the actions to make it a reality. He had the idea, the plan, and the financial backing, yet his self-doubt got in the way. To him, it made no sense since he was already so accomplished. We unlocked a part of him that needed to be freed from the past. Within a short time in coaching, he was feeling great and moved forward with his business plan to amazing success!

Or Carrie, who was having trouble unwinding, shutting off her overactive mind, and sleeping at night. The stress was getting in the way of her personal happiness and professional relationships, and stagnating her business growth. As we worked together on both her life and business goals, her company expanded and launched a new online division. Self-worth directly correlates to your belief of who you think you "are." It's a state of being rather than a state of having. In my experience, solid self-worth is made up of the following common elements and I AM statements:

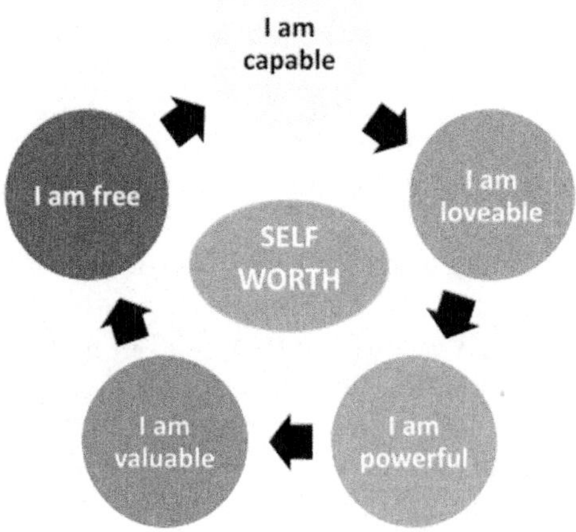


The next time you notice that you are feeling stress, overwhelm, doubt, or hesitation, gently notice which I AM statement feels like it is in play and then consult the free resources on my website, www.lisacavender.com, or drop me a line by email, lisa@lisacavender.com, and let me know how I can help.

## Lisa Cavender

Lisa Cavender is a highly experienced Transformational Life and Success Master Coach and Business Mentor who works with people all around the globe to grow their net worth with more ease, passion, and purpose.

She is an international speaker who has shared the stage with business development legends such as Kevin Harrington, Jack Canfield, and Brian Tracy. Lisa is also the international best-selling co-author of two books with Brian Tracy.

Lisa Cavender is the CEO of Innergy Ltd., a company located in the Turks and Caicos Islands dedicated to empowering people to go from stress to success in their businesses and personal lives through the company's signature coaching and mastermind programs such as: ***Chaos to Calm Masterclass***™, ***Passion***, ***Purpose and a Plan***™, ***Self Worth to Net Worth Masterclass***™, and ***The Enlightened Entrepreneur Mastermind***™.

Lisa loves to give back and has mentored many young entrepreneurs in developing their vision and executing their plans. You will also find Lisa on ***The Uplifted Entrepreneur Podcast***™, a show which brings inspiring and empowering wisdom, knowledge and support to entrepreneurs in today's ever-changing world.

Lisa is also a graduate of the Richard Ivey School of Business, a CPA, an accomplished entrepreneur, and the proud mother of two daughters. Walking in nature is one of her favorite places to be.

**Contact Lisa Cavender:**

www.lisacavender.com

www.facebook.com/Lisacavenderofficial

@lisacavenderofficial

www.linkedin.com/in/lisacavendertci

# Rising to Your Soul Blueprint

## By Anaelle Coulon

"I love you, you can rest and sleep now." Those were the last words of my mother before the blackout. I felt sucked in a golden light tunnel. It was like I was the Universe, immersed in pure unconditional love. I met a guide who told me that I was here to support the transition to the New Earth, that I would help humanity to upgrade, ascend, and bring new ways for humans to live and thrive on the planet. Then, I had the choice to come back to my body or not. Finally, after a deep coma and even experiencing a prolonged clinical death and the other side, I came back to life.

I was twenty years old and was in Milan for my studies in fashion when I had a tram accident that left me with two broken ribs that had pierced my lung. Totally bedridden for weeks, I had lost all my muscles and was rapidly losing the ability to walk, stay seated, and even hold my head up straight. I was like a puppet, kept between life and death. Repatriated to France, the doctor said that I needed another surgery but he was unsure whether or not I would survive it. Just before the operation, he looked at me and said: "Goodbye Miss."

Finally, after many hours and many complications, I woke up with a grave infection and one lung removed. But I was alive. The surgeon told me that I was the miracle of his career, and that if I was alive, it was really thanks to God. After four long months at the hospital, I was able to breath and walk again, so I came back home. But after only six months, I had a grave parasitic infection caused by ascaris worms. I couldn't digest anything anymore. After a few weeks, I was nothing but skin and bones, weighing just 22kg. I was meditating a lot to escape the pain in my body. I lived an out-of-body experience, explored other dimensions, and connected to my astral body.

Then, I fell into a coma and was hospitalized again for three months. At the hospital, I received a lot of visions, new codes, and upgrades. I was visited by my guides, by cosmic light beings who offered me an energetic surgery to recalibrate my brain and my entire being. This marked a profound rebirth and a real identity shift. It was the beginning of a new chapter of my life. After a decade of transformative experiences, I definitely left behind the old version of myself, the one who had been suffering from a restrictive eating disorder since she was twelve years old. I healed the little Anaelle from her suicidal thoughts, the feeling that she would never be "enough", and the belief that she would only be loved when she died. All these things had led her to maintain a rigid and destructive self-discipline in order to feel safe.

I dreamt again and embodied an updated and upgraded version of myself, and I reconnected to my Why, to my soul purpose. I wanted to contribute, to help people and so I left my fashion career despite the resistance of my ego: "You're twenty, fashion journalist and invited to all the fashion shows, so many girls would dream to be in your shoes!" But inside, I knew that I was here for so much more; to impact more, to contribute more, and to receive more.

Things happen for us and not to us. And today, I wouldn't trade all the challenges I went through for anything. The last three years have represented exponential growth. I have been guided, divinely supported to manifest a life I couldn't imagine possible before. I feel grateful for all the miracles, synchronicities, and the incredible people I continue to attract in my life. I commit to constantly upgrading myself to embody my highest potential in order to serve more.

I have been obsessed with learning coaching, quantum modalities, energetic healing, neurosciences, fitness, nutrition, biohacking, shamanism, and breathwork, to heal, upgrade myself holistically, and be able to help others to accelerate their own holistic enlightenment journey. Now, I would like to come back to the biggest insights that have created the most significant shifts in my journey.

It all started with a deep spiritual awakening when I was thirteen. I had very profound experiences and connections. But honestly, I was lost in my spirituality, thinking that matter was bad and the body impure. I was blinded by my spiritual ego using spiritual practices to escape my body, my emotions, my feelings, and my human life. The shift happened after the accident. Being about to die reminded me how to live. I realized that my body was as essential a facet of my being as my soul was, that I needed this vessel to manifest my purpose and enjoy life.

When I started to be connected but grounded, and to embody my spirituality, my external reality shifted so fast. It was the beginning of mind-blowing manifestations, synchronicities, miracles, and opportunities flowing into my life. Some experiences have also led me to deep, uncomfortable self-inquiry and to learn how to be raw and real with myself.

I realized that I have used my body as an excuse to refuse my soul purpose that I felt was too big for me. I had to be honest with myself and admit that I found benefits in my situation: I had attention, care and love, I had justifications and reasons if I failed, and I had an escape from responsibility. I saw all the situations where I had used my frail body as an excuse, even as a way to manipulate, and I clearly heard a voice say: "Stop playing the victim, you are stronger than you think. It's time now; we need you".

When you feel stuck in a challenging situation that you don't feel like you're able to change, be raw and real with yourself about the benefits that situation is giving you. I have also experienced energetic healing and the power of frequencies. I'm passionate about quantum sciences and how to use frequencies in order to accelerate healing and the manifestation process. Humans are a lot like radios.

How many of your dreams are flying through the air in the quantum field? They are already there, it's just up to you to tune into the right frequency to receive and manifest them. It works the same with healing frequencies. Using quantum tools and modalities has been a real accelerator in my recovery and is now part of my daily life.

On an energetic level, I also had to face my emotions after years spent stifling them as a sort of spiritual bypass. I learnt how to navigate my emotional waves without giving any attachment or identification to them. Now, I let them come through me, I feel them, and I transform them. It's a real pathway for enlightenment. Your emotions are your doorway to Heaven if you know how to alchemize them. It has accelerated my manifestation process and helped me to connect deeper with my intuition and my inner guidance. I also went deep into neurosciences and learned how to use the superpower of the mind in order to manifest real miracles in my life.

When I was at the rock bottom, not able to move anymore, I visualized myself walking again, feeling the weight of my body on my legs, and the floor under my feet. In just two months, I was able to stand up and take my first steps. Recently, after four years, the major part of my lung that had been taken out, has extended and grown again in a miraculous way. This surprised even the doctor who asked me what I have done to grow a new lung. You have the most amazing computer in your brain, you've just forgotten the password to access all its powerful programs.

It has been also essential for me to clear my unconscious mind and all the things underneath the surface that had been influencing my life. I was making choices from this unconscious, conditioned, autopilot-survival-mode part of my brain. With the power of awareness, I rewired my nervous system and upgraded my processing system to make new conscious choices.

I have biohacked my mind to align my conscious, unconscious, and my supraconscious, in order to manifest my dreams using my soul and not my ego. When the three minds are aligned, you feel blissful, aligned, and fulfilled in your life. Finally, this journey has guided me back to my physical body, causing me to admit that in order to embody my soul purpose, to contribute, and enjoy life, I needed a strong and healthy physical body.

I realized how ungrateful and careless I had been with it. So I began a new relationship with it based on unconditional love, respect and trust. Before, I tried to change my body to fulfill my unmet needs. You know when you don't feel confident enough, when there is something that you feel you miss, and so you look at your body and ask it to give you this thing, this feeling?

That's what happens when you identify yourself to your body. Instead of transforming your body into something that you can accept, the shift is to transform it into what it wants to become, in what it is meant to be, letting it reveal its highest potential. Your body is not just a thing, it's not a meat suit that you can change or throw away.

I have also learnt to listen to my body intelligence. My choices about my health no longer come from my mind or from external dogma, theories, or gurus. Now, I listen and trust my body to guide me to make the best choices for my health. Every day is different, Life is movement and impermanence. I have learnt to navigate without attachment and comparison because we are all unique with our own needs. I have finally released my strict control and learnt how to intuitively and intelligently use all my knowledge to biohack and optimize my body and health. It has been a deep journey of releasing, recalibrating, and surrendering.

The real intelligence comes from accepting that you don't have the truth and being able to listen, trust, and act from your intuition and body intelligence to tap into your own current truth. This whole journey has given me the tools I need to thrive, upgrade, and embody the best version of my multidimensional self to serve and contribute more. Every day, I continue to ask myself: "How can I upgrade and amplify my highest potential, how can I step into the next level?" This is what I help my clients to do too.

As Pablo Picasso said: "The meaning of life is to find your gift, the purpose of life is to give it away". So now, my mission is to help humans to remember their gifts and their purpose and to guide them to accelerate their holistic ascension journey to embody their Light Soul Blueprint. It's time for humanity to upgrade and thrive. It's why I guide people to update their system and make new, empowered, and conscious choices to become the Superhumans that they are.

All your life happens only between B and D: Birth and Death. In between, there is only C: Conscious Choices. So if you choose to commit to embodying your highest potential, tapping into your soul leadership, and if you feel that you are here for more, connect with me on my social media and message me to receive a very special gift created only for you. Remember, your optimal w(h)ealth, your greatness ascension is always one conscious choice away.

## Anaelle Coulon

Anaelle is a global expert in holistic ascension transformation. She has inspired and helped thousands of people to embody their highest multidimensional potential in order to thrive and contribute to the New Earth, embodying the new Superhuman blueprint.

She guides people to upgrade holistically to the next level. Her clients optimize their body and health, improve their mind capacities and performance, amplify their energy, and connect deeper to their soul's purpose and to their inner guidance.

At only twenty-five, after a decade of deep personal experiences and learning physiology, holistic health, biohacking, nutrition, fitness, breathwork, quantum modalities, energetic healing, shamanism, neurosciences, and coaching, she has created her own unique way of unifying ancestral wisdom and new advanced technologies to help people to accelerate their ascension journey.

She has been certified in holistic health and fitness coaching by the world's most powerful life transformation company, Mindvalley, being taught by top experts like Vishen Lakhiani. She has also been mentored and certified in coaching and quantum modalities by the global leaders Regan Hillyer and Juan Pablo Barahona.

She helps conscious people who feel stuck, stagnant, who feel that another level is available for them, who know that they are here for more: more impact, more contribution, for receiving more, and ready to embody their soul leadership.

She is here to support the ascension of (the) Earth by helping humanity to upgrade to its highest potential to thrive. She is convinced that together, we can change the world and create the New Earth.

She has a big vision of creating holistic centers giving access to the best technologies, tools, practices, wisdom, education, and expertise to support people in their transformational journey. Her biggest dream is to co-create conscious communities in the world.

**Contact Anaelle Coulon:**

- www.facebook.com/anaellecoulon.flow
- @anaellecoulon
- coulonanaelle1805@gmail.com
- www.linkedin.com/in/anaelle-coulon

# Who Do You Think You Are?

## By Nina Deissler

"Who do you think you are?" It was not a real question. It was more likely the expression of total despair and frustration my mother must have felt when I became a teenager: I was clever but lazy, stubborn, messy, and like many teenagers, full of myself. I only realized many years later that many people have heard this "question." And I never imagined how much impact it has: in my case, it taught me not to think too much of myself, that not only was I "nothing special," but that I was nobody at all.

Secretly, I thought that I was somehow special, but I wanted to avoid hearing that "question" ever again—while still repeating it in my head like a broken record for so many years into my adulthood. I did not have a bad life in particular, but I was playing small and often enough fell short of my potential. On the other hand, I was curious, playful, and outgoing, so it was easy for me to meet people and to flirt. That was very useful in my side-hustle job as a bartender on the weekends in my early twenties, and as male guests and friends started to ask me for advice on love matters, I thought to myself, maybe I could offer that as a "service?"

After a stock market crash, the internet company I worked for in the early 2000s fired hundreds of people, including me. My life started to change. My idea to coach people on how to get better at dating, overcome shyness, and find love was an easy decision. Not so easy was actually being an entrepreneur. There it was again in my head, that question: "Who do you think you are?" I haven't even studied psychology, so how can I dare to coach people on their problems? How can I "brag" about my ideas? How can I even think that I will be able to help others?

It turned out that I had exactly the same problem as the people that I wanted to help, just on another level. I was shy! It wasn't that I thought particularly badly about myself. I just thought I wasn't good enough. I did not dare to approach a magazine, a newspaper, or a possible business partner. I felt not educated enough to really go out there and be a successful entrepreneur, let alone a thought leader. I was not good enough... so I just sat there, working hard without doing a thing that really made a difference. My first idea of overcoming it was the "fake it till you make it" approach, so I changed my age from twenty-eight to thirty-two and denied my origin. Then, I read even more books, trained as a systemic coach and NLP Master. Even after all this, I was still feeling anxiety before every (rare) new client. And they were so rare, I could hardly pay my rent. On my thirty-second birthday, the ATM swallowed my card as my account was overdrawn. Two days later, my electricity was cut off as I hadn't paid the bill for three months in a row. I sat there in my small apartment, single, broke and doubting myself. "Who do you think you are?" my inner voice asked me.

On this day, maybe due to the amount of despair and distress I felt, I did surrender to that question. For the first time I really thought about it as an actual question: Who am I really? Who am I if I leave out all the stories I tell myself, and tell others about myself? I was a thirty-two-year-old woman, sitting on her sofa by candlelight. I had no university degree in psychology and, nonetheless, I had already helped many people. I could not help everyone, but for God's sake, who can? Nobody!

Realizing this was like opening a new door; I remembered I'd once heard that if you had your own bed, a bank account (no matter how overdrawn), and a phone, you belonged to the top ten percent of the richest people on earth. I had all of this and more. I had things that even the top one percent did not possess, like real friends and a loving family that (despite the fact that they had accidentally placed that self-doubt in my head years ago) would never let me down if I was in real trouble.

These thoughts made me burst out in laughter: I had exhausted myself for four years without any major success and I was absolutely broke. So, what would "real trouble" look like? All of a sudden, I found myself entirely happy and giggling, with a feeling of excitement within me that I hadn't felt for a long time. Rock bottom turned into a wake-up call to a new confidence. It was not about where I came from, it was about where I wanted to go, and who I wanted to become! I felt rich and blessed, and started acting according to these feelings.

Change did not come overnight, but it came. A year later, all my debts were paid, my workshops were well-attended, and I could actually make a living from what I was doing. The only area in my life I was still struggling with was my own love life. My "kind-of-boyfriend" just didn't really want to commit to me.

When I met men, many ran away when they heard what I did for a living. It almost felt like a curse. I, of all people, who help people find love, couldn't experience love myself? And there it was again: "Who do you think you are?" And again, the moment I really asked myself the question, the answer amazed me.

Because, in truth, I was the one who didn't want to fully commit: Not to a partner, nor to my business or even to myself. This time, however, I didn't start to laugh; I cried. I realized that I did not act like I was loving myself fully—so why should anyone else do so? I had always kept my options open so I wouldn't have to endure the fear of not being good enough. If you did something half-heartedly, there were many reasons why you failed besides your own inadequacy. It was me who didn't go all in, ever!

When I finished sobbing, I made a promise to myself and I didn't wait long before I followed up with action: I ended the half-hearted relationship, and all projects that didn't support my heart business, and I finally reached out to the magazines I wanted to be featured in. I put up a photo of myself on my MySpace Profile that I might have abandoned before my epiphany of self-commitment: one that showed my true self.

Not particularly pretty or sophisticated, but lively and laughing. Around this time, I also discovered a fancy shop in my neighborhood selling magical rituals. Although I was skeptical, it intrigued me. I definitely didn't want my love life to be "bewitched," but a money ritual... why not? It came with a big candle and the indication of the appropriate moon phase.

The instructions asked me to carve into the candle what I wanted money for. Good question: Shoes? Vacation? Fancy dinners? Yes, that was all good, but somehow it seemed small and shallow. When the thought struck me, I thought I was crazy—but I carved the word "wedding" on the candle. The fact that I didn't even have a partner seemed almost a minor matter to me. I wanted someone who really wanted me and I was ready to commit. Weddings are expensive—so here we go! I finished the ritual, put away the candle and forgot about it.

A few weeks later, my phone rang. A publishing house had found me via the internet and wanted a flirting guide in their new series of self-help books. The timing was divine; I had already outlined an idea for such a book, which was exactly what the publisher wanted.

And a few days later I actually had my first book deal. As much as I had forgotten about the candle, I had also forgotten about my MySpace Profile. And, to my surprise, I had received a message from a musician I had learned about just weeks before in my favorite live music club: "You have to check him out. You're gonna love this guy!"

And I did. We started talking about music, then about life, and as well about love. And something really amazing happened: We literally fell in love over a couple of emails and a phone call. After we met for the first time, I "knew", and I told my friends, "I will marry this guy." To be honest: It was still a surprise that he dared to propose to me with a song he had written for me on our second date.

I thought, "This is what you wanted! So why not?" And I agreed. I know this sounds strange but I just knew this was right. A few days later, a magazine that's displayed at every seat on every train on the Deutsche Bahn agreed to feature me in their Christmas issue.

The trains were full of singles making their way home for the holidays and within the next few months before our wedding, my love workshops were sold out, and I even had to schedule extra dates. There it was; the money for the wedding I had carved into that candle.

Don't get me wrong: This story is not about magic wishes and getting married to the love of my life. And this is also not the "happy ending" of the story—it was just the beginning. Since that day, I have learned and practiced it over and over again: life is an adventure! It asks you to commit to yourself and act upon it.

Asking myself who I think I am and who I want to become is my guiding star. Needless to say, this question has made its way into my work, my speeches, is part of my identity-reframing coaching method, and has inspired thousands of people to date. I hope it will also inspire you!

So: Who do you think you are and who do you want to become?

## Nina Deissler

Nina Deissler is referred to as "Germany's Date Doctor No. 1", and is a renowned expert in finding love, and overcoming shyness and self-doubt, with over twenty years of experience. She has published thirteen books, and created the Identity Reframing Method, which has already helped thousands of people to see themselves in a helpful, growth-oriented perspective, to develop their full potential, and create the love life they deserve.

Her clients include millionaires, celebrities, and CEOs as well as major brands who also benefit from the love expert's knowledge about attraction and appearance. Her workshops and online programs about dating, flirting, and finding love have reached more than ten thousand clients.

As the go-to person when it comes to dating and confidence, she has done more than one thousand interviews and been featured several times in every major magazine and newspaper, as well as dozens of podcasts in Germany, Austria, and Switzerland. For several years, she had weekly appearances as a relationship expert on the morning show of German TV channels SAT.1 and NDR.

Her podcast, "Mission: Liebe!", has more than one million downloads and will be—together with her YouTube channel—soon available in English.

Nina Deissler was trained and/or influenced by NLP co-creators Richard Bandler and Robert Dilts, as well as Ajit Nawalkha, Dr. Joe Dispenza, and Byron Katie, among others. She is also a certified Mindvalley Coach, a member of the German Speakers Association, and the Association for Transformational Leaders—ATL Europe, founded by Marie Diamond.

She has been married since 2008, is a passionate cook, and an explorer who has traveled to over thirty-five countries.

**Contact Nina Deissler:**

- www.ninadeissler.com
- @nina.deissler / @ninadeissler.datingexpert
- www.youtube.com/@nina.deissler

# The Power of Forgiveness: Free Yourself to Find Yourself

## By Channin Dionne

It felt like time had slowed down. I heard nothing. The scent of lavender in my diffuser filled the air as if the universe knew I would need calmness for this moment. I could feel my heart begin to beat faster as I found myself holding my breath in apprehension. "Wait a minute," a voice said, "Be present. Feel what is going on in your body. Now, take a few deep breaths before you look any further." I placed one hand on my heart and the other on my womb. Then I inhaled, filling up my belly. I picked my phone back up.

Only five minutes ago, I was getting ready to close my laptop for the night, eager to be a part of the *Conscious Global Entrepreneur* book. It was just after midnight when I searched for something on Google, Trending Searches came up, and I saw a name I recognized. Nope. Clearly there's like, 20 million other people with this name too. UFC fighter? No way! Just to prove myself right however, I got ready to click on it... and paused. Here I was, excited to share with the world how Holistic Healing had helped transform my life and my clients, when a flood of memories suddenly came flashing back. I thought I had dealt with everything in that dreadful box hidden away in my mind. The box at the top of a closet in a room locked off with the words "Danger, keep out!" on the door.

The box was a coping mechanism created as a child to feel protected. I became good at it. I grew up in a family that did not discuss feelings openly to help identify and process an experience. There were no tools or resources provided to me. Just two hardworking, endearing parents doing the best they could to raise four children and manage their own experiences in the world whilst still trying to shield us from any perceived harm. They did an excellent job with what they had been given, better than their own upbringing. I'm quite sure their parents had done the same, and so on. No one realizes that if you do not talk about things, you cannot have the awareness of patterns, generational afflictions, and pain being carried and passed on.

As I pulled back the layers, I discovered it was him. The world hadn't stopped. Not then and not now. Apparently, it had gone on for him, and quite well actually. My own life had felt frozen in time for years. Unable to feel safe, I felt a part of my life had been stolen, killed. Not knowing that, years later, all of it would have to die in order to be reborn in the knowing of who I really am and what I came here to do. This baggage was not mine to carry. Whilst this man carried on, making the best of his life after such destruction, I was weighed down by the burden of my brother's horrible accident that left him forever changed by a traumatic brain injury before I got to talk to him and make peace.

Then, even years later when he died, I still carried this weight. The heaviness of shame, guilt, pain, and so much loss. The compassion and the forgiveness and the grace that is practiced to my clients. This was the final test in my healing journey. Yes, this was shocking. Now what was I going to do with this newfound information? How was I going to show up? Would I curl up in a corner and die? No. This story is not about him, but it is about me using my voice which I didn't do then, but today I will liberate my soul for me and my healing.

I know the symptoms of trauma very well and what it does to the body. The poison released through the chemicals of the fight, flight or freeze response. By being silent for so long and subjecting my body to whatever was inflicted upon me, I unintentionally committed self-harm. I took this pain and I stuffed it deep down until I almost forgot it. My body could never forget about it though. I absorbed so much trauma in my body, not to mention my ancestor's trauma that I've worked diligently to clear. Now I had a decision to make. A teenager hanging out with friends, sharing their life's dreams. The caller's tone became more distressed and pleaded "Please, I just need to talk, it won't be long." Need. Anyone who ever needed me, I would be there.

Like a trickster you hear about in African folklore, luring his victim under the false pretense of needing help. That night, I witnessed the ugliest violent side of the world. My big brother, who I grew up very close to, tried to warn me about this person. Of course, not heeding the wisdom of my elder brother whose shadow I was always in, I did what I wanted. When you're one year apart, he's always there looking over my shoulder, bossing me around. This person said he needed help and I could help whoever I wanted to! Besides, he really opened up to me and explained that he's just misunderstood, that the things people said about him weren't really true. I took pride in not judging people and forming my own opinions. The detrimental effects of sexual abuse and racism has on a person's self-esteem. Growing up in predominantly white spaces, nobody looked like me. I was being constantly reinforced with what the standard of beauty was and success was, and it looked the opposite of me. At five years old while playing at Chuck-E-Cheese being told by another child "I can't play with you because you're black." The violence perpetuated in the media against people that looked like me, and then add that up with daily microaggressions or being sexually harassed at work and told "Who do you think they're going to believe?" as if my female blackness meant that any harm could be done against me because society does not believe or value me.

Over time, this affects all areas of being including psychological, emotional, and physical. I began to shrink myself down more and more each time, trying to become invisible, not wanting to be seen or take up space. When more abuse would be added on, so would the weight as though it would build layers of protection as a failed attempt to feel safe. Contradictory, I would gain weight while trying to shrink so as not to be seen. At an early age, I did not feel like I belonged and was constantly receiving messages from my environment that there was not enough space for me to exist. If you do not exist, if you don't have any value, if there is no space for you, then the next question is: "Why am I here?" Even though my way of coping with trauma as a child was not healthy, locking it away in an invisible box permanently so as to pretend it didn't exist.

I had not yet learned how to receive support. This didn't mean support wasn't there, it means when it did arrive, I was unable to receive it. However, after years of studying and training, I gained tools and resources and practiced them daily. I realized it was not permanent. I went into that garden, where a lifetime of seeds of doubt had been planted and were becoming poisonous, prickly, painful plants. I now had an antidote to the root poisons, so I pulled up all those weeds of limiting beliefs and I planted new seeds. The journey to healing is a process. A lot of this path is about being and less about doing. Be kind, be gentle, have compassion. Be present. Celebrate small wins.

Tantra has helped me and my clients to heal trauma through integration. Connecting with the five elements and grounding myself, learning to be fully present while weaving light and sound with form has been life-changing. Instead of shutting down, I communicate with love and compassion what my feelings and needs are so that I can form healthy boundaries. I am now able to have a balanced life that includes a harmonious sexual expression. I taught myself to be the support I needed when I was younger. To go into as many dark places as possible for anyone who needs support and compassion.

Here, I found in my clients some of life's most precious gems. I no longer fear the shadows because that is where I supported myself in communion with my soul. In those places, I saw that separation was only an illusion. You can never separate from the One heart, the infinite essence of Being. I utilized these modalities of healing including Reiki to raise my vibration at any given time to remain in the vortex. Despite what is going on externally, my internal state remains in harmony. This story is not about the moment I discovered my abuser was trending on the internet for being a celebrity. This story is about how I reclaimed my power. This step in my healing pushed me even further on my mission to evolve into my highest version of self in order to add light to the world.

I made a conscious decision that night after processing the feelings that showed up in that moment that I would allow myself to feel whatever it was that I needed to feel. When I watched an interview and read an article about his difficult upbringing, I put the needs of the young girl inside of me first. Then I spoke with the abuser's broken child-self and I empathized. At that moment, I truly forgave not just him, but myself for carrying the world on my shoulders, so gracefully and for so long like so many women do. Women like my niece, who had shared her own stories of trauma and abuse. I knew this generational suffering was to be broken at long last.

Although my brother is gone, I still feel him. The morning he left this earth, the most beautiful sunrise I've ever seen peaked through the window as I awoke, not knowing this was his last day. I had dreamt about my brother the night before. He was encouraging me to climb the highest building. I was terrified, I was told I had to overcome my biggest fear. As I walked, there were plums and peaches along the pathway. Now here I am in the kitchen, slow-dancing with my beautiful niece to Frank Sinatra's "That's Life." As I take a bite out of a plum being totally present, I notice the bitter tartness and then the sweet juiciness spills over in my mouth. I laugh as I can hear my brother's voice say "Girl," as he lovingly called me, "That's Life."

He was a rose that grew from a crack in the concrete and he not only survived the unimaginable, he fought to stay here longer to teach. Now I too am a part of that rose that continues to grow despite its conditions. I hid beneath the layers of dust that hides the glow of a rose. He taught me to blow that dust off and shine like the Sacred Treasure that I Am.

## Channin Dionne

Channin Dionne is a Tantra Healer, trained at the only government accredited, professional institute using the Tibetan Five Element Tantric practices for trauma-informed holistic healing of the mind, body, and spirit. She connects spirituality, sexuality, womb, and energy medicine so that her clients can create the healthy, whole, balanced, and expansive life that they desire. Through compassion, grace, gratitude and support, she walks together with her clients to free themselves from living a life of shame, guilt, depression, or low self-esteem. She is a reiki practitioner, energetic coach, naturopath, vaginal steam practitioner and a teacher of presence, training with Eckhart Tolle. Trained by Paul McKenna as trauma informed NLP and Havening Technique Certified Hypnotherapist. She founded Sacred Treasure Temple. With over a decade of experience and training, she expertly combines these modalities of healing with Tantra to help countless clients move from simply surviving to thriving by first building self-love and compassion to supportively guide them safely to the unveiling of the hidden treasure buried within.

**Contact Channin Dionne:**


- www.sacredtreasuretemple.com
- Support@sacredtreasuretemple.com
- www.instagram.com/sacredtreasuretemple
- www.linkedin.com/in/channin-dionne-a40589265
- www.facebook.com/channin.dionne

# Origin Of A Sound Therapist

## By SueZee Finley

I couldn't help but feel intrigued as the man handed me two music CDs and a note that read: "Relax and listen to this music twice a day. Wear the color green. Look at the color red. Buy yourself some roses, get yourself an emerald necklace, and call me in the morning." I re-read the note and thought: "Was I just handed a prescription to go shopping and relax?" Yes, I had! I will remember that joyous moment for the rest of my life because that was the day I decided to become a sound therapist. That was the day everything changed!

Prior to sound therapy, I was suffering from extreme fatigue from Lupus and Sjogrens, both auto-immune diseases that I was struggling with. I had maybe three hours' worth of energy a day and the attention span of a narcoleptic flea. I lived in a state of heavy brain fog and had trouble staying awake in the evening. I could no longer work as a sculptor or do martial arts and yoga; all the things I had loved to do. All that changed one magical weekend when my friend Marla invited me to a dowsing convention in New Paltz, upstate NY. I wasn't sure how I would feel traveling but I was so eager to get away. I decided to take a chance.

The convention was amazing. Speakers and vendors from all over the world had converged there and I was having a great time attending lectures and workshops. I was feeling good, but then it hit me. All at once, I was smacked with a wave of exhaustion. Think of Superman when he comes into contact with kryptonite; it was just like that. I felt like everything was shutting down simultaneously. I broke out into a cold sweat and was just moments away from passing out, when I saw in the back corner there was a guy with a massage table, a chair, and a computer.

I remember thinking: "I don't care what that guy is doing over there, I have to get over and lay down before I fall down!" With all the speed and grace of an arthritic snail, I made my way over to the table and collapsed into the chair. The man sitting there smiled and introduced himself as Greg. He handed me a microphone and told me to speak into it so that he could record the frequency of my voice. I was slightly delirious at the time and I couldn't really comprehend anything he was saying. All I heard was: "Blah, blah, blah, speak into the microphone." So I did, and then I crawled onto the table which had been my main goal all along. He handed me a headset and a blanket and I laid down.

Sci-fi, kind of new-age style music played softly through the headset and up through the table. I was laying cocooned in sound and vibration and I drifted off into the calmest, most blissful slumber of my life. Twenty minutes later, I woke up. Well, actually, Greg woke me up. I felt so amazing though that I thought I was still dreaming. My energy was completely restored. My mind felt a sense of peace I had not experienced in twenty years. All I can remember is blurting out: "I feel awesome! I need to know everything about this; what just happened to me?"

Greg explained it like this: "Your voice is the composite of all the frequencies in your body. The program I had you speak into using the microphone tells me what frequencies your body needs. and I simply play them back to you. Frequencies are like nutrients to the body, I simply played the music your body needed to hear." Greg then handed me two CDs and instructed that I listen to them daily and gave me (and this is my favorite part!) a wonderful list of recommendations; my frequency prescription for fun, happiness, and health!

Each item on his recommendation list had been selected because it vibrated in my frequency; foods, supplements, music, and essential oils. He even told me some of my personal traits, based on the program's analysis. He recommended an emerald gemstone, green colored clothing, peppermint and cedarwood essential oils, and music in the notes of C and G. These things, Greg said, would correct my frequency imbalance.

I was in my glory, filled with newfound energy and joy. With my prescription in hand, I started out on a hunt to fill it. I carefully scanned the room to see where I should go first and suddenly found myself drawn in by the most beautiful sounds coming from across the room. I followed the sound until I came to a man playing a hand-hammered and engraved brass Himalayan singing bowl. I had always wanted one of those, and as it turned out, it was in the note I needed, G. I took that as a sign that I needed to buy it, and so I did!

The vendor was extremely kind and threw in two tuning forks in my notes as a special thank you gift! There wasn't a bag big enough for the bowl but I was happy to hold it as he put my tuning forks in a red velvet pouch and tossed them inside the bowl. Hugging the bowl joyfully, I left and continued my hunt. At the next table, I found a beautiful hand-painted green silk scarf. I'm supposed to wear green; check mark! I bought it and put it into the singing bowl. I continued to circle the dealers room to see what I could find and was drawn to the most heavenly scents coming from the essential oils booth. This was too easy! Both scents I needed were there; peppermint and cedarwood. Boom! All went into my singing bowl. I started to feel like I was trick-or-treating as I added more and more items to my magical singing bowl. There was just one item left, an emerald. I found a vendor that had raw, uncut emerald stones. What are the odds?

I bought one and, you guessed it, that went into the singing bowl too! When my bowl was filled up and my pockets were empty, I glanced into the singing bowl. Just looking at my emerald, tuning forks, essential oils, and green scarf, I felt this amazing energy and was hit with a lightning bolt of clarity; I want to be a sound therapist! I want everyone to feel how I did in that moment! I want to write prescriptions for music, color, essential oils, and gemstones! I want everyone to know there's an alternative to prescription drugs out there, especially for depression. Sound therapy has no side effects. Oh wait, yes it does, let me clarify that.

Sound therapy has a major side effect and that is; happiness! Holding my Himalayan singing bowl with its magical contents made me feel like some sort of superhero who had just discovered her powers and been given her cape, magic amulets, and her mission. My journey as a sound therapist began that day. My mission: happiness, rejuvenation, and connection through sound therapy. Within a week I got my dream office, enrolled in a three-year sound therapy program, and purchased an acoustic sound table and frequency test equipment.

I thought getting the equipment was going to be the high point of it all, but it was the teachings that followed and the endless journey into the depths of this amazing field that keeps me so riveted, excited, and passionate about each day ahead. Over the first three years, I learned about sacred geometry, color therapy, light therapy, tuning forks, singing bowls, toning, humming, and drumming. With each class I grew more and more excited. All I kept thinking and wondering was how had I gone so long without knowing this whole field existed? How had I not known that everything is frequency and that we're all electrical, light, and magnetic beings? Life changing for me!

One moment I will never forget was when my teacher, Vicki Dodds, came out and said: "Of all the tools in your sound healing tool box, your voice is the most important. You can use it to heal others and you can use it to heal yourself." My first thought: "My voice is more likely to make someone sick!" My second thought: "Couldn't someone have told me that before I spent a fortune on sound therapy equipment!" Vicki taught me otherwise and explained that our voices are the exact frequency our bodies need to heal, so we should sing and hum as often as we can! Have you ever noticed how happy people are who hum? When was the last time you saw a grumpy, humming person? So, yes, humming is one of the most healing things you can do for your body.

Everyday since, I have new respect and appreciation for my voice, for humming, and for how it can heal and harmonize you as good as, or even better than, some of the most expensive high tech equipment out there. I can't speak enough of all the fun and exciting ways to incorporate sound into your life.

I am going to leave you with a fun, yet life changing fact from Jonathan Goldman: "Vibration + Intention = Manifestation". Think about that, and try it! It's a very important part of the whole manifestation puzzle showing again the importance of sound and vibration.

Since I have been consciously working on tuning my frequency and learning to love my voice (something that, up until recently, I used to be embarrassed by), the most amazing people and opportunities have been drawn into my life.

I now host my own podcast *Suezee's Happiness Hive* and have been invited to host a live show with the same name every Sunday morning on the *WinWin Women Network.* I host in-person sound therapy retreats, virtual events, and just wrote my first book *The Blueprint of Happiness* and have been published in *Creations Magazine.*

The coolest thing about incorporating sound practices into my life is that it gives me an abundance of energy to fuel my mission as I help others (that's you!) to discover fun and exciting ways to bring the power of sound into your life to create the happy and vibrant life you deserve!

Every day is a new adventure, a new day to learn, and that's why I made it my mission to share everything I discover and bring people with me on this magical journey so that we can all grow together.

So, I invite you to come and join me on my exploration into the exciting, healing, and happy world of sound therapy and frequency medicine. I look forward to meeting you.

## SueZee Finley

SueZee Finley is on a mission. A mission to help people tap into their own healing abilities and enhance them with the power of sound. After battling Lupus and Sjogren's (two debilitating autoimmune disorders), sound therapy gave SueZee her happiness and vitality back and changed her life forever.

It has been an exciting, never-ending journey of learning and healing for SueZee. As she learns, she shares her experiences in all different formats so that she can help as many people as possible.

SueZee is the owner of Acoustic Therapeutix, her private practice, where she does sound therapy. She hosts a weekly *Happiness & Sound Therapy* show on the *Win Win Women* network and she created and hosts SueZee's *Happiness Hive Podcast* where she interviews experts in sound therapy and frequency medecine.

She's been published in *Creations Magazine* and is the author of the book *The BluePrint of Happiness* which is her own unique system that combines sound therapy, frequency medicine, happiness mindset training, and art to give you a happy and vivacious life!

She also hosts sound therapy and happiness retreats in Woodstock NY. She continues to study and learn and has had the most amazing teachers; Vicki Dodds, Diana Domingo, Dr. John Beaulieu, David Gibson,

John Stuart Reid, Peter Blum, Richard Feather Anderson, and Randy Masters. Each one has their own amazing abilities and gifts that have influenced and inspired her.

She's grateful for this expansive field and the amazing people in it. SueZee wants to share every step of her journey and welcomes all that wish to join her.

**Contact SueZee Finley:**

- www.facebook.com/SueZ.Finley
- www.acoustictherapeutix.com
- www.linkedin.com/in/suezeefinley
- @suezeequest

# Lie Not?!

## By Myrna Flick

"She's lying." "You're lying." Sitting at the table with two team members, the tension grew as they glared at each other. I couldn't help but wonder what could have happened to bring them to this type of conflict. More about this later on. Why do people lie? After all, most people are honorable and well-meaning. Right? Not always. Most times people tell white lies, to not hurt the feelings of others. Other times we tell lies to make ourselves feel or look better, and to prevent conflict or avoid embarrassment. Social media and the news are continually uncovering blatant liars, whether it's a politician, a leader, or an influencer. What must our children think when they see people getting away with it? Do they think everyone lies? Who are they to trust and believe? Honesty is crucial. We need to be able to trust each other. Children need to see honest, trustworthy people. After all, they will grow up and become our future leaders.

Neuroscience research shows that the brain adapts to lying. Telling even small lies conditions our brains to tell bigger and bigger lies. Researchers studied the Amygdala, the part of the brain that deals with emotional responses. Sadly, as you lie more frequently, the Amygdala is tapped less and less. Our feelings of guilt about lying tend to weaken, causing us to feel okay bending the truth. What a scary thought for society! Research points out that we don't like thinking of ourselves as liars. It chips away at our self-esteem and self-worth. Lying has been a part of society since the dawn of time. The term, prosocial lying, describes lies used when one wants to prevent harm to another individual. It is commonly used to facilitate uncomfortable conversations, and to build and maintain relationships. It often occurs in the workplace, as managers seek to encourage growth in coaching situations, but must be used cautiously.

When commenting or providing feedback, it's so much easier to point out something that is going well. To promote growth, the person needs to hear about the areas to improve. The sandwich technique can work. First state a positive accomplishment, then an area to improve upon, ending with encouragement and appreciation. At home, you seek to calm fears and prevent your children from worrying, so you tell age-appropriate truths. Children are exposed to prosocial lying at a young age as we seek to instill politeness. When grandma asks, "How do I look?" You don't want your children to blurt out, "You look fat in that dress." You want them to comment on something nice that won't hurt their feelings.

To maintain our authenticity and preserve our mental health, it's important to look at the intention and size of the lie. There is a line between showing empathy and compassion vs. harmful, selfish lying. Consider your words and ensure the lie benefits the other person. If not, and you benefit more, it's best to tell the truth. Think of the fallout when you are found out. Think of the quote by Mark Twain, "If you tell the truth, you don't have to remember anything." A good friend, Debbie, and I recently exchanged Christmas gifts. With excitement, I opened the bag and removed the tissue paper. It was a wall decoration with frayed dish towels. Even with its beautiful wooden adornment, it sparked a bad memory from my childhood. At the time, I graciously accepted it.

However, I decided to return the gift. At our next outing, I explained the old memories of how my grandmother, when she was upset with us kids, would wind a towel up and snap it at us as punishment. I thanked my friend for her thoughtfulness and said how she should give it to someone who could genuinely appreciate it. She said she was grateful and happy that I was honest and returned it instead of giving it away or hiding the truth.

Since I didn't want to hurt her feelings, I was nervous. In the end, we talked about how we will always be completely honest with each other. That day, we both felt our friendship and trust in each other deepen. There are several ways to help prevent and limit lying. Just as in the workplace, where you have a code of conduct, you can establish guidelines at home for your family or with your partner. Our goal as parents, mentors, and educators is to create an environment where children don't feel the need to lie.

Several resources state the main reason that children lie is to avoid punishment or shame. Other reasons are the ***ABCs of Why Children Lie:***

1. Attention seeking
2. Bragging
3. Covering-up
4. Don't want to hurt the other person and are being polite
5. Exploring what they can get away with
6. Fantasizing about the situation
7. Guarding or protecting themselves or others

What are we to do? One of the greatest legacies you can leave is modeling and mentoring positive life skills. Utilize the ***ABCs of Handling Lying:***

- Acknowledge the issue
- Build the relationship
- Communicate with empathy
- Discuss to resolve
- Empower them and teach emotional intelligence

Children can be taught about telling the truth at an early age. Would you rather influence a child to seek out the right thing? Or do you prefer one who does what is considered right only to avoid trouble? Choose as a parent or mentor the extent to which you will involve punishment and consequences. Research shows that punishment will erode the relationship if too severe and not understood.

To encourage honesty, here's a simple framework to follow:

1/ Set rules, promises, and commitments.
Define them together whenever possible. Print a poster or photo of them. Explain that in sports and games, there are rules and proper ways to achieve victory. Talk about your expectations.

Examples of family rules. *In Our Home We*:

1. Treat each other and our property with respect
2. Always tell the truth
3. Clean up our messes
4. Knock on closed doors before entering
5. Openly share our thoughts and feelings without judgment
6. Follow schedules, including electronics
7. Take care of our bodies

2/ Role model honesty.
Others need to see you being honest even in difficult times. Parents are often the child's first and most important life model. To build trust is to honor our word and not lie. When overheard lying to others, parents unintentionally encourage their children to lie. If you get caught lying to them, continually let them down, or don't keep your word, they will likely do the same.

3/ Reward honesty.
Encourage honesty whenever possible—don't punish them for coming forward with their feelings. When you catch someone lying, don't get

overly angry or overreact. Being calm, patient, and persistent will keep you focused on resolving the issue. If you catch someone lying, try not to be too critical or harsh in punishment. They need to know a single lie doesn't break your trust forever. For some of the rules and severe situations, you will want to set appropriate consequences.

Research points out that children lie or withhold not only because they think they may get punished, but because they want to avoid a long lecture. Unfortunately for them, research shows that lectures work, but only when trust is established. Trust doesn't come from just lecturing, but it is nurtured through open communication. Lying in the workplace can erode a team and even damage the entire company, so honesty is crucial to success. When it starts to appear, those who can be trusted and relied upon will emerge, and those the team doesn't trust will soon be avoided and isolated.

At the extreme spectrum it's important to acknowledge that there are pathological liars who are stuck in a pattern of habitual lying. Something has happened in their lives that wounded them, and they haven't gotten help to resolve those feelings. When you encounter this, show compassion. Recognize your ability to interact, but seek to protect yourself. So how did I resolve the two employees bickering? Having spent over thirty years in leadership and human resource positions, I've encountered numerous conflicts. In this situation, I reassured them that together we would find a resolution. Allowing each person to email me an account with dates, times, and a list of the individuals involved gave them a chance to gain clarity.

Upon confirming the accuracy, I was able to determine who had initially come up with the idea they argued about. After first talking with the one who lied, together we crafted a plan and conversation to have with the team. The team met to discuss how we would move forward. When the meeting ended, several employees stated it was difficult, but they felt the team had grown and would be more open and effective. Some lies may not just hurt, they can haunt us. If there is an incident you recall, simply tell yourself, "I didn't know what I know now. I've grown, and I won't make that mistake again." The best thing is to forgive yourself and release it.

As you master honesty, it's much easier to mentor your teams and children. When you can be trusted and believed, others will want to build a relationship with you. Commit to a day of complete honesty. If you catch yourself starting a white lie, stop, and don't say it. Look for the positive in the situation and stay focused on that. We can all help to create value-driven future leaders. To keep your kids from lying, teach them as young as possible your thoughts about honesty and lying. Remember that repeated conversations (aka lecturing) actually work. Ask questions, and in necessary situations implement consequences or punishment. So, ultimately, we must ask... is it ever okay to lie? Completely avoiding lying may seem difficult, as it has become commonplace to allow mistruths. Because of technology and social media, lying gets easier, more prevalent, more public, and sometimes more complicated. There will be lies you cannot stop. Accept that white lies are bound to happen. Lying can be acceptable for safety reasons, protecting yourself, others, or securing confidential and important information. We all know it's difficult to admit to lying. Knowing that lies can destroy relationships will help us understand the importance of insisting on the truth. Whether it's difficult or not, it's beneficial and a requirement for growth.

Realizing that we want the best life possible for everyone, it's important to stay focused on telling the truth. So why not tell the truth immediately with honorable intention? Lie not.

## Myrna Flick

Myrna Fay Flick spent over thirty years in human resources and leadership positions, coaching, and training employees. She found not everyone grew up with strong role models, and key values such as honesty, integrity, kindness, and compassion.

With that in mind, she formed The Mind Heroes, LLC, and wrote the *Discovering the Difference* book series to help children... our future leaders. Book one, *Being Silly, Not a Bully,* helps children learn valuable life skills about kindness, diversity, cultural differences, and inclusion. Book two, *Being Proud, Not Loud,* shows children the difference between being proud and bragging.

Myrna held several leadership positions, including:

- VP of Training and Workplace Communications
- VP of Human Resources for a $100 million subsidiary of a $1 billion corporation
- President of a technology company
- Chief Services Officer for a large satellite TV master system operator

Myrna was an associate producer of the movie *Three Feet from Gold*, an interview with transformational leaders. The Napoleon Hill Foundation commissioned the work and is best known for the book *Think and Grow Rich.*

Myrna is a Certified Family Coach with ACPI; Senior Professional in Human Resources/SPHR with HRCI; Senior Certified Professional/SHRM-SCP with SHRM.

Connect with her at www.myrnafayflick.com and on Facebook, Instagram, LinkedIn, and Twitter.

**Contact Myrna Flick:**

www.myrnafayflick.com

www.LinkedIn.com/in/myrna-flick

@myrnafayflick

www.facebook.com/themindheroes

# The Sustainable Foodie

## By Nicole Frith

My journey towards Food Sustainability started about fifteen years ago. At the time, I owned an internationally recognized gourmet food retail store. I was dealing with regular media from around the world, film crews, magazine write-ups, and TV and radio interviews about my unique store and its contents. Within the store I had a delicatessen, back of house kitchen, butchery, cheese and wine section, local and international selection of food, and a gourmet food catering business as well as running cooking school classes on premises. I was already passionate about supporting locally produced food and ingredients with an emphasis on sustainability and my store reflected this. My background had been in the French wine industry so I stocked some beautiful French wine along with some exceptional Tasmanian wines.

My life was busy, full and fun, all until chronic fatigue. I was allergic to everything I ate and I couldn't drink a drop of alcohol. My world had blown up. Or, more accurately, it had imploded. It's challenging for me to talk about this period of my life as I still feel like there's healing to be done, but here we go. I ended up with an extremely severe case of chronic fatigue which lasted for about five years. My food allergies were so immense, I could barely walk because my muscles became so atrophied. Going from my bed to the toilet was about as much as I could manage. None of my organs were working properly, I had heart palpitations, severe brain fog, nervous system issues, and major digestive issues which lead to malnutrition. I lost 20 kg and was housebound. I could barely talk and my parents had to look after me. I felt like a pair of eyes.

Here I was, a food and wine expert who couldn't drink a drop and whose diet was limited to a few steamed vegetables and boiled chicken. I'd always loved engaging with people, I loved diversity and connecting with the thousands of customers who came through my doors, and some close to me may say that I didn't mind the odd party (or two!). I loved being outdoors, going for long walks connecting with the environment, and climbing mountains to breathe in the fresh air. I was now housebound and could barely walk or talk. All the things I loved in my life were no longer there. I'd lost my business, my marriage and my much-loved grandmother. Who was I? What was I? I could see the fear in my family's eyes... Would she ever recover? I felt that fear too, constantly. Every. Living. Breathing. Moment.

Modern medicine offered me very little so I turned to alternative options. I researched as much as I could and went on my journey of self-healing, using as many modalities as I could. During this time, I felt like a chrysalis, learning a new way of Being and Transforming. I developed a greater appreciation for the simplest things in life–the sunshine on my face, a flower in the garden, and the beautiful simplicity of a single fresh, organic vegetable! My perspective had shifted. Simple was beautiful and I was really tasting the purity of a single ingredient. Part of my healing was simple, fresh, organic food and the nutrients they contained. It was also a time for contemplation and as I started to heal (emotionally, energetically, physically), I started to ask myself some questions. I cared so passionately about the environment, so how could I be of service? How could I address climate change issues?

I'd always been an advocate for local, organic and sustainable produce but the ramifications of the alternative, industrialized food production, hadn't really sunk in. It was more subconscious, like knowing that it wasn't good but not understanding quite why. When you look at the facts and figures in more detail however, it's really quite terrifying. The appreciation of local, sustainable and organically grown produce to heal not only me but the wider collective of the ecosystem, the environment, the planet. This was it! I'd found my true purpose in life. This leads me to the subject I'm most passionate about and is my life's purpose: Food Sustainability! This refers to food grown in a sustainable and environmentally friendly way rather than food grown using industrial food production processes.

The industrialisation of food has a huge and vastly negative impact on the environment. There is a huge amount of waste created by the industry, largely driven by big supermarket chains demanding perfect, spot-free fruit and veg with a long shelf life. Because they are mass buyers, they have the farmers at their mercy and can essentially dictate the price they want to pay, driving down the profit margins for the farmers. It's a vicious cycle as the farmers then, trying to make a living, seek out the cheapest options for growing fruit and veg which consists of using pesticides and chemical sprays in the attempt to reduce crop loss due to pests. The pressure placed on the farmers by the large supermarket chains also leads to farmers breeding crops for one quality only–to have a long shelf life.

This results in loss of flavor and nutrient value, and it's also a false economy. The sprays and pesticides used destroy the soil microbiome and the natural ecosystem which leads to poorer quality fruit and veg prone to more disease. The naturally beneficial insects have been wiped out which leaves the crops even more vulnerable and exposed to pests and disease, and the cycle continues. More sprays, weaker vegetables, and poorer soil quality. This is just the tip of the iceberg though. The food waste that is produced from crops that are discarded upon harvesting is massive. Huge piles of perfectly good fruit and veg that don't even make it to distribution because of a minor 'spot' or imperfection, like a carrot with a bump on it, or two legs.

Then, after the aesthetically perfect (but flavorless) fruit and veg make it to the supermarket chains, there's the huge amount that's discarded after its Best Before Date. Once again, that expectation of perfection is the cause of so much waste. On top of that, when the produce does make it home to our refrigerators, there's always something that gets forgotten in the back of the fridge and therefore adds to the potential for more waste.

Here's a staggering figure: If food waste was a country, it would be the third largest producer of greenhouse gasses in the world! Here's another–one third of all the food produced globally never gets eaten.

When I heard this, I thought: "Wow!" This is such a massive problem that's so easily fixed. We don't have to be supporting these businesses with their extensive waste problems. We as consumers have the power to change this! What if most of us bought local, sustainably produced food, or even, grew our own? The environmental impact would be huge! Less waste, less chemicals in the environment leaching into the ground and waterways, healthier bio-diverse ecosystems, and better health for all of us!

It's really quite simple. It's all about the food choices we make daily. Not all of us have the luxury of choosing where we buy our food and how much we pay for it, but for those of us who can, I encourage you to pay those few extra cents or dollars to give back to the soil, the farmers and the environment. Also, what if we as small communities all around the world took growing into our own hands? Community gardens, swapping produce with our neighbors and friends, supporting local farmers markets, organic food retail stores in our area, permaculture businesses, local growers and producers, even urban foraging.

My mission is to encourage everyone from around the globe to grow their own food. It can be anything from growing a few herbs to planting out a whole veggie garden. A lot of us live in apartments or have no access to soil. I have some great foods you can grow, some even soil-free! For those of us who are time poor, I have some great tips and hacks. For those of us who have access to a bit of soil and a bit of spare time, well, the possibilities are endless!

I also think it's important to mention that for those of us who enjoy the beautiful aesthetic of ornamental gardens, there is no need to fear. Edible gardens can be just as beautiful, spectacular, and whimsical as ornamental ones. I have a huge amount of edible flowers in my garden including roses and peonies as well as chamomile, cornflowers, calendula, violets, lavender, elderflowers and borage flowers, and there's many more to choose from. I also believe that when we take the time and energy to grow our own food, we value it more, which also equates to less waste. Fresh apricots off our tree generally end up in my family's tummies pretty quickly as opposed to sitting in the back of the fridge going stale.

Even just being outside with your hands in the soil is so healing and it's definitely contributed to my recovery. Even when I couldn't do anything, just sitting on the ground breathing in the fresh air, I found it so healing and energizing. I'm now an avid gardener and have found so much satisfaction from growing my own produce–tomatoes, zucchinis, pumpkins, edible flowers, lettuces and a huge array of herbs just to name a few. Life can be busy and I've found that if ever I'm feeling a little ungrounded, I just go out and pick some herbs from the garden and make a tea. It reconnects me back to my sense of place.

I believe by eating food that's grown in the land around you, you're resonating with the energy of your environment. The vibration of the food you eat ultimately has an effect on your own vibrational frequency. I also believe that when you eat food from the land that surrounds you, whether it be from your own garden or locally grown, that land becomes more meaningful to you. You value and respect it. Indigenous cultures have always had this connection to the land and we need to regain that connection as a collective.

If any of this resonates with you and you'd like to assist with eating our way to a cleaner, greener planet, please sign up to my website newsletter for more information and visit my online store. Let's change the world, one mouthful at a time!

## Nicole Frith

Nicole Frith is a leading expert in food sustainability. Interviewed for her expertise in this area by numerous media corporations including: ABC Australia (The Australian Broadcasting Corporation) for both TV and radio, *Brilliance Business TV*, *Gourmet Magazine* (Times Square, New York), *Country Style Magazine* (Australia), and many more.

She is the producer and host of the podcast *The Sustainable Foodie* and is currently creating a TV series that will introduce you to some of the world's most talented and sustainable chefs and food producers, inspiring us to eat our way to a cleaner and greener planet.

She's owned and run an internationally renowned food business promoting local and sustainably produced food to thousands of customers, and helped small producers build and promote their brand using her connections to food media such as *Gourmet Traveler* magazine, TV, and radio.

She's a sustainable food coach incorporating her energetic and intuitive training of over ten years with her practical knowledge of how to live more sustainably.

She's worked with celebrity chefs such as Shannon Bennett (of *Master Chef* fame) and Kirsten Tibbles (from *The Chocolate Queen* series)

Nicole's message is clear "Food is a part of everyone's life and the choices we make around what we eat can have a huge impact on the planet.

I want to encourage, inspire and educated people so that they can make informed decisions and eat cleaner, greener and more sustainably, not only for our own health but for the health of the planet"

**Contact Nicole Frith:**

- www.nicolefrith.com.au
- @thesustainablefoodieofficial

# I Am the Baseline

## By Liah O. Goldenberg

The journey of building your own business is fantastic. With the bravery to follow your dreams, you leap into unknown territory. You give physical form to what were previously bright, beautiful thoughts. You breathe the essence of your vision into the company and support it in growing. Yet how do you architect your business into being a source of energy, inspiration, and fulfillment, rather than allowing your creation to imperceptibly push its needs to the forefront, with your needs becoming buried underneath? How do you ensure that the company you have founded does not subtly evolve into a sweet monster that drains your life energy?

The key is to be honest about the price you pay for not serving your needs on the entrepreneurial journey. Finding your path to inner and outer authenticity gives you the gift of inner balance. My entrepreneurial journey began with my unwillingness to accept the idea that there are seemingly irreconcilable opposites, which leave me with only one option: choose one side or the other.

I felt committed to replacing the misconception of lawyers being a necessary evil with a new idea of lawyers being a valuable part of the client's success team. I wanted to create a different concept of the lawyer-client relationship as being one between human beings who care and where the individuals on both sides feel seen, valued, and understood. Though being in a profession that seems callous and harsh, I wanted to create a working environment where every individual finds a safe place to be able to develop in every aspect and facet of their being. In a profession characterized by fight or defeat, I wanted to prove that it is possible to have a team of top performers that draws its motivation and strength from mutual support, not from the competition.

Amid a professional lifestyle that seems inherently stressful and unforgiving, I wanted to create a place where you go not just because you want to earn a living, but because you create value and thereby have a great time, with like-minded people. And I was convinced that it must be possible to achieve great commercial success, even though the industry I am entering has been oversaturated for years. There were no blueprints, no examples of successful law firms where the employees were truly happy and satisfied.

Instead, the deeper I dug in my search, the more it became apparent to me that there seemed to be another rule that nobody was questioning: Being a successful lawyer comes with the price of accepting that you do not have a life outside work, that the answer to all demands of your profession is to put in even more hours, that you have to accept a broad range of stress-based diseases, even if you are in your twenties or thirties. Realizing this, I fell even more in love with my bold ambition to whip the legal industry into a better-feeling shape. So, I quit my safe job in a law firm, gathered the few thousand euros that I had saved while still paying back my college debt, and founded my own firm from scratch.

The firm began to flourish quickly, and my team grew. The success was breathtaking, and my experiences exceeded my expectations. But there was something that I felt strange about. A feeling grew inside that something was wrong. Looking at it from the outside, our beautiful office space, the growing numbers of clients and revenue, everything was more than just fine. Only it did not feel to me the way it should have, the way you would expect such success is supposed to feel. It felt as if there were sand in the gears somewhere. Although we put all our heart into making our clients' projects a success, there were still clients who expressed dissatisfaction. Though we always went the extra mile for our clients, making every effort to find an even better solution, to deliver real value, there were still clients who complained about the prices and blackmailed us into giving them more and more discounts.

Though I implemented every idea I had to make the workplace as stylish and comfortable as possible, to create an open culture of appreciation, and always to be sensitive to the individual needs of the employees, there were still dissatisfied employees, employees who concealed mistakes, who took advantage of me and the company, who betrayed the company. I began searching for the sand that was crippling the gears. I have read hundreds of business development, mindset, and leadership books. I attended countless courses and seminars, and implemented a myriad of great systems and tools in my business that I learned there.

But the only thing that changed perceptibly was my health and mental condition. It exhausted me to wake up every morning with worries, despair, and negative thoughts. To escape it, to finally find solutions, I went deeper and deeper down the rabbit hole of more reading, more learning, and more attempts to change the systems in the company. The days were getting longer and longer; the weekends had long ceased to be a time for rest. I remember one rainy evening when I called my mother and shared my despair. "I have followed every tip and tried to implement every system that came my way. Nothing seems to work; there is always just a little piece of progress, no breakthrough, nothing lasting. I do not know what to do anymore. Maybe my vision was too big, too unrealistic?"

Waking up the next morning, I observed my thoughts for a while. There was nothing beautiful, nothing hopeful. I felt that I was deeply tired of fighting my way through the day with such thoughts in my head. I packed a few things and booked a quiet hotel in the mountains, a tiny hideaway surrounded by lush nature and fresh air, without any mobile phone or internet connection.

Arriving there, I asked myself one single question: What is the price I pay for my success? The moment I was brave enough to take a clear look at the price tag of my success, frankly, I was shocked. Constant sleep deprivation, poor personal relationships, a persistent feeling of guilt about all the things that were not yet done on my to-do list, evenings, nights, and weekends spent working, the ever-present inner restlessness, and the feeling of never having my needs met.

At that moment, I understood something that changed not only my entrepreneurial self-image but my whole life: There is a significant lack of balance between my outward and my inward focus. I realized that despite all my efforts in making the company a better place for the clients and employees, I, myself, was still the lawyer that is callous and harsh, in constant fight mode and unforgiving, though not towards the outside world, but towards myself.

I was still someone who accepted not having a life outside of work. Someone whose answer to all the demands of the firm, the clients, or employees was to work more hours. Someone who accepted stress-based diseases as part of the game. Even financially, I had demoted myself to the very last spot. I reinvested every cent I earned in the company, in nice comfortable furniture for the employees, the newest and best technology, and the most up-to-date legal tech tools for the clients. I considered it natural and normal to allow myself the crumbs left over once the cake was shared.

I realized that I had misunderstood the concept of serving. I had confused it with self-sacrifice. By disrespecting my personal needs, by not valuing and taking care of myself, I was embodying the very opposite of what I simultaneously tried to establish as the company's vision. As a result, I was broadcasting contradictory energies that spread throughout the company, which everyone consciously or unconsciously sensed as being inauthentic. I had found the sand in the gears. I aimed to create a perfect environment for my clients and employees. **But I forgot that I am part of the system.**

The growth journey that followed these realizations was profound and genuinely transformative. For the first time in my life, I have been thoroughly enjoying the whole process of learning and growing. It felt right, and it felt like pure fun. It felt like this was the missing link I had always been looking for in my life.

I understood that I have meticulously learned how to function perfectly in this world, but I never learned how to take care of myself. I began to focus inwards. I made myself the starting point for comparisons as to whether decisions are aligned with the company's vision. I began to pay attention to treating myself the way I have dedicated myself to treating my clients and employees. I learned that I am the baseline.

The rewards were enormous. The employees were happier and more relaxed, we received more and more words of appreciation from our clients, the law firm's revenues went up, the company began attracting even more outstanding people, and the whole atmosphere developed into something extraordinary.

All the beautiful words describing my vision for the firm became finally shaped into reality. As an entrepreneur, you are crucial to your company. You are the visionary, the driving force behind your company, and every single product and service. You are the essential element in aligning the company's systems with its vision. It is vital for your company that you feel good.

Compare all the unique gifts you give to others with what you allow yourself to receive. Even if self-sacrifice seems noble at first glance, and even if there are enough people who have taught us, and still do today, that altruism characterizes a truly good person, it is not true. There is not enough action in the world that can be taken to remove the sand from the system that is spread through the imbalance between your vision and your very personal alignment with it towards yourself. No amount of success can ever reward you for exhaustion, deep sadness, and loneliness.

Consider what your personal price for your success is. You can have the right mindset, you can make all kinds of helpful systems work in your company, and you can be successful. But if doing so comes along with a constant state of anxiety, pressure, and sacrifices, this is choosing the hard way. And it does not have to be this hard. When you find ways to serve yourself and start measuring everything from the perspective of your inner balance, magic starts to happen. Not only do you feel happy and fulfilled, but at this point, your business success quickly begins growing into dimensions far beyond what you ever thought was possible.

Do not follow the fallacies that claim "profound change takes time," "you are who you are," or "either you succeed, or you have fun." Whatever you discover in yourself that does not serve you well, know that change is possible. Even more, it can happen in a brief period of time. Seek the tools that help you make changes easily, quickly, and sustainably. Your business will always grow as you grow.

There is nothing you cannot be or achieve. There are no opposites that cannot be balanced. Remember: **You are the Baseline.**

## Liah O. Goldenberg

Questioning the status quo in the legal industry inspired Liah's vision to create a space of value and care, with the bold ambition of making the legal industry a better-feeling place. This vision was the basis for founding the now flourishing law firm, LEGE ARTIS IP.

LEGE ARTIS IP is specifically focused on innovative, disruptive start-ups that are dedicated to making our planet a more beautiful, comfortable, and sustainable place through their ideas.

Liah and her team support these companies by registering their brands and product designs in more than 140 countries across all continents, and by developing brand development strategies according to each client's unique vision.

The second area of expertise of the firm is in contracts in the field of research and innovation. Liah guides her clients through contract negotiations with international companies and research organizations, as well as through the processes of research project funding. In recent years alone, over fifteen hundred contracts with project values of several hundred million euros have been successfully negotiated.

She particularly appreciates the fact that each of the R&D projects has contributed to making the world a brighter and more innovative place.

Inspired by her personal journey to transformation and inner balance, Liah has followed her second dream of inspiring entrepreneurs by sharing the lessons of her journey, which resulted in a company today operating under the brand IAMGOLD.

Liah's mission is to share the most effective, easiest, and fastest tools she has gathered on her journey that enable aligning the needs of businesses with the needs of their founders.

The focus of IAMGOLD is to share ways for business owners to balance business success with inner peace and harmony, transform non-well-serving beliefs and step out of the hustle loop, without sacrificing business success.

**Contact Liah O. Goldenberg:**

- www.artip.law
- www.iamgold.world
- @lege.artis.ip
- @i.a.m.gold

# Looking For the Light: Finding The Light Can Lead to True Healing

## By Sarah Preston Hesler

What does it mean to truly heal on all levels and to identify the root cause of sickness, disease, pain and trauma? My own journey through health struggles and trauma have helped me to better understand my patient's experiences, and to help them to experience true healing. When I was quite young, I was vibrant and full of life. My grandfather said I was "a little ray of sunshine" when I was born and each day of my childhood, I saw light and love all around me. The colors were so bright and I delighted in exploring my world, making up games, learning how things worked and making others laugh. Each moment was better than the last.

In high school, I was diagnosed with a severe case of mononucleosis that kept me out of school for over two weeks and almost landed me in the hospital. I remember being incredibly fatigued and even after I returned to school (part-time at first), I could not sleep enough. Where once I had seen vibrant color around me, everything was less vibrant and much less captivating. It was difficult to focus, I no longer cared about spending time with my friends or about after school activities, I just wanted to take a nap every day after school. My parents took me to our family doctor and she diagnosed me with an autoimmune condition (which I now know was likely kick-started by the mono) and depression.

I began taking medications, which helped, but I was always cold, tired and mostly apathetic. The richness, vibrancy and joy of life that I basked in as a child was mostly gone and looking back at this time now, it's foggy. In college, I was on the pre-medtrack and I was still much more fatigued than others around me. I spent a lot of my free time sleeping and would joke that naps were my favorite activity. I experienced a sexual assault during this time and experienced PTSD with worsening depression and anxiety. Roughly one week after I graduated from college, I started Naturopathic Medical School in a new city. It was here that I met my husband and learned how to help others to truly heal on all levels.

Ironically, in my professional life, I help my patients learn to live a more balanced life, but going through Naturopathic Medical School is anything but balanced. There is no time for this because it is the rough equivalent of three full-time jobs. This incredibly stressful journey took everything I had just to get through it, though I learned more about the relationship between the mono diagnosis and the autoimmune disease. I made some progress in my own healing in some ways, but the experience of going through school compromised my health even more. It took roughly two years post-graduation before I began to feel more like myself again, but the little girl who saw light and love everywhere I looked was still far away.

After my husband and I had been married for about five years we decided to start trying to have a family. We got pregnant quickly but our first ultrasound didn't show a heartbeat and we had our first miscarriage a few days later. Lying on the bathroom floor with our faithful dog by my side, I rode the waves of pain and blood as my body processed the loss. I immediately became obsessed with getting pregnant again. I worked again and worked with fertility specialists, acupuncturists and naturopathic physicians, but unfortunately, we went on to have two more losses. I felt numb and depressed most of the time during this period of my life and the world was even darker, mostly shades of gray. I remember the day when Beth (name changed for privacy) walked into my office for the first time. She could hardly get out of bed, she was 40 pounds overweight, her blood sugar levels would spike and then they would crash, she had polycystic ovarian syndrome (PCOS), PMS and her periods were irregular and painful.

She was depressed and anxious. She and her partner longed to have a family, family and despite trying for two years, years they had not become pregnant. She had seen fertility specialists with several rounds of IUI and IVF without success. Her thyroid labs were normal, but suboptimal, and her progesterone was lower than it should have been. We began to work on balancing her hormones, menstrual cycles and blood sugar. I asked her to eat a whole foods diet, and she began to move her body, meditate and journal every day. She began to lose weight and her depression and anxiety began to lift. Each day she would imagine filling her womb with pure light and she would envision holding her baby in her arms.

She came to see me every two weeks for acupuncture treatments and each session she released more fear and self-doubt, and she began to believe in her body and to trust that her dream of becoming a mother would come true. One day she called me with the exciting news that she was pregnant and we had a joyful cry together. Now she and her husband are living their dream of raising a beautiful little boy.

Even after more than thirteen years in practice as of this writing, it never gets old to experience the thrill of watching my patients achieve true healing on all levels: physical, mental, emotional and spiritual. Now that I have healed from my experiences, the colors are vivid and vibrant again.

I have a better understanding of what my patients are going through and how they need to be supported. I have sat with many friends and patients through the trauma of their sexual assaults, pregnancy losses and infertility, and have helped them to find true healing. When we finally heal from sickness and trauma, we can realize our purpose on this earth and we can start showing others how to do the same.

Those who have been through the lessons can reach back to help those who are walking through the darkness and help them to find the light again. My journey to become a physician led me to my passion for humanitarianism and teaching.

I am a co-founder of the charity, Naturopaths Without Borders, and have been providing free integrative medical care here in the US and abroad, for over sixteen years. We hold clinics in some of the most underserved regions on earth where many patients eat once a day and might only make $1-2 USD/day. We recruit volunteers to expand our capacity and continue to train community health workers to serve their local communities.

I have found great delight in teaching the next generation of providers what it means to really walk alongside their patients as they heal from their pain and trauma and to utilize the most efficacious techniques and therapies medicine has to offer.

For many years, I threw myself into my work, dedicating every ounce of my energy to helping those in need. I saw the worst of humanity–war, malnutrition, disease–and felt a deep sense of responsibility to make a difference. Wearing all of the hats that I wear became particularly challenging to balance self-care when it is my job to care for others. As time went on, I realized that I couldn't keep up the pace.

I was exhausted on every level and no amount of coffee could keep me going. That's when I realized that I needed to focus on self-care if I was going to continue to make a difference. Every parent, caregiver, teacher and healthcare worker can relate to this first hand. It's important to remember that there will be periods in our lives where it is more challenging to find balance between care for ourselves, ourselves and care for others. It can be helpful to zoom out a bit and see that this is just a period of time and that it will not be like this forever. Seeking support and ensuring you are doing what you can to meet your basic needs during times like this is crucial.

When the opportunity to contribute to this book came up, I was hesitant to say yes because I didn't feel like I had arrived at the end point of being perfectly balanced, never burned out and always steadfast with my boundaries. When I meditated about it a bit more, I realized that none of us is at the end point just yet (if ever), and if my experience so far can help someone else on their journey, then this is all worth it, and I have succeeded.

In thinking back over the years and how I have consistently recovered from pain, trauma and sickness and that each time I wanted to give up, I have realized that when I am able to remain consistently detached from needing to be perfect and I implement radical self-care, that is when I am at my best.

No matter what is going on, no matter how much I have failed or how many tasks are still on my to-do list from the day before, I try to look at each new day as an opportunity to start over again, to try again and to continuously hone my skills and abilities to continually improve and get closer to my goals.

If I become too attached to the outcome, I can experience analysis paralysis and essentially stay in the same place. If I am unable to remain consistent, I can fall off the wagon and may not get back up for several weeks or months. However, when I let go of the ropes and trust myself and the universe, I know that as long as I keep going, I am making progress.

If I fail, I can start again tomorrow. This is my story of how I have learned to heal myself while teaching others to do the same, and each day, I know I am moving closer and closer to my goal of helping 100 million people to heal mentally, emotionally, physically and spiritually.

I hope my story inspires you to begin your journey to true healing, so that you can fully experience the beauty, love and light that is all around us.

## Sarah Preston Hesler

Sarah Preston Hesler, NMD is an award-winning expert in the regenerative medicine field, is an author, business owner, humanitarian and internationally recognized trainer, instructor and speaker. She has helped tens of thousands of patients to lead healthier, happier lives and has trained thousands of students to provide practical, real-world tools they can use to help their patients.

She is a co-founder of the charity Naturopaths Without Borders where she served as the Director of Operations for over 10 years, and has raised hundreds of thousands of dollars to provide integrative care to underserved populations in the US, Mexico, Haiti, Thailand and India.

She is the co-owner of Phoenix Natural Family Medicine in Chandler, AZ and is passionate about helping her patients not only to heal but to achieve their optimal health using regenerative therapies.

She received her medical degree from the Sonoran University of Health Sciences (formerly Southwest College of Naturopathic Medicine), she is on faculty at AT Still University and is a co-founder and trainer with the Naturopathic Mastery Courses. She was the 2011 co-recipient of the Southwest College of Naturopathic Medicine Alumni Award for Community Service, the 2018 co-recipient of the American Association of Naturopathic Physicians' President's Award and the 2019 Impact LIVES' Abundance Award Recipient.

Dr. Preston Hesler believes in helping her patients to heal on all levels by finding the root cause of their concerns, that her role as a physician is to walk alongside her patients as they journey to better health.

Her life mission is to help 100 million people to heal mentally, emotionally, physically and spiritually.

Dr. Preston Hesler loves to listen to music, play the piano, sing, travel to new and exciting places, read, cook, practice meditation, exercise and spend time with her family. She and her husband have two well-loved dogs.

**Contact Sarah Preston Hesler:**

- @dr.sarahprestonhesler
- www.linkedin.com/in/drsarahprestonhesler
- www.facebook.com/drsarahprestonhesler
- www.phxnfm.com

# Conversations With Teeth

## By Dr. Kathrin Huzelmann

Once upon a time, there was a magic land where Dentistry was known as a healing art. Every single tooth was revered as a keeper of great wisdom. So when a tooth made it known that it had a message to impart—often in ways impossible to ignore — one would make a pilgrimage to the Dental Sanctuary to understand the message of the tooth in order to restore health on all levels of being. Happy tooth and happy human would leave the sanctuary with a restored mouth and radiant smile, feeling empowered and transformed in life. No, this is not some sort of fairy tale. This is my day-to-day reality for the patients who choose to see teeth for the magical things they are and are ready to embark on a journey of rebirth through the most powerful portal of transformation that I know: the mouth!

So, what are the stories your teeth have to tell? And why is their home in the mouth so powerful? Think about it. You take food in, you chew and transform it in the mouth, breaking it into micronutrients so the body can use and absorb them. It is the interface between the inner and outer world: you smile, kiss, and communicate. You merge emotions, thoughts, and breath in the mouth to speak your reality into existence. You sing the songs of your heart! It's a very, very powerful place of transformation from the outside in and the inside out. Imagine how life could be if your food were to come into your body through a clean, healthy and conscious environment, if the words that come out of the mouth were formed in a space free of trauma and filled with consciousness and light. The mouth holds a very special place for the power of your transformation—and it is the home for your teeth.

Teeth are the hardest structures in your body, like crystals. This crystal armor protects the precious insides: the blood supply and nerve connection, lymph flow and stem cells, which connect the tooth to every system in your body and allow for self-repair. Could the teeth be messengers of the soul as well as the body? The mouth is a precisely connected space. We know through traditional Chinese medicine that specific teeth are linked through meridians to specific organ systems, vertebrae, joints, and sensory organs of the body. As such, they also link to specific emotions, which bring specific messages. Knowing all this, I feel the mouth deserves to be treated like a temple, YOUR temple, in which you can be magnificently empowered. And to this temple, all my beloved clients come with different stories.

To give you an example, Lisa, a forty-four-year-old BBC producer with an impeccable mouth, wanted a second opinion on her only treated and painful tooth, which was her lower left first molar. It had been bothering her for four months, in which time it had broken several times, been fixed, then the nerve was removed and the tooth crowned. Still, it hurt. Her dentist recommended an extraction and implant. I explained to her that the Lung and Large intestine meridian ran through the tooth, and the connected emotion was grief and letting go. I had lovingly called it the "mother grief tooth." She burst into tears as she revealed that she had lost her mother four months before and had never fully allowed herself to grieve. She listened to the message of her tooth, finally grieved, and as if by a miracle, her tooth recovered and did not have to be removed.

Though I have known this forever, I am always newly astonished at just how precisely teeth communicate with us. Another patient, Katy, had a life-threatening infection in her lower left jaw which required several hospital visits, with no resolution. The surgeon, unsure of what was causing her recurring condition, booked her for another surgery. The message I received was, "I do not deserve this." She powerfully clenched her jaw on a regular basis and was deeply angry. I recommended that she see my dear friend Gosia Gorna (whom you might know from her best-selling book, *The Expansion Game*).

As Katy worked through her anger, hurt, and fear, the life-threatening infection in her jaw healed within days and she was able to cancel the surgery! After not speaking to her daughter in ten years, she subsequently healed the rift in her family. This shows how utterly important it is to release trauma before surgery. So, how exactly do we talk to your teeth? Have you ever considered talking to your teeth? No? Have you ever asked your heart what it needed when you felt heartbroken? Why not your teeth? They are living structures in your body, and to me, they are like family members all living in the same home.

First of all, I would like to invite you to close your eyes for a second and please relax your jaw! It does not need to be tight. I encourage you to place your awareness with your teeth and relax your jaw for the rest of this chapter (or for as long as you can). Ask your tongue to gently and lovingly say hello to your teeth, one tooth at a time, just like you would greet a long-lost lover, a hurt animal, or a scared child. After all this time, show them some love and appreciation, the basis for any kind of healing and transformation. If you asked what they needed (and I officially give you permission to do just that), what would they say? Sometimes they come in niggles or pain, sometimes teeth respond to specific or difficult situations. Sometimes people hear very clear messages and get instructions on precisely what to heal. I have collected my favorite transformational healing journeys of my patients and am in the process of publishing it as a collection of short stories called *Conversations With Teeth*. I feel certain this will be helpful and inspiring for your own journey with your teeth.

So, how did I get here? For those readers who associate dentistry with pain and fear, allow me to assure you I have felt both in spades. I was born with the rare condition of not having enamel on my teeth (amelogenesis imperfecta). For much of my youth, they were both very sensitive and ugly. I suffered tremendously at every dental visit and social encounter. I was unable to enjoy hot, cold, sour, and sweet foods. Sometimes, even breathing cold air was painful. And the silver fillings on my front teeth glittered every time I smiled, so I did not smile that much. Kissing was out of the question. Then, I embarked on a two-year healing journey and came out mercury-free, with a restored smile and bite, restored health and kissability. I confidently followed my heart, ditching my university studies in Intercultural Management, French, Russian, Economics and Law—to master and revolutionize Dentistry!

I decided to share the gift of life and transformation through dentistry with the world. Little did I know just how powerful this portal was, or how much transformation life had in store for me. I learned the trade and many other useful tools, and became a skilled craftswoman. I traveled the world and studied with all the medical people I could find: stem cell surgeons, integrative oncologists, professors of applied cellular medicine... as well as enlightened beings in India and Shamans in the Amazon and Mexico.

Outside the dental office, I gave healing treatments, and yoga and meditation lessons. I offered cacao and other ceremonies, and sang. Yet, I still failed to live up to my own expectations. I had NOT revolutionized Dentistry... But a tooth came to the rescue! On one occasion, I fractured my mother-grief tooth so badly that I nearly died of blood poisoning. I had to travel to Spain to have the tooth removed and a ceramic implant inserted. Though my mother is still alive, I had not learned to mother myself in a way that allowed me to dare to step out and really live what I came here to do. With the dead tooth removed, my system was clear again and I could easily make decisions to bring my life back into alignment with my true soul's purpose. I realized that having a conscious relationship with my teeth opened a portal to great spiritual, physical, and ancestral healing. It became clear that being in ceremony or performing a surgery or playing a symphony in an orchestra hold exactly the same energy: total focus and presence, while feeling connected to the divine. It fulfills my life purpose to be in service in this way and for that I am ever so grateful. This one little tooth powerfully led me to finally putting everything together: my love for surgery, singing, plants, medicine, cacao, ceremony, healing, NLP, Hypnosis, Mantra, blessings, intention, and much more. Four years later, I've put together a whole methodology that can help you to use holistic dental treatment to transform your whole life, and that any conscious dentist can learn and apply to transform the lives of patients.

It is the product of my mission to create awareness to reintegrate the mouth into the whole being. This will allow you to successfully walk through your teeth's hero's journey and physically heal much better and faster. At the heart of my system is high-quality biological dentistry, which is the removal of interference fields and triggers, and the subsequent rebuilding of your oral health, with materials that are in alignment with your system. My tools and resources guide you through every dental visit, allowing you to feel safe, grounded, in control, and clear to make good decisions that are in alignment with who you are.

The moment you start listening to the call of your teeth, an opportunity is created to release trauma and consciously reintegrate lost parts of you. Real healing takes place with the integration of all parts of your being, even the ones that have departed with lost teeth. Reintegration helps the whole being to realign. The regained clarity helps you to easily access your intuition and restructure your life where it feels out of balance. I have created a set of resources, tools, and meditations for patients, so you can do this yourself, and I offer bespoke guidance throughout your treatment. I'm also developing an online academy to teach practitioners in general to treat the whole person, and dentists specifically to consciously go through the process with their patients of integration and creation of wholeness.

The teeth don't know borders, or countries, or nationalities. They all speak the same language. They try to communicate with you and teach you what it is that you need to learn. If you are ready to embark on this magnificent healing journey, it starts on my website, www.conversationswithteeth.com. Download the free tooth love meditation and start cleaning your teeth every day with mindfulness, awareness, and joy! May you smile always, outside and in.

## Kathrin Huzelmann

Dr. Kathrin Huzelmann is a highly qualified and experienced holistic dentist with over twenty years of experience. She holds a degree in dentistry from the University of Hamburg and has a PhD in mouth cancer. She is also a licensed Cranial Sacral Therapist, yoga and meditation teacher, and NLP practitioner, and is currently studying to become a naturopathic doctor.

With her unique approach, Dr. Huzelmann has merged her toothy wisdom with her knowledge of the connections between the mouth and the rest of the body. Her understanding of the human condition to create a truly holistic approach to healing through the mouth has inspired and helped thousands of patients to lead a healthier and more aligned life.

Dr. Huzelmann is an international practitioner, having lived and worked in different countries. She is a member of ATL Europe and has been featured in podcasts and panel discussions. She has volunteered her healing services in the Andes and the Amazon, and co-presented at the Health Optimisation Summit 2019.

She is in the process of publishing her first book, *Conversations With Teeth*, and setting up an online academy to teach her approach to patients, practitioners, and dentists.

Her website (www.magicteeth.co.uk) hosts many resources for patients. She also offers a tailored service where she accompanies patients in a personalized way during their dental treatment.

Additionally, Kathrin is an accomplished organic chocolatier, creating delicious chocolates and medicines, and offering healing ceremonies.

You can follow Kathrin's work on her LinkedIn (Dr. Kathrin Huzelmann), YouTube (Magic Teeth 8), and Instagram account, "Magic Teeth", where you can see her creative expression and sense of humor.

**Contact Kathrin Huzelmann:**

- Me@conversationswithteeth.com
- MagicTeeth8@gmail.com
- www.magicteeth.co.uk

For dentistry only:

- www.Mariposadental.co.uk
- www.facebook.com/DrKathrinHuzelmann
- @magicteeth8
- www.youtube.com/@MagicTeeth8/featured
- www.linkedin.com/in/dr-kathrin-huzelmann

# Designs On Success: Just Get Up and Keep Going

## By Angela Jones

"Angela, please come to the guidance office." Career Day with my high school guidance counselor. I handed my slip of paper to the secretary and then sat in the uncomfortable plastic chair in front of a stern-looking guidance counselor. I waited for the fateful news of my career path.

"Angela, you are just not smart enough to become an architect. Your math grades are not there." I was crushed. Everything I always dreamed about doing. Poof. I became complacent, just grateful to graduate. I carried on, got married, became a professional figure-skating coach, and worked as a secretary at a local school. I just rolled with the easy path.

Then the irony. I was placed as a secretary working in the same office with the guidance counselor whom I let determine my future. Being in this environment and seeing him every day made me think, Was he right? If I wasn't smart enough to do my dream career, my gut was telling me there was more for me than this job. I always visualized myself being successful in a career, no matter what.

In a stunningly fateful moment, I decided to take charge of my own destiny. I packed my bags, two kids, and moved six hours north to help manage a vacation resort that my parents recently purchased, for their next venture in life. This was the fork in the road that changed everything.

**The Fork Turned into a Life-Changing Opportunity**

On a tranquil Canadian lake, surrounded by nature's beauty, I saw the architectural possibilities in the idyllic lakeside cottages. It was here that I started my entrepreneurial journey. While I was managing this lovely resort, I started to flourish. I helped grow the property from eight rustic seasonal cabins to a year-round twenty-cottage destination and marina restaurant.

Little did I know this was the foundation to my growth—that seed inside of me sprouted. For every challenge that came my way—and there were plenty—I figured out solutions. I learned about building, site planning, construction, renovations, and working with municipalities on permitting.

I thrived. My newfound confidence sent me back to school to get smarter about the world of my dream career in interior design and décor. I craved to learn more and received my diploma. Success. Like Mom always said, "Where there's a will, there's a way." Then life hit a bump, as life tends to do! Divorce. Not me, but my parents. Our resort was sold. I needed another plan. I applied for the perfect job. After the final interview I was driving through the downtown area feeling confident about my chances. And then the call. They chose a different candidate. Disappointed, I strolled through a local store and glanced out the window. Across the street, there it was. A vacant building. Suddenly, it occurred to me that I knew the owner of that building and a spark ignited. I called him with my new plan, made the deal. And so, my vision began anew—my design studio.

With a good friend and barely any credit left on my credit card, we painted, laid new floors, and purchased furniture for the grand opening. My sister and I had figure skated with determination as our driving force while growing up. But it was Shelley Simonton, our tough, world-class coach who taught us many prophetic lessons (not just about skating): Keep your eyes and head up, if you fall get up quick and keep going, keep smiling, visualize yourself completing your routine perfectly in your mind, practice and repeat, eyes up, train harder than your competitors, focus. To this day, those lessons ring true in every one of my skills, in business and life.

So, when we turned on the "open" sign in our new design studio, I got my first $20,000 client. In the beginning, I didn't pay myself for the first year. Everything rolled back into the company. If I didn't know something, I would figure it out, like my figure-skating coach had advised: visualize, head up. The jobs started coming in. One day I searched for an area rug supplier, and not five minutes later a salesperson walked into my store with exactly what I needed. The power of thinking. Could this be how it works? My angel fairy delivered.

Shortly after opening my new business, that fork in the road popped up again. Another divorce. This time, mine. I moved back into my mother's home with my children, Jeremy and Samantha. And there I was, starting over, picking up the pieces. If you fall, get up quick and keep going. Right. I reached deep inside to find that driving force. Some of those days were tough, but I wanted to show my children I could do this. Well, it was either train harder than your competitors or curl up under a blanket.

## Dreams Do Come True

I sought counseling. Some of the best advice I received during the first sessions was to do some homework: watch the movie *The Secret* and make a dream board. Off I went, rushing out to get supplies of Bristol board, scissors, glue, and collect some magazines. Sitting with my kids, we watched the movie, cutting and pasting at the same time. And on my board, I remember putting Carrie Underwood on there because she had great hair. I had a picture of Jack Canfield, trips, money, jewelry, motivational words, awards, trophies, and happy people. The statement from Jack Canfield during that movie stood out to me, still to this day. He used the metaphor, "When you are driving from California to New York in the dark, with your headlights on and you can only see 200 feet in front of you, and then the next 200 feet appear and then the next, as he explained, that is how things will unfold for you."

Oh boy, could I relate! My dad always said, "Life is in front of you, look out the front window not through the rearview mirror." I shared my dream board with my counselor, Kim, who noticed I had Jack Canfield on there, and said, "Did you know he is coming to Toronto?" Immediately after my session I ordered tickets. I took action! When I went to Toronto to see *The Secret* on tour. To my surprise, I bumped into Jack Canfield in the lobby of my hotel. I mustered up the courage to say hello. We posed for a photo, and he signed my business card. Yikes, was my dream board manifesting? Yes, I could hear that angel fairy wand ringing in my head. Continuously improving every day, I was on a mission to become the best version of myself that I could be. I took courses, read books, attended seminars, and studied directly with world-renowned personal development experts such as Marie Diamond, Tad James, and Stéphane and Shalee Schafeitel. My daughter also joined me in these training sessions, which has been one of the best experiences we could share together. Watching her excel and have a natural gift for coaching people to their potential is gratifying.

Creating a success mindset is definitely the key to perseverance and overcoming obstacles that show up in daily life. Even though I often hear people say, "You are so successful, how do you do it? You are so calm and make it look easy." Believe me, the skills I have learned over the years have shaped me, starting with the sharp edges of figure skating learned on the unforgiving ice: if you fall, get up and keep going, look ahead of you. Awards started to come my way, along with magazine and television interviews, with clients flying me to help them with their secondary home locations. I am so grateful for the success and opportunities I have. Being honored as Business Woman of the Year was a bonus. Humbled, and reflecting on my success of how I brought my company from a dream to now a multimillion-dollar company, and now expanding with another location is an achievement that brings the utmost satisfaction.

**What? Elton John!**

"Would you be interested in putting in a proposal to decorate a dressing room for Elton John?" What? I was invited to show our design skills when my childhood rockstar idol came to town. "Absolutely!" I called my sister, Jacqui, and she immediately stepped up to help me pull off the biggest transformation for a Hollywood green room. I mean, we turned a stinky hockey locker room into a glamorous scene out of a Hollywood movie in less than two days. My team worked through the night and pulled off a magical transformation.

We also had the privilege of working as the dressing room attendants, steam cleaning his iconic suits, and preparing them pristinely for Sir Elton John. We were like little kids, giggling, and filled with excitement. After the amazing show (unfortunately delayed by two weeks because Elton was ill), we received a handwritten note and gift from Elton's personal assistant for how grateful they were for our beautiful space we created and our help. Priceless. The celebrity experiences didn't end there. I have worked with many celebrities, rock stars, and NHL icons, even Carrie Underwood and her husband, Mike Fisher. Remembering how I put her picture on my dream board because she had great hair, who knew—boy, that angel fairy wand really worked. What a powerful exercise!

Helping people reach their highest potential is, for me, amazing. Such experiences, combined with my own training as an elite athlete, inspired me to become a personal and business coach where I could help others release limiting beliefs, negative emotions, and teach them skills to level up their mind power. With my daughter, we align on our global mission to help people live a life of possibility and joy. Because we have found both. It is okay to say you are struggling, but know that you have the power inside you to start over. Sometimes circumstances don't go the way you want, as it is not what happens, but how you respond to that. Having the ability to learn new skills is your powerful gift. My mission and goal is to help anyone wanting to overcome their limitations and achieve their most important goals.

I didn't let a guidance counselor derail my dream. If you are ready to make some changes and commit to yourself, then take the action.

## Angela Jones

Perseverance describes Angela Jones, who owns and operates Lakeshore Designs—her Canadian company creates dream homes for thousands of clients. She has grown from a small start-up to a premier, multimillion-dollar interior decorating and design firm with an impressive celebrity client roster. Her firm is the official designer for Canada's world-famous Princess Margaret Home Lottery to Conquer Cancer.

Angela's successful career in the design business is highlighted by her many awards, TV appearances, interviews, and weekly TV design tips called Let's Talk Design.

After winning a Canadian Gold Medal in synchronized figure skating, she began professionally coaching elite hockey players to refine their game and mental toughness.

Always committed to growth, Angela joined Marie Diamond's Feng Shui training program and implemented everything she learned to complement her design business. She also studied NLP, Time Line Therapy, hypnosis, and Huna with Tad James.

She is coached privately by Stéphane and Shalee Schafeitel (Stéph & Shay), best-selling authors of *Master Your Mindpower.* They helped her break through to a whole new level of excellence and taught her their highly effective Mindpower Coaching system.

Despite early discouragement of her career choice, Angela persisted and developed into an elite-level coach ready to help anyone overcome their limitations and maximize their potential.

She coaches alongside her daughter, Samantha, who is also an elite-level coach, and both help business leaders and high performers achieve their personal and business goals.

Reach out to admin@aspiredmindcoaching.com and visit her website for design projects at www.lakeshorehd.ca.

**Contact Angela Jones:**

www.lakeshorehd.ca

@lakeshoredesigns

Coaching Instagram

@Aspiredmindcoaching

# Nurture Your Mind & Find Your Path To Happiness and Contentment

## By Charmaine Lang

I was twenty-one years old, desperate for something new and far away from my current life. There I was, driving on the highway in a snowstorm, my two babies strapped into their seatbelts in the backseat. I was determined to make it to Vancouver BC in search of a better life; and I did. My first thought was, I want to be an interior designer! I loved the idea of one day helping clients with their homes. After a few days of searching, I applied for a kitchen designer job at a cabinet shop, among dozens of other applicants. I waited all day to have my interview and that's when I had a stroke of genius! I decided to look in their showroom for some samples and put together color schemes while I waited to make a lasting impression.

To my relief, I got the job! My first step towards my dream had been a success! With that successful first step, I was ready to take the next one. Immediately I enrolled into a kitchen design course and began selling cabinetry to clients so that I could get the hands-on experience I needed to become the designer I wanted to be. Every single step I took brought me closer to realizing my dreams and I refuse to give up until I do. Retrospectively, I can say this was the moment that changed my life. I was now on the path towards achieving what I had set out to do and I could not be more eager to see how far I could take it. Years had gone by; I wanted to grow further in my career, so I decided to enroll in a program to earn a diploma in interior design and project management. After graduating and getting set up with all the basics for a successful career, I eagerly began taking on small jobs to renovate my clients' homes.

Before I knew it, I had successfully taken on larger projects, such as being the Interior Designer and Project Manager for a 250-lot subdivision. I was ecstatic with the challenge and felt that my career was finally taking off. My curiosity and ambition kept me going and I ended up spending years gaining further experience and knowledge such as the fire and flood restoration industry as a contractor, a salesperson for doors and windows, a kitchen designer for a few different cabinet companies. I even managed a flooring business, had my three of my own retail furniture stores, and a staging business. Later, I won an award for "Best Modern Renovation" for a Spa and

Salon. I built out a 5,000 square foot Medical Center & Pharmacy. I provided Interior Design and on-site Project Management for several 15,000 square foot luxury homes, and a multi-residential condo building. I felt proud as I looked back on my thirty-year career journey. After all the obstacles I had faced and the successes I had achieved, I had made a name for myself in the industry. Along the way, I had taken up so many unique opportunities, allowing me to gain invaluable experience and knowledge, especially as a woman in the construction industry, to gain such experience. It was my passion!

The more I reflected on what I had been able to achieve, the more I felt a desire to give back. I wanted to package up my knowledge and experience and help other designers and construction industry professionals learn from my lessons and save them time, money, and years of learning the hard way. It seemed like a noble goal, and I set about creating courses and mentorship programs. I started teaching my business/client process and practices', sharing templates I had created, contracts and more, with my students, helping them with the tools they needed to become more successful.

However, I soon realized that this ambition was a lot of work and it was starting to take a toll on my health. Creating meaningful courses and mentorship programs requires a lot of time and effort, and on top of that I had to keep up with my own projects. It was a balancing act, and I wondered how long I could keep up this pace. Before I knew it, I was being approached by property investors and homeowners, asking if I could provide a course for them on how to plan a renovation from an interior designer's perspective and method. Surprisingly I was quickly gaining popularity. I felt a sense of pride at the knowledge I had been able to pass on to others.

My success with the courses I created made me realize that helping others through my knowledge and experience was my real passion. I realized that I could make a living out of this if I was able to continue this path. My company was growing so fast; it was hard to keep up with all the projects. Even with a team of staff behind me, I was juggling long work hours and weekends. My health was suffering from lack of sleep, and I was desperate for a change! Even my relationships were challenged! I not only needed help with balancing my business life, but my personal life was also suffering. A transformation is exactly what I needed! I was feeling overwhelmed and spread thin–like my life was a web of broken and frayed strings, flying every which way chaotically! Have you ever felt like this? I knew I needed help. I didn't know where to look. I did not want a low-level coach and really wanted the very best coach I could find. I had heard every business owner needs a coach to be successful in the long run. Even coaches have a coach. Despite the initial hesitation, I decided to look for a coach to help me gain clarity and balance. After several weeks of searching, and more sleepless nights, I finally found my perfect coach; a Certified High-Performance Coach with an acclaimed program heavily focused on neuroscience tools and techniques and rated having the highest satisfaction curriculum in the world. Who knew this type of coaching even existed! Did you? I was so excited with a sense of hope, but still a little unsure of what would happen.

From the very first appointment I knew I was going to be in good hands. My coach was patient, kind and supportive, and she had a knack for helping me to find the clarity, focus, courage, and the balance I had been desperately searching for. I was able to implement new habits which made such a difference to my results. I literally felt like my energy was renewed and I wasn't so stressed out. I was better equipped to make better decisions. I found myself making progress with my goals, each week building on the previous one. With every achievement, I could feel the wave of accomplishment wash over me. It was like I was on the journey of my life, and I was finally able to take control of the wheel. I discovered some deep insights and made some major breakthroughs that I didn't even know were holding me back.

I was so inspired by the progress I had made in just twelve short weeks that I decided to become a high-performance coach myself. I had an unquenchable curiosity to understand how much more I could help others reach their goals. I decided to dive deep into the training and certification process, to see how I could make an even greater impact with my newly acquired skills. As I worked through the training to become a certified high-performance coach, I started to notice how differently I felt. Like I was on a higher vibration. I felt happier inside. This training continued to be a healing journey for me.

I soon launched my new company called The Certified Coaching Guru, as my unique method of coaching my clients. I'm now proud to say I have been working with my clients as a certified high-performance coach helping many over the past four years, helping others reach their goals and guide them to their new reality. It's incredible to witness the transformation in another person's life, especially in such a short time. It's amazing what you can achieve if you invest in yourself, and if you just give it the time and effort.

I am grateful for the amazing transformation that comes with this certified high performance coaching method through sessions that focus on achieving results. People who had previously felt stuck, hopeless, even suffering from imposter syndrome, suddenly felt more confident, focused, and motivated. The transformation that I watched was nothing short of miraculous and there was no doubt in my mind that this was exactly why I had wanted to start this journey in the first place. I was determined to do more than just watch these transformations. I wanted to actively nurture their minds and help these people find their path. With that thought in my head and my newfound mission, I set out to become an agent of change.

I remember the feeling of elation when my first mentee finished the course and made a career switch. Seeing the newfound energy and joy in their eyes was amazing. They had conquered their fear and were now tackling their goals head-on. As I thought about my other mentees' progress and the progress that I had seen in those months and years, I knew that I had finally found my purpose in life. Hi, I am Charmaine Lang. Looking back, I had been working as an Interior Designer for more than three decades, aiding my clients in creating the perfect home and work atmosphere. But now I am able to assist you in another way, by helping you understand your internal world and mindset. Are you ready to find the sense of purpose you have been looking for? Helping you reach your full potential is my calling, a mission I was meant to embark on. I find joy in knowing that I have managed to make a real difference in people's lives and that's a feeling I wouldn't trade for the world. It is an amazing journey, full of emotion and power, and I would love to work with you too.

I am forever grateful for the amazing results of this Certified High Performance coaching method and for the chance to help you reach your dreams. There is no limit to the types of people I can help. I hope to continue this mission of helping thousands of others including you, and I look forward to the challenges and rewards that come with it. I believe that the ability to reach a level of excellence while still prioritizing one's health and relationships is the secret to surpassing the ordinary and achieving exceptional results. Just imagine how your life would be improved if you were to live up to your highest potential. Are you ready to revolutionize your life and career with the help of a Certified High Performance Coach? If so, I would be thrilled to be working with you. I welcome you to reach out to me. You can contact me by email using the contact info at the bottom of the chapter to book a sixty-minute call. I can't wait to hear from you!

## Charmaine Lang

Meet Charmaine Lang, DID, IIDA, CHPC, who is both an Award-Winning Global Transformational Interior Designer and Certified High Performance Coach.

Charmaine believes in living an inspired and fulfilled life. The Certified Coaching Guru, her Certified High Performance Coaching Program combined with her more than three decades of experience as a luxury interior designer and project manager has mastered how to help individuals combine their home atmosphere with their internal state of mind.

She believes that by prioritizing one's health and relationships and reaching a level of excellence, one can surpass the ordinary and achieve exceptional results. Charmaine's strength lies in her ability to really understand what her clients are wanting to achieve.

She spent over thirty years providing interior design and project management for luxury 15,000 sf residential homes, $30M+ multi-residential luxury condo building, hundreds of renovations, and 5000 sf medical & pharmacy.

Her coaching began four years ago. Charmaine has helped hundreds of homeowners, business professionals, interior designers, property investors, and construction industry professionals.

Charmaine Lang mentored with Brendon Burchard (High Performance Institute), Ona & Les Brown, Kane Minkus (Industry Rockstar), Kevin Harrington (Original shark from *Shark Tank*), John Assaraf (from the movie *The Secret*), and Certified Design/Build Contractor by Bryan Baumler (TV Host *Island of Bryan*).

Charmaine holds a Diploma in Interior Design, and a designation of a Certified High Performance Coach from High Performance Institute. Awarded Best Modern Renovation of the Year Award–Spa and Salon

Charmaine has two up and coming books: *Think & Go Renovate – Makeover Your Mindset Before You Begin* and *Interior Design Success Habits – How to Take Your Client on the Decision-Making Journey*

Certified Coaching Guru—Business and Life Coaching, *Home Renovation Mastery*, and *Mentorship Program for Interior Designers* Contact:

Charmainelangdesigninc@gmail.com
Charmaine Lang, CHPC, DID, IIDA
Global Transformational Certified High Performance Coach and Interior Designer

**Contact Charmaine Lang:**

- @certifiedcoachingguru & @charmainelangdesigninc
- www.facebook.com/CertifiedCoachingGuru
- www.facebook.com/charmainelangdesign8
- www.LinkedIn.com/in/charmaine-lang
- www.CharmaineLang.com & www.CharmaineLangDesign.com
- info@certifiedcoachingguru.com
- Charmainelangdesigninc@gmail.com
- www.Calendly.com/charmainelangCHPC

# Life Is a Story of Love and Appreciation

## By Altantulga (Tulga) Mandakh-Ayush

It's 8:45AM in Ulaanbaatar. The city is enjoying one of its bright, sunny summer days. I walk through the doors of a Central Tower building and head to my office. My heart is singing, my steps are light; going to the office is one of my favorite parts of the day. I get out on the tenth floor and am met by a familiar smell of my favorite morning coffee from our office. After a couple of minutes of small talk, I head toward my desk and open my laptop. Boom, I am now completely blown into my job as a lawyer; my mind restlessly travels to Hong Kong, Singapore, and many other international clients to prepare for their next deals.

When the end of my workday comes, unbelievably, it is already 9PM. I am reminded of my kids when I receive a call from my son. Time to finish my job. After supper and evening routines with my kids, we go to bed. My sweet family are all deep asleep, all except me. Every night I read Wayne Dyer's books until dawn and get so much relief and wisdom from him. Whilst I love what I do as a lawyer, I still feel something is missing in my heart and Wayne Dyer's books seemed to fill that empty space for me.

I got up each day and had this same busy routine for five consecutive years. One day, I felt this unusual calling from within me saying: "There must be something bigger for you in this world. You need to open yourself up. You need to travel the world. You need to write and inspire people around the world. You need to disseminate insight to people to help them become aware. If you wait until all important deals and contracts are completed, it will be too late to live your own life to its fullest". Later that week, I submitted my termination request and left my job. The next day, I drove my kids to the countryside to sunbathe and play around as much as I wanted to celebrate my newfound freedom. Bryan Adams' song was playing loudly on the car radio, the wind through the window was ruffling my hair, and my kids were laughing happily in the backseat. I felt completely in control of my life and was filled with an overwhelming sense of freedom. If only I knew that this was just the tip of an iceberg!

The first month of being a stay-at-home mom felt like a honeymoon. The kids were happy to have me around, and my husband's satisfaction was through the roof. We were optimistic about our prosperous future together when suddenly one day, I was informed that my husband's business had collapsed and were having to deal with a substantial yet completely unexpected court payment. That wasn't much of a concern to me until I discovered that I was pregnant with our fourth baby. "What an irony", I thought as the timing couldn't have been worse. The pending business payment combined with my having just left my job could have halted my plans, but yet I chose to move forward anyway.

I committed myself to a *My Business* coaching program provided by Monica Batsukh, a successful Mongolian coach living in London. Having admired Monica's own success story and her having worked with Tony Robbins, Roger Hamilton and many more global entrepreneurs, I realized that getting a mentor was an absolute must if I wanted to transform my life. I was amazed at how unpredictable life was getting from moment to another. I had been contracted to translate my first novel and, being a warrior-spirited woman, I had also decided to study to get my LLM degree. When I was five months pregnant, I was offered a full-time job at the Constitutional Court of Mongolia. Although the timing was not convenient, I did at least feel a deep relief that I had gotten an offer. The world had not forgotten about me!

The family financial battle was underway, our baby was born, and the second volume of the novel was being translated. Life seemed to be a struggle with all the bills and kids' tuition fees yet still no budget at all for our own dreams, such as world travel and moving to a bigger house. I wasn't just focusing all on the problems though. I was also searching relentlessly for big ideas that would transform my life. I was an educated woman who had completed three universities, two Master's degrees, and who had an enormous experience with UNFPA, UNDP, World Bank and US Embassy. If I was finding it hard to sit at home, then what about other, younger women with children? There must be an empowering option out there to help young women and mothers, and I was determined to find it. My goal was to one day tell my story to inspire other mothers who were desperate to go back to work but were instead stuck at home with young kids.

It has been twelve years since I graduated from Hiroshima University of Japan. In order to celebrate the last decade and to make an appreciation trip to Japan, in May 2016 I decided to attend His Holiness', the 14th Dalai Lama Buddhist, teachings in Osaka. The trip was amazing. All participants of that global event listened carefully to the teachings by His Holiness the Dalai lama and were blessed to learn how to raise our awareness in order to extend love and wisdom to the world. The closing day supper in particular was extremely impressive; all the guests were wined and dined like kings and queens on a special retreat. After the luxury supper, we all were invited to an open onsen on the surface of Japan sea where we were witnessed by the luminous light of an amazing full moon. An unforgettable view, an unforgettable night. Suddenly, I felt that there was something not quite right with my body. Upon arrival in Ulaanbaatar, I headed straight to the hospital and was exposed to the heartbeat of our fifth child. It took me six months to stop crying my eyes out. Why me, why did this happen to me, why did God want me to be at home again? Why does God not allow me to pursue my career and be successful? Why, why, why?

One day, I received a call from the United Nations Human Rights Commissionaire office to inform me that I needed to meet with experts coming to Mongolia from PRC and Malaysia who wanted to interview me. I did an amazing interview and the following morning, I was at the hospital holding my dearest fifth baby. Another case of wrong timing for my career success! This is a story of a woman, representing millions of women worldwide, who sacrificed her career for the sake of her kids and families. Women have to endure much more to gain their place in business and work. After my fifth child was born, I was asked by a prominent Member of Parliament to translate the autobiography of Eleanor Roosevelt, the First Lady of the USA. It's passion that uplifts us, not just money or career progress alone, so I was happy to translate the words and wisdom of this brilliant lady. Working through it, I became so inspired. I learnt that leaders are not just prominent women like Hillary Clinton, Michelle Obama, and Sheryl Sandberg, but that there is that leader spirit in everybody and in each and every mother.

Then the pandemic happened. One late November night in 2020, there was a World Without Limits event online. The weather outside was chilly and people were in a gray mood due to the lockdown regime. After a less-cheerful-than-usual dinner, my family went to bed but I stayed up. I'd secured a place to attend the event which was due to start at 1AM Mongolian time. I felt my husband's empathic glaze and declined his offer to go to bed to get warm. The event started. From the moment it started, I knew that I had found my tribe, that it was my place to be. I laughed and cried together with Jack Canfield, Ken Honda, Erve Hacker, Jay Abraham, and many others. God sent me that night Janet Attwood, a woman with the biggest heart and passion in the world. I was totally mesmerized by the power of these world transformational leaders, by their kind hearts, and by their resilience to keep going, no matter the ups and downs.

The following day, I was registered for her certified Passion Test facilitator course. This course has transformed me deeper and deeper, day by day. I was blessed to serve hundreds of people worldwide in helping them find their passion. There is nothing more joyful than watching my clients' eyes sparkling after they learn to tune into their hearts, finally spotting their passions! This was followed by Mindvalley courses. I was always fascinated by reading the stories behind peoples' success. I was amazed to learn about the key turning points in their lives. I learnt that you have to take proactive decisions in life and that the key behind these actions is your passion. Any goal fueled by passion will take you to greater, longer, and more fulfilling destinations.

So, my friend, you are a born leader. You have an amazing impact on this world, just by your breath and presence, given that you already know what your passion is. In hindsight, I now realize that every challenge was indeed a true blessing for me! You just have to keep going. Let me conclude my story with Janet Bray Attwood's words: "When you know what you want clearly, everything comes true in your life, and how clear you know it will come true".

## Altantulga (Tulga) Mandakh-Ayush

Altantulga is a former international lawyer and a UN translator from Mongolia. She has translated dozens of international best-selling books. Her mentors are global. She has been a loyal student of Debra Poneman, Janet Attwood, Marie Diamond, Dr. Joe Vitalle, Mindvalley, and more.

She is an expert in helping people gain clarity and to help them define their purpose in their lives. She left her successful career as a lawyer in search of her deepest "Why". Her search for "Why" challenged her to test her resilience as a stay-at-home mom for nearly a decade.

Together with her beloved spouse Bayanmunkh, she has raised five wonderful children, one girl and four boys, all whilst connecting herself constantly to the wisdom of the global renowned transformational leaders. Eventually, she found her life path and pursued her career as a successful Passion Test facilitator and a business coach.

Tulga was mentored personally by Janet Attwood as a Master Trainer and has discovered the importance of encouraging people to find their truest passion. She has already helped hundreds of Mongolian people and has published the New York Times best-selling book *Passion Test* in Mongolian.

She currently resides in Ulaanbaatar, Mongolia and became a global transformational leader herself. As a Mindvalley certified business coach and life coach, she provides personal and group coaching sessions globally to encourage people to find their passions.

Her visions are to help thousands of successful entrepreneurs around the world and to bring huge impact by just being a "happypreneur" mom herself and a global best-selling author. Her motto is Live Happy, Work Happy.

**Contact Altantulga Mandakh-Ayush:**

@altantulga_passiontest

www.facebook.com/Altantulga.M

www.facebook.com/AltantulgaCoach

www.linkedin.com/in/altantulga-mandakh-ayush-58383957

www.altantulga.mn

www.youtube.com/passiontest

# Believe And It Will Happen

## By Maria Matias

From being a little girl, I've always leaned towards something that is positive, exudes light, hope, compassion, and joy. In my most profound essence, I've wanted to share with the world that we are all one with our creator. Now, as a Registered Dental Hygienist, and certified Feng Shui Expert, I am manifesting this message and connecting with individuals who are seeking the same vision. One such individual is Yusuf Bakaki from Uganda, Africa, who contacted me in search of oral health education. The relationship started out with me sharing my expertise of dental oral health, and was later transformed by me sharing my knowledge of Feng Shui. We had sessions every Monday for eight weeks, and I was implementing specific Feng Shui principles that would help him manifest his goals.

Yusuf already had faith in God, yet he was also learning the art of manifesting via Feng Shui, and gave me permission to share his story. Yusuf explains, "In Uganda, opportunities are hard to come by, and meeting Maria Matias really impacted my life. She has been my mentor in visualizing and implementing Feng Shui, and to envision that I would be nominated to be one of ten winners for the Future Africa Leaders Award. She taught me to take a leap of faith and go to the embassy to acquire a visa even though I still had not been nominated." Yusuf is the co-founder and director of "World for Life," my passion and mission has always been to share my experiences for social and emotional learning, and to create a conscious global awareness through philanthropy. My organization is nonprofit, and strives to empower and improve the socio-economic status of vulnerable children, especially girls, and their families, through entrepreneurship, mentorship, provision of education, health services, and sports.

So, it was vital for me to attend the event and accept the nomination as it would bring light and focus on the communities of Uganda. My heartbreaking dilemma was that my visa application was rejected at the Nigerian embassy in Uganda, and I walked out of the doors heartbroken. How was I going to claim this beautiful moment in my life that I had visualized so many times in my heart and mind? If I received this award and attended the event, that would shed light and awareness on the needs of my community. It would propel my core beliefs of giving light to the world. At this time, Maria was working with me on visualizing that I had the visa and the award in my hands. We initially connected on oral hygiene, but the conversations also geared toward Feng Shui, which is something that Maria is also passionate about. Like me, she has a strong faith in God and how the universe works, and that connection gave me faith in her. Her oral health course was very helpful. Maria is very knowledgeable, has great humor, and is an excellent oral health and Feng Shui teacher. She was so patient with me, especially when I was working with her online, and she knew of my struggles with internet access because we had many sessions together where I would lose my internet connection. She would still be waiting for me, even though I would sometimes have to go to different areas to reconnect to Wi-Fi. Through a donation that she sent me, I went to a dentist for dental work.

If a picture is worth a thousand words, then my smile must be worth ten thousand! While talking to Maria, I was inspired to tell her about my nonprofit organization and my desire to educate the children about oral health. So, Maria worked with me by collaborating and creating personal vision boards on oral dental health and personal topics for the children from my organization. I was impacted by some of the results as one of the children had been abandoned by his parents and he rarely smiled. He created his vision board on the relationship side and he wrote a sentence that he wanted to be in a happy family, and to be loved. We finally found his family and are in the process of a reunion, and he is starting to smile again. Once I saw how these vision boards were created and how impactful they were, I asked for a personal one, and Maria customized my vision and goals. After walking out of the embassy without my visa, everything that Maria had taught me came to me in a flash. My mind shifted to the present moment and the fact that I had no visa in my hand. The personnel at the embassy had informed me that the only visas they were issuing were for delegates, with a cost of $300.

I only had one hundred dollars. I left the embassy in Uganda dejected. I went to church and prayed, and I received a message from God that I needed to go back to the embassy. I remembered what Maria taught, and to visualize and have complete faith that I had the visa and the award with my name on it. So, with my faith and determination I returned to the embassy, and a man approached me. He was the ambassador of Nigeria, and he stated that I looked like his son. He asked me what I was doing at the embassy, and I explained my work and mission, and my dilemma of not being able to obtain a visa. To my surprise he went and ordered the staff at the embassy to expedite a visa for me, and he even paid the extra $200 needed. So, I walked out of the embassy with my visa. I was grateful that Maria had taught me to visualize and manifest that I had already received the visa. Back at home, my pastor found out about the nomination and asked me if I had my flight ticket ready, and I told him that I did not, and I didn't ask him for anything as I really didn't want to put a burden on anyone for financial help. I prayed and implemented what Maria taught me, and a miracle happened, because my pastor surprised me with an $800 plane ticket to Nigeria. I jumped for joy and let out a big celebratory yell. I then contacted my teacher, Maria, and told her that I had been nominated for this prestigious award, and the roadblocks that I had faced. But, with faith in God, and by implementing the strategies Maria had taught me, I was tenacious enough to not give up on my vision and dreams. Maria was so supportive and proud that I was going to make this dream a reality.

She asked me if I had the right attire to receive this award, and I told her that I only had limited items. Right away she wired me the funds to purchase all the items that I needed. The day finally came when I boarded the plane to Nigeria. It was an exhilarating emotion as the plane took off and, as the plane ascended, so did my dreams for a brighter future. Looking out my window, I saw the clouds below me and knew that I was on my way to brighter days. That evening, as I was preparing my clothes for the ceremony, Maria called to check up on me. She gave me the wonderful news that my story would be featured in a book. Could life be any better? At that moment, I wanted to jump up and scream. As I entered the venue of the award ceremony I was in awe of the grandeur of this event, and it dawned on me that I was one of ten young leaders chosen to appear before millions of people from across the fifty-four countries in Africa.

This worldwide televised event would shed light on my community, and I was representing the future as a leader and innovator. The Future Africa Leaders Foundation celebrates the positive impact of youth who create healthy communities and nations in Africa. Being named and awarded meant that I would continue to grow and be mentored and supported on the initiatives that I started. As my name was called out to receive the award, a surreal sensation and out of body experience came over me. I listened to the narration of the speaker stating my accomplishments: "Yusuf Bakaki is an avid nation-builder. He implements project programs, he started a five-hectare farm, where youth and women led modern farming methods; over 50,000 farmers from the region have visited the farm. He distributed thousands of sanitary products to young girls from Uganda, and donated three hundred baby kits to mothers in a maternity ward. Yusuf offered services in many districts that included dental health care. Over 25,000 people were served with free medication worth nearly $30,000 US dollars. He assisted in improving housing conditions for the elderly." As the speaker kept stating my accomplishments, I was reminded that I had visualized this reality.

This was all for my community, for the greater good of my people. They are deserving and worthy of the resources that will give them a life worth living. After the award and $10,000 was given to me, there were many pictures, congratulatory handshakes, and further celebrations. Afterwards, I went back to rest, and in the middle of the night, my coach Maria sent me a video and pictures of the award ceremony. I felt joy that she was there in spirit right along with me. I was not surprised by her kindness and generosity in recording the event for me. It gave me great joy to see her cheer me on as all the accolades were being presented, and I remembered all of the coaching sessions that helped me stand proud in front of millions in this ceremony. All the sessions with Maria brought me to this motto that I hold dear to my heart: "Let your light shine."

## Maria Matias

Maria Matias is a prominent and influential entrepreneur, registered Dental Hygienist, passionate Diamond Feng Shui Consultant, and board member for Cavity Free at Three since 2009, possessing twenty-nine years of diverse experience in healthcare services, living in Denver, Colorado, U.S. She recently signed on to be a show host for the Win Win

Women Network, and a contributor to an e-book with Marie Diamond. Maria went from being a homeless refugee to a successful business owner and is now living the dream in her American home.

Her transformation to a successful life began thanks to Feng Shui, and she has found purpose and fulfillment through this practice.

Maria has helped thousands of families to improve their general health and well-being through her dental hygiene services and education.

To date, she has donated $50,000 in dental equipment and hundreds of hours on oral health education in schools to serve her community.

Her company, Global Smiles, has reached globally, living up to its name Global Smiles and has created professional videos in English and Spanish for Delta Dental for PBS.

She was part of a pilot for Delta Dental Foundation nonprofit, published in the American Association of Public Health Dentistry.

As an individual, Maria is result-oriented, selfless, and caring, and has assisted many people in improving their quality of life through Feng Shui.

Seeing their transformation gives her immense personal satisfaction, and her vision going forward is to help others realize the many benefits this ancient art offers.

**Contact Maria Matias:**

www.linkedin.com/in/mariamatiasofficial

www.facebook.com/mariamatiasofficial

@mariamatias_88

www.mariamatiasfengshui.com

# The Comeback Trail

## By Maximilian Messler

Transforming adversity into growth, inner peace, and purpose. Embracing a new path to success and happiness that nourishes the soul.

On a Tuesday morning, I had just arrived at my work desk and felt exhausted. My energy was strangely low and I had a busy day ahead. So, I got myself some coffee, yet I realized how hard it was to walk the 150 meters towards the cafeteria on campus. My legs were heavy and every step I took was a burden, yet this day was only about to get started. It was around 8:24 a.m. and meeting after meeting was on my schedule. I was thinking to myself, how can I get through this day? Little did I know, this moment would start to lead me down a path of self-discovery and transformation.

I was climbing the ladder of success as an ambitious professional at a global fashion brand, constantly striving for validation. My work was my first love and I defined myself by what I did. But my addiction to success and constant need for validation came with a hefty price, self-doubt. I often felt like an imposter and struggled to balance my life. Despite receiving compliments and rewards, the feeling of accomplishment was short-lived. Being consumed by work, my relationship started to take a hit; my partner and I struggled to connect, and drifted apart. I felt more isolated and doubted myself even more. Was I still attractive? Who would like me anyway? I'd lost the sense of knowing my worth beyond my work.

But, I lost the connection to my heart almost twenty years earlier. When I was only nine years old, my mother died of cancer. I remember that day when the phone rang. It was a Sunday, we didn't know what was going on. *Get into the car.* My uncle was driving my sisters and me to the hospital where my mum was. Once there, I watched her lying in this cold room on a hospital bed, just skin and bones, breathing so heavily I could still hear it in my ears. I was terrified; the person I loved most was about to leave this world and I would be left alone. Left alone with a father who wasn't emotionally available and two sisters that were dealing with their own struggles. This was the very day when my heart started being in pain. I grew up to be confused about who I was and how to deal with my emotions. A young boy finding out he was gay, living in a little village, not feeling his grief, not knowing what life would bring. Feeling lonely, disconnected, different, and betrayed by life. I just went on. Life goes on, that's what they said. I lost touch with my own needs as I became a yes man, but this mindset made me also more resilient. I thought that no matter what challenges came my way, I could handle it all, making me determined and adaptable. Twenty years later, this hurt little child was still inside of me trying to get that feeling of being loved, connected, and seen, just the way I was. Working hard, being successful, and getting praise was my coping strategy. Trying to fill that dark hole inside of me; it came at a high cost. Being at work became challenging, as my focus got worse. Everything took me much longer, but I kept it to myself, it was my secret. Something within me couldn't accept what was going on, so I looked away, I blocked it out. I kept going; that's what I've learned. You keep going... so I overstepped each sign of my body, pretending everything was fine. In the beginning, the signs seemed to be subtle, but got louder as it went on.

I had this voice within me, telling me, *you can't go on like this anymore*. Yet I did not listen! One day I received a present, a book on life's purpose, from a friend, which sparked an internal struggle with my current way of living. Despite feeling trapped in my successful career, I still felt a sense of belonging and recognition in my job. I forced myself to go on, put on a mask doing the work, and just keep going, even if I knew deep inside me something was wrong, that this job was not fulfilling me and my heart's desires anymore. But could I really trust this feeling? Descending into my inner world felt like venturing into a dark and ominous basement filled with buried secrets and fears that threatened to consume me and unravel all I had built. I worked so hard on building this perfect version of myself that my ego did everything to keep it going. I was afraid. Afraid of being weak, allowing myself to take a break. It was no option, so I did what I've learned and remained strong.

My greatest teacher, my body and intuition, showed me many signs, like the lack of mental concentration, the physical fatigue, and the missing joy and fulfillment, but I ignored them all. I shut them down, in fear, in desperation, and not knowing what to do. I was at war with myself. Not by conscious choice but by being unconscious of it. The battlefield was between my ego and my heart. The environment at work got even more challenging; being successful at what I did, I got more responsibilities and was trying to deal with them all, though already feeling overwhelmed. However, as my energy level got lower by the day, I had to start making changes, like coming in to work later and leaving earlier. On a summer night in July something happened that shook me up. I was lying in bed and my heart started pounding strongly. I got nervous and anxious, believing I was having a heart attack. These were moments of extreme desperation; fortunately, it wasn't real, but yet another sign. My body was screaming, telling me to listen and to look deeper into what was going on and to make a change. This was the moment when I slowly started to wake up to what was going on. My heart was sending me a clear message: you've been pushing yourself too hard for too long.

Reaching rock bottom, climbing just three steps to my apartment felt like scaling Mount Kilimanjaro. Exhausted, out of breath, and depleted, I felt like an elderly man despite my youth. Sleep evaded me, leaving me with physical, mental, and emotional exhaustion. My body forced me to stop doing what I was doing, as I simply couldn't function anymore. A time of extreme doubt and insecurity started. What would happen? Could I ever recover? Who am I without my job? All those questions were running through my mind and hunting me like a shadow. Feelings of being anxious about my health, my future, my job, my relationships, and the life to come were bothering me and flying around my head like a heavy cloud.

On a quest for recovery, I found solace in nature. Soaking up the warm rays of the sun, I felt a glimmer of energy return. I turned to meditation, connecting with an inner wisdom and searching for a path to healing. Over time, my inner voice grew stronger and a deep sense of knowing and trust emerged. I knew I would recover, even if I didn't know how or when. I realized that I had been so focused on achieving success and external validation that I had lost touch with my heart, and my body was screaming for a change. Embarking on a journey to rediscover myself, I was faced with a harsh realization. Was I truly living for myself, or just existing to please others? Guided by therapy and coaching, I bravely set out to make the changes my soul craved. As I delved into my subconscious, I uncovered patterns formed in childhood that were slowly tearing me apart. But with each insight came a newfound strength.

The basement lost its fear factor. No longer was I navigating the unknown depths alone. My guide held a shining torch, illuminating the path and giving me the courage to face the shadows and demons within. Together, we tackled the fear and discovered that reality was not as intimidating as fantasy. I had to rediscover self-love and accept myself beyond work and image. Unlearning societal beliefs that tied my worth to my actions and earnings was crucial. It was a journey of letting go and embracing my true identity as a human being, not just a human doing. My intuition grew louder, guiding me towards a brighter future. I shed the shackles of my past and embraced the person I was meant to be. The journey was not easy, but the reward of inner peace and authentic living would be worth it all. With a year of growth and challenges behind me, I was ready for a change. So, I pursued my passion and dived into the world of psychology. I was on a mission to understand the human mind and why so many struggle with mental wellness. But the answers I found were unsatisfying and left me wanting more. I found out that there is a dangerous myth out there that's holding people back from living their best life: the idea that mental health struggles, limiting beliefs, and self-destructive habits can only be slowly overcome, or maybe never overcome at all.

Unsatisfied with the notion that it would take a lifetime to understand the complexities of the human mind, I embarked on a quest to challenge and delve deeper into the story that has been told. Determined to find a faster path to healing and transformation, I set out on a journey to uncover the secrets to a successful transformation. Years of studying and personal growth led me to seek a quicker solution, one that could benefit others and help turn their struggles into lives that are vibrant, inspired, healthy, and successful. I refused to give up until I found the answer.

Meditation sparked my interest even more and opened doors to exploring altered states of mind. The trail of mystery led me to hypnosis, an ancient technique at least 2,500 years old, with a rich history of transforming the mind. Could this be the key to my search for a faster, more successful way of healing and transformation? I don't know if it was luck, fate, or meant to be, but I found the teachings of Marisa Peer, a renowned expert therapist and a pioneer in her field. She had developed a revolutionary method using the power of hypnosis, honed through thirty years of working with clients. I knew in my heart that I had found what I was looking for. The Lao Tzu quote, "The teacher appears when the student is ready," rang true for me.

With the help of her method, I skyrocketed my own personal growth journey and realized the root cause of my own issues: that I was living according to an outdated story in many areas of my life. Like a computer that hasn't been updated in a very long time, full of bugs and slowed down. Finally, I was able to replace outdated belief systems and negative behavior patterns with new life-affirming beliefs almost in an instant by reframing my core beliefs, values, habits, and emotions deep in the subconscious. I uncovered my true self integrated, healed, and empowered. A transformed version of myself, now living a joyful, lighthearted, and healthy life with purpose. With gratitude for the support and guidance I received, I now stand empowered to take on new challenges. A Global Conscious Entrepreneur spreading inspiration, reminding others to live from the heart. Start by changing yourself, and watch as you make a positive impact on your life and the world around you, with ease. Make the subconscious mind work for you, attract and manifest what you desire and deserve: happiness and success that nourish your soul.

## Maximilian Messler

Maximilian Messler is an international transformation creator helping people to deliver extraordinary change using the multi-award-winning method called Rapid Transformational Therapy (RTT®) and proven coaching methods. He also holds a bachelor of science degree in psychology.

As an expert in the world of personal development, he is trained by the globally acclaimed therapist Marisa Peer, with her clientele including Hollywood celebrities, CEOs, royalty, sports stars, and many more. With a deep understanding of human psychology and a big heart, Maximilian has helped hundreds of people in their personal growth, breaking free from their limiting beliefs and behaviors, paving their way to a happier, more fulfilling life.

From overcoming feeling burned out and depressed to weight management and finding one's purpose, Maximilian's approach is tailored to meet each individual's unique needs and desires. He leads with intuition, leaving those he works with feeling uplifted and empowered, with a newfound sense of confidence and self-esteem.

Maximilian has a deep-seated belief that within each and every one of us lies the power to create change and unlock our full potential. He knows that by bringing awareness to our subconscious patterns and beliefs we can break free from the limitations that hold us back. With his unwavering guidance and support, he empowers individuals to overcome any obstacle and live the life they've always dreamed of. Maximilian is on a mission to unleash the untapped potential within us all and guide us towards a brighter, more fulfilling future for a life guided by the heart, filled with happiness and success.

Maximilian's mission is to inspire and guide thirty million individuals and beyond to become conscious change-makers who live and lead with their hearts. Together, they will spread joy and creativity, and make a positive impact on the world. Join him on this transformative journey, unlock your true potential and achieve your goals today.

Are you ready to experience extraordinary change from emotional, physical or psychological pain? Letting go of limiting beliefs to unlock your potential for vibrant health, success, and purpose. Imagine waking up each day feeling energized, living a life that's filled with joy and abundance and that is aligned with your true self. It's all possible, and I'm here to guide you on this amazing journey towards your dreams. I warmly welcome you to explore my website to discover more, get free resources, or to book your free discovery call with me. Let's start this incredible journey together.

**Contact Maximilian Messler:**

- www.maximilianmessler.com
- @maximilianmessler
- www.facebook.com/maximilian.messler
- www.linkedin.com/in/maximilianmessler
- www.calendly.com/maximilianmessler/discovery-call

# A Wounded Healer's Path to Wholeness

## By Jocelyn Michel

The hot tears streamed down my cheeks as the biting cold winter wind blew. It was a particularly dark and snowy winter in Wisconsin, but the energy in the house was darker and heavier than the oppressive cloudy night sky. The pain of shame, fear, loneliness, exhaustion, heaviness, and anxiety bubbled up uncontrollably as I shoveled one more pile of snow, trying to prolong my reprieve from the family drama. My mind raced with thoughts of having no way out and plans to end my life. I just couldn't take it anymore; all I wanted was for the pain to stop. Out of the ocean of drowning emotions a voice of reason said, "We haven't tried therapy, let's at least try, before we say goodbye."

It wasn't supposed to be like this, I had recently graduated with two degrees. A bachelor of science in nutrition and a master's degree in Oriental Medicine, above and beyond my previous bachelor of arts degree in psychology. The plan was to heal the world, and here I was; I didn't even know how to help myself. My office had been open for three months and I'd had to close the doors because the panic attacks were so bad. I would wake up in the morning trembling and my eyelashes would be stuck together from the tears I had been crying in my sleep. I didn't have high expectations for therapy, but I decided in my heart that I would give it up to one year.

That if I was still in the same place in a year, I would take my life. This was my lowest point, the breaking point, and the decision that changed everything. I had tried self-help, and it did help, but it wasn't enough. Shame immobilized me and only the internal threat of death was strong enough to overcome the fear of revealing my shameful self and ask for help. I needed to find my healing path.

It was in therapy that I learned a great lesson: we don't get emotionally wounded alone and we don't heal alone. The second great lesson I learned was that not all of our "stuff" is actually ours. I learned, what intuitively seems obvious, but was shocking at the time, we carry the unresolved traumas of our ancestors.

My own path to healing had often been slow, rambling, uphill, in the dark, and alone. I've also experienced the treasures found only in the dark places. The deep satisfaction of pure authenticity from facing painful truth. The freedom from fear that comes from trusting others to touch and assist in the healing of deep trauma wounds. The breakthrough that comes from rising courage that shatters the silence to speak my own truth.

The knowledge, deep inside, that only comes from taking the risk to do what you think you can't do and seeing yourself succeed. The bond of humanity that we all share. My ceaseless curiosity always has me asking the questions, "Why?" and "What is real?" I have always been sensitive to the spiritual realm and somehow knew that the truest answers in life come from a spiritual perspective on life.

As a Christian, I was taught to have faith and live by faith, but struggled greatly to know how to apply those truths in practical ways. It was my therapist who introduced me to the law of attraction. The law of attraction was a missing key for me. It provided some of the how-to steps that allowed me to put my faith in action and see tangible change in my life. I never thought I would ever be an acupuncturist.

I was sick a lot as a kid with ear infections and strep throat, and that meant getting a lot of shots of antibiotics. I hated needles! Little did I know that acupuncture needles or pins, as they are often lovingly called, would change my life and the lives of my future patients.

Backtrack several years after our opening scene; I was working as an employment support specialist and trainer in social services and dealing with what was becoming chronic pain from an automobile accident. It was a co-worker who invited me to a class on cleansing, led by a local acupuncturist, that first exposed me to the power of this ancient medicine.

Though never confirmed by a traditional medical doctor, I had symptoms consistent with fibromyalgia and chronic fatigue. I had worked with a chiropractor who used nutritional therapy in his practice. He helped me overcome the chronic exhaustion and achiness that I had all over my body.

Now, here I was in another painful situation; I was living in fear of pain after an automobile accident. I didn't know when I would be in pain, where the pain would be, how severe it would be, or how long it would last. Sometimes I would be fine and then a seemingly normal activity like reaching for a pen, or bending over to pull a blouse out of the dryer would end up with horrible pain.

It might only last for a moment, or it might take me down for the day–I never knew. Sometimes I would wake up in the middle of the night with excruciating cramps in the bottom of my feet. Chiropractic had done wonders for me, but it wasn't able to help me with this residual accident pain.

I couldn't handle much in the way of manual therapies like massage because my muscles were still so tender to the touch. I was in the same situation that many of my patients are in when they first come to me–I didn't know what else to do but I knew I had to do something. I was willing to "try" acupuncture out of pure desperation. I went to the acupuncture clinic thinking I was going to see a "witch doctor". I needed relief from not only the pain but from the chronic stress over fearing the pain. I didn't really feel the needles; I just laid on the treatment table hoping this was going to work. When I got up, I thought I was floating because it didn't feel like my feet were touching the ground.

Although rare, that one treatment totally resolved the lingering accident pain I had. I was hooked. The practitioner I saw didn't educate me, so at that time I didn't know I could go back and get more acupuncture or use it as preventative medicine. I didn't know how at the time, but I knew this medicine had to be a part of my life. It was about two years later that I found out there was a school for Oriental Medicine closeby and knew this was for me. 2023, the year of the first publishing of this book, will mark ten years of practice for me. Acupuncture is so deep, wide, and layered that I always find new things to love about this medicine.

I never thought of myself as an artist, but that is what medicine really is; an art form. I read a definition that said art is: "learning the fundamentals and then practicing." Holistic medicine is a form of collaborative performance art. It is something we do together. I tell my patients all the time, "I'm dancing with you." Change is predicated by some level of pain, discomfort, and/or distress–there is something in your life that you know could be better.

Holistic healing is for when your mind needs clarity and focus, your heart needs peace and calm, your body needs relief and rejuvenation, and your spirit needs reconnecting. My professional life has blossomed very organically to include five powerful modalities to help my patients find their healing path: acupuncture, whole food nutritional therapy including Chinese Herbology, craniosacral therapy, life coaching, and hypnosis. I began professionally as an acupuncturist and herbalist who utilizes whole food nutritional strategies for healing. Sometimes my patient and I would never make it to the treatment room because we'd spend the whole time talking instead. My patients would say, "I could just come here and talk to you all day, this is better than therapy!" They offered to pay me for this and so, out of demand, I began offering coaching.

Coaching is phenomenal for our conscious mind, but sometimes it isn't enough to recalibrate our subconscious programs–this is where hypnosis makes a huge difference in shifting what couldn't be changed with coaching alone. As an acupuncturist, I'm usually the last person on the list after you've tried everything else. And, as fantastic and powerful as acupuncture is, sometimes it doesn't make the difference that we expect.

So, what do we do now? This is where craniosacral therapy and dynamic body balancing came into my life, first as a patient receiving these therapies and now as a practitioner. Fascia is what unites the whole body. Structure affects function. When fascia is twisted, it binds muscles, causing strain on the skeletal system and generally disrupts our optimal functioning. Releasing the fascia is a very gentle, hands-on process that has profound effects.

You can start or accelerate your journey with these five steps:

1/ Make a decision and commit to your healing

2/ Be open and willing to try "out of the box" modalities

3/ Acknowledge and appreciate the inner resources you already have

4/ Ask for and get help–don't try to do it all alone

5/ Find a way to give or give back to others–as you heal, share your story and help others connect with the resources you used to heal. As you give back, it brings everything full circle and it reinforces the results you have gained. This also plants the seeds for you to receive help you may need in the future

Join me on the Healing Path by enjoying a free guided meditation at www.healingpathacupuncture.info

## Jocelyn Michel

For over ten years, Jocelyn Michel has been a noteworthy leader in the holistic medicine space. You may know her from her work as an acupuncturist at Healing Path Acupuncture, but Jocelyn is also known for her work in CranioSacral Therapy and life coaching. She specializes in Chang Weike, which is ingestion and digestion of physical and experiential input.

She takes pride in providing personalized treatment to a growing number of over five hundred clients. She holds a bachelor's degree in psychology from the University of Wisconsin at Milwaukee and a dual degree in Nutrition and Oriental Medicine from the Midwest College of Oriental Medicine. She is also a certified life coach and certified hypnotherapist. She currently resides in Marshfield Wisconsin where she works as clinic director and clinician at Healing Path Acupuncture.

**Contact Jocelyn Michel:**

- www.linkedin.com/in/jocelyn-michel-c-ac-msom
- www.facebook.com/pinandplantdoctor
- www.youtube.com/@healingpathacupuncture

# Heal Your Home with Feng Shui & Diamond Dowsing Techniques

## By Deborah Miller

One day, twenty years ago, a series of related events changed the course of my life and my family's life forever. My husband and I moved to Minnesota in the early 90s, purchasing a relatively new house in a Twin Cities suburban neighborhood. Our oldest daughter was three years old when we moved in, and we welcomed another daughter shortly afterwards. My girls are now sixteen and twelve. That morning started like any typical weekday morning. Both girls had left for school, and I was cleaning up around the house. While cleaning the bathroom floor in the girl's bathroom, I had the distinct impression that a young girl was standing outside the door.

She looked a lot like my youngest daughter. I started to say something to her but remembered that my daughter should have been at school. Had she come home from school early? When I looked again, the hallway was empty. I checked to see if there was anyone home. That image of a girl was so clear that I could have sworn it was real. Once I realized what I had seen, a chill went up my spine. Was it a ghost? My husband and I were out for dinner with friends that evening when we received a frantic call from my youngest daughter. She had a friend visiting while we were out. Our dog had started barking at something up the stairs causing her to wonder what it could be.

When she looked up the stairs, she saw the figure of a girl standing in the middle of the hallway. She screamed and ran back outside with her friend. I told her to stay at her friend's home until we could get home to figure out what was happening. Later that evening, my older daughter was doing homework in a lower-level room in our house. It was used as an office then, so it had a separate phone line for business. She used that phone to call the home number, which rang in our bedroom, waking me up. I immediately knew that something was wrong from her frantic tone. She explained that a ghost girl was standing at the office door and that she was too afraid to leave.

She asked if I could walk with her from the office upstairs because she didn't want to walk alone. Keep in mind, we had yet to share any information about each of our interactions with this ghost. The same chill ran up my spine that I had experienced earlier in the day. I couldn't fall back to sleep that night. My mind was spinning over the events of the day. Was this a ghost that we all saw? The same ghost? Where did she come from? Why was this happening now? Doesn't this usually occur in older homes? What should I do? Who do I call? While trying to figure out my next steps, I started to pay better attention to things that were happening around our house.

Items would be missing and then appear in very unusual places, lights and other electrical appliances would be turned off and on by themselves, doors would swing open by themselves, and objects would move without anyone touching them. These things seemed random and insignificant before, but I began to see a pattern develop. All of this continued to escalate until I could no longer ignore it. The most disturbing thing about this was that most of these events revolved around my youngest daughter. I was very fortunate to receive a recommendation for a "Ghostbuster" who came to our home. She connected with the girl spirit and helped her to cross over.

She not only cleared our home, but took the time to educate us about why this had happened in the first place. We all tried to go back to our normal routines, but couldn't deny that we were changed by this experience. A few months later we had more paranormal activity in our home. I called the same medium to come back to our home that previously was so helpful. She informed me that we not only had another spirit in our home, but this time we had three. She explained to me that both of my children were very intuitive and that children with this gift have a kind of light or glow around them. This bright aura acts as a beacon and is very attractive to spirits.

The fact that these children can sense the presence of a spirit around them is also very attractive to ghosts. The challenge is that children do not know how to protect themselves or how to prevent these "hitchhiker ghosts" from following them home and attaching to their energy. The medium also shared with me that she felt I could do this clearing work myself. I had always known that I was intuitive, but I put all those ideas aside while delving into my career and parenting. Now it was time to learn more about it. I signed up for a psychic development class, my first of many. That week I also signed my youngest daughter up for a psychic development class designed for intuitive children.

There, she learned how to protect her energy, create boundaries, and deal with what she was psychically seeing, hearing, and feeling. The medium and I became friends and colleagues. I continued my studies with her through the healing center where her office was located, such as energy clearing, energy healing, the law of attraction, and past life regression. In addition, she invited me along on many of her ghost-clearing appointments so I could learn firsthand the process she used to clear homes, businesses, and parcels of land. While working with her, I gained a better understanding of ghost energy and learned different approaches to clearing it.

I then understood that ghosts, especially spirits that have been in a space for a long time, created a lot of heavy, dense energy and how it affected those who spend a lot of time in those negative energies. They would carry that energy with them, even when they were away from their homes. I had a better understanding about what was happening in my own home. In my daughter's case, the origin of that ghost energy was a negative vortex located in her bedroom. It had become a "worm hole" allowing spirits to pass back and forth. She was surrounded by this dense energy even when she was sleeping. Spending a lot of time in this dense energy will drain your physical and mental health.

It also affects the way others react to you because of all that negativity surrounding you. For example, I discovered that teachers and friends were bullying her in school, excluding her, and harassing her on social media. I watched my happy and confident youngest daughter sink into a mild depression in a short period of time. I needed to find a solution to clear and heal my home. It was becoming critically important for the health and well-being of us all. I focused on mastering the practice of Feng Shui, which is an ancient Chinese art of arranging buildings, objects, and space in an environment to achieve harmony and balance. I have completed all levels of Feng Shui training at the Wind & Water School of Feng Shui, including their Master's level.

A few years later, I was introduced to Marie Diamond's programs. As a result, I was one of the first to be certified as a Diamond Dowser in my area and later certified in Diamond Feng Shui. Using a Diamond dowsing technique, I completely cured the negative vortex in my daughter's room and changed it to a positive energy flow. Dowsing is especially critical when clearing homes of negative energy and has become an invaluable part of my Feng Shui work. That once negative dense bedroom space is now my office, where I meditate, write, create, and conduct my Zoom meetings. After clearing the energy in our home, specifically my daughter's room, she did a complete turnaround.

She was happier, more social, and thrived in sports as well as academics. Another important concept in all of Marie Diamond's programs is the use of quantum energy and quantum colors. Each of the twenty-four quantum colors has a unique healing quality that can be used for self-healing in meditation or as a cure in Diamond Dowsing, Diamond Feng Shui, and any energy clearing. Since I started working in and understanding how the quantum field of energy works, I am not limited to only seeing clients locally. I can connect energetically with clients in their homes or offices worldwide working through programs like Zoom or Facetime.

A few years ago, I was working with a woman who had a very intuitive daughter around the same age as my youngest. We were comparing stories and realized how similar our experiences were. Our daughters even had the same first name. Unfortunately, she didn't see that her daughter was highly intuitive and had difficulty understanding what she was experiencing. As a result, her daughter chose the path of self-medication, drug addiction, and became a runaway. If this parent had recognized that her child was struggling with her gifts, she might have been able to intervene before things went too far in a negative direction. I realized this could also have been my story, but I had the tools to change the ending to a positive one.

Through awareness and understanding of the situation, I could better support my daughter as she learned how to navigate through life as an intuitive person. Today, both of my daughters are very successful young women raising families of their own. They embrace their intuition and have the necessary tools to protect their energy and deal with any situation that may arise. These combined experiences have led me to do this work that has become my passion. I am especially focused on helping families create safe healing spaces and become advocates for their intuitive children.

I can share my personal experience and knowledge with parents, giving them the tools to help their children live happy, well-adjusted lives. My Feng Shui & Dowsing practice supports not only individuals & families, but also architects, realtors, interior designers, developers, partnerships, organizations, and businesses to help them find solutions that increase harmony, success, and abundance.

## Deborah Miller

Deborah is a Global Transformational Energy Worker.She has a Master's Level Certification in Feng Shui with the Wind & Water School Center and has successfully practiced with residential and business clients worldwide since 2008, bringing a new level of harmony and beauty to the places they live and work.

She more recently was certified in Diamond Feng Shui and was certified as a Diamond Dowser in 2015. Deborah has been working as an Interior designer for more than 4 decades.

Her work was first published in "Designed in MINNESOTA, An Exquisite Collection of Minnesota's Finest Designers (2007).

Early in her career as an interior designer, she was sensitive to how different the energy felt in each of her client's homes.

She took years of classes to fine-tune her intuition and psychic abilities to understand this better.

Deborah also has extensive knowledge and years of training in the law of attraction, inner diamond meditation, color frequencies, space clearing, and healing dowsing.

She intuitively combines all these healing modalities to create nurturing, supportive environments that promote Happiness and Health.

Deborah incorporates the principles of Feng Shui and dowsing in all aspects of her life and has witnessed the dramatic, positive transformations they have made for her clients, friends, and family.

To learn more about how she can share her knowledge to help you transform your Success, Health, and improve your Relationships, contact her for a free 15-minute consultation at one of the links below.

Deborah Miller
Domicile Design, Inc.
Interior Design, Feng Shui & Dowsing
Allied Member ASID, IFSG, FSIM
President of the Feng Shui Institute of the Midwest (FSIM)

**Contact Deborah Miller:**

www.facebook.com/Domicile.Design.Inc

@DomicileFengShui

www.linkedin.com/in/deborahmillerdomiciledesign

@Design_FengShui

www.pinterest.com/deborahkmiller

www.youtube.com/@deborahmiller4626

www.domicilefengshui.com

# A Letting Go Miracle

## By Anne Moore

My healing journey began in my mid-forties. I had been a medical provider for about ten years by that time, I had gotten divorced, had been fired from my job, was taking medication for ADD, was experiencing chronic pain and obesity and I felt like none of my relationships were working. Especially my relationship with my mother. My parents adopted me from an agency when I was just two weeks old. They had a son nine months later. I do not remember a time when I did not know I was adopted; my parents likely told me when I was very young. I remember telling a classmate in grade school that there was something wrong between my mother and me. I expressed my thoughts in childish terms but the observation was accurate. I had something to do with the two of us being so very different from one another and in a way that was not harmonious. As I write this, I am amazed to realize that I did not take our differences personally at that time.

By the time I was a teenager, I was very much taking her behavior personally. Her dismissive approach to each and every thing I did or said was irritating and suffocating. I moved out two weeks after graduating from high school and never looked back. I swore to myself that I would live under a bridge before I would ever live under her roof again. As I settled into adult life with a marriage and a career, I concluded that my mother did not love me. How could there be love when everything she did and said enraged me? It required an enormous amount of energy to prepare for and recover from each visit with her. I set extreme boundaries like limiting visits to seventy-two hours. That was the limit of my patience; I would turn into a She-Hulk/vampire/werewolf hybrid creature in the seventy third hour because I had been biting my tongue for three days. I chose to go no contact for a few years once just because I could not stand the way I acted around her.

Amidst all this fury, there was a quiet whisper in my heart that told me not to give up completely on my relationship with my mother. My journey to heal myself began in earnest right before my forty-fourth birthday. I had gotten divorced, was in a rebound relationship, was taking medication for ADD and had been fired from my job. I had plenty of time to look closely at the choices I had made. One day in late August of that year, I woke up with the worst headache of my life that lasted until bedtime. I couldn't fall asleep, I couldn't stop crying. I felt so lost, sad and frustrated about everything. I got up and searched the internet for "spiritual healing". The first thing that came up was a chakra quiz. I had heard of chakras and thought they sounded cool so I took the quiz. It showed my crown chakra was completely closed. That made me cry harder. So, I enrolled in the chakra healing course right then and there, listened to the first lesson and was able to calm down enough to fall asleep. I completed that course in a week and started learning how to heal my childhood wounds. It felt like a new beginning!

There were many more "A-Ha!" moments after that as I dove into energy healing, meditation, astrology, and biohacking. It got easier and easier to let go of limiting beliefs and habits that didn't serve me. At the same time, I was finding work that paid better, bosses who appreciated me, friends who supported me and effortless mental and physical well-being... Then on January 1st, 2021, when I was fifty-one years old, I started my first Feng Shui course. And then things happened very quickly. I hadn't spoken to my mother in three years, having gone no-contact for a second time. As my life had gotten better, the difficulty between us seemed more palpable and less bearable. But that whisper in my heart persisted: "Don't give up on your mom." In December of 2020, I told a meditation teacher that I was impatient to let go. He had replied, "Let go of impatience." So, I did. I relaxed. I started my Feng Shui course on January 1st, 2021. At the end of January, my boyfriend got sick. It turns out my mom had been emailing his mom without my knowing. So, my boyfriend's mom had told my mom of his illness. My mom emailed me on March 3rd to ask how he was doing. She closed by saying that she missed her daughter.

At first, I was mad. How dare she email me when I had told her no contact? Then I quickly let go of the anger, realizing that my power had not actually been taken away. I realized that she was free to send an email if she chose and I was free to not respond. So, I didn't. Three days later, I was changing from my indoor pajamas to my outdoor pajamas to go for a walk. As I was bending over to put my boots on, the words "Email your mother" came to me. I halfway said out loud, "Oh.... ok.... wha?" Then these words filled my brain: "YOU'RE GONNA EMAIL YOUR MOTHER RIGHT NOW AND HERE'S WHAT YOUR GONNA SAY!" At this point I was halfway yelling at my bedroom ceiling, "Okay! Just lemme get my boots on! Okay, okay! I'm going. GEEZ!" I went downstairs, fired up my laptop and started typing an email to my mother. Normally, writing to her would be a doubt-filled ordeal but that day, my finger effortlessly composed the following: "Dear Mom, Larry is much better, thank you for asking. As far as missing your daughter, the experiences you miss are no longer an option. If you are interested in exploring a new, healthy relationship with the person who also happens to be your daughter, I invite you to explore a new experience with me. Here is what I will need from you and what I am able to give you" Then I went on to list things like mutual respect, mutual accountability, no more trivializing each other, etc. I clicked send and went for my walk, confident that I would never hear from her again. Whew!

But the next afternoon, I got a reply: "Wonderful. Thank you, Anne: sounds like a good plan. But whenever I am out of line, I ask you to kindly tell me as I have much to learn." My first thought was, "Oh, crap! Now what do I do?" I was convinced that my mom's words were hollow, that having her in my life again would be an infuriating, toxic disaster like before; I was afraid it was a trick to get me back into her life. So, I decided to call my meditation teacher, who is also a psychologist, who knows all about my family dynamic. I knew she would have solid advice and I trusted her implicitly. I was truly ready to surrender.

My teacher and I had a Zoom call that evening. I told her everything that had happened: my boyfriend's illness, the emails, the voice. I told her my fears, that this was a trick, that nothing would change if I let my mother back into my life. She listened very patiently. Then she told me that she didn't get that from my mother's email at all. She told me that to her it sounded like my mother was genuinely ready to have a new experience with me. And she told me that everything was going to be ok. I could not breathe at that moment. My brain was formulating a protest along the lines of "But what if she can't/won't/doesn't?" As I started to speak, I was overcome by the sensation of something leaving my body. From my left upper abdomen, I sensed a dense ball of heavy gray energy the size of my fist floating painlessly out and away, taking with it all the anger, hurt and resentment I had been carrying for decades. I started crying; I saw that my teacher's jaw had dropped. We were both amazed by what had just happened. I suddenly felt lighter and I knew that everything really was going to be ok.

I reached out to my mom right away. We had a great phone call a few days later. I thanked her for not giving up on me. She welcomed me back wholeheartedly. We have Zoomed regularly and I visit her a few times every year. I can now receive her love fully and I appreciate her role in making me the person I am becoming. Our relationship isn't perfect; we are still very different people. And in truth, she hasn't changed. But I have. I don't take her stuff personally anymore. And the anger, hurt, and resentment have never come back. That's the real miracle!

Letting go has been such a vital part of my story. Fully accepting my mom's love has opened me up to receive abundance on a level I did not know existed! I have mastered a core set of techniques and tools that have been key in my journey to let go and heal. In my medical career, I have helped thousands of patients recover from physical and mental illness. I now offer an online course in Getting Unstuck in which I teach one of the techniques

I have used to heal my life. The course can be learned in the time it takes to make dinner; I teach why our brains resist change, then I demonstrate the exercise I have used over and over to heal my relationships with family and friends, unhealthy eating habits, chronic pain and financial struggle.

Students will be taught how to customize this technique for any problem they want to work on and will have access to the content indefinitely. There is also a private Facebook group and the opportunity for one-on-one coaching with me for further support. I look forward to helping you heal your life!

## Anne Moore

Anne Moore PA-C has been a medical provider for over twenty years and has helped thousands of patients manage and overcome physical and mental illness.

For over ten years, she has provided free medical care to the uninsured through community outreach and has coached and mentored dozens of students pursuing medical education.

In her mid-forties, she struggled with obesity, attention deficit disorder, job loss, divorce, toxic relationships and chronic pain.

In her journey to heal her life, she mastered powerful tools and techniques in energy work, meditation, Feng Shui, personal coaching, and biohacking to transform her life from an experience of struggle and lack to one of abundance and empowerment.

Her highest desire for humanity is peace and clarity. She offers personal coaching and online courses to professional women who seek a transformation that touches all areas of their lives, who know they are meant to do something special with their lives, who are hungry to fulfill their life purpose and experience more meaning.

**Contact Anne Moore:**

- @gerdesmoore
- www.facebook.com/Anne.MooreTheKey
- www.linkedin.com/in/beautifulhealth
- www.mykey.love

# Strategies To Build A Purposeful And Profitable Business Start With "Passion"

## By Wendy Nguyen

Strategies to build a purposeful and profitable business start with "PASSION".

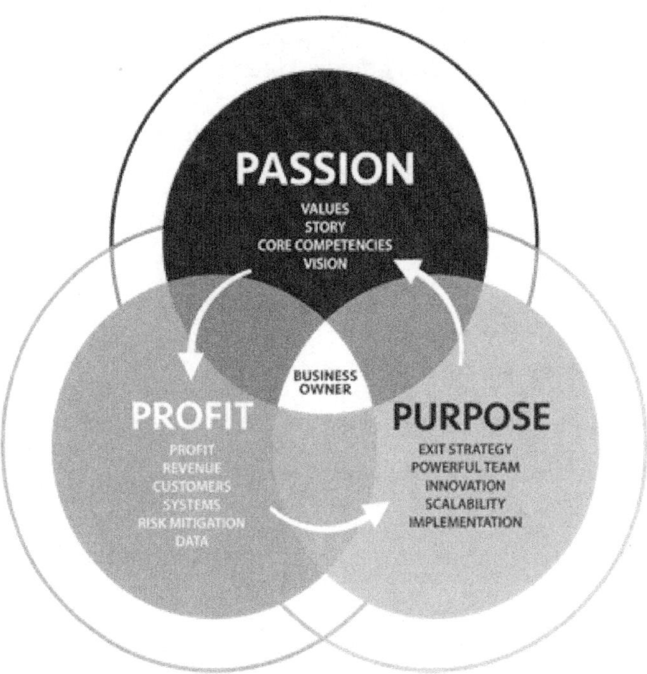


As a business owner, you don't know what you don't know. I certainly didn't when I started. Although I've spent almost two decades serving as auditor, controller/CFO, and CPA, and have founded and owned multiple businesses, I was once clueless about what it took to build a thriving business. I know what it's like to be so enthralled with a business idea that you charge full steam ahead—only to plateau and wonder what went wrong. Because in business, it's not enough to solely have passion; your profits will suffer, and you'll ultimately wander aimlessly without purpose. Purpose is wonderful, but without a tie-back to your strengths and a sound means to generate revenue, you'll be frustrated and stalled. And even profit alone won't work when your heart and talents aren't engaged in your business.

For your business to flourish, you need to view it through a different lens that aligns passion, profit, and purpose—what I call the "3P Formula."

But first, let's define what each of these elements means:

**1/ Passion:**
This is about leveraging your talents and interests, and relates to your core competencies. To determine your passion, ask yourself what you love to do every day—and what you are good at. The intersection of these two areas is where your passion resides.

**2/ Profit:** This is about generating revenue. But be forewarned: This is not just net income; it's about the cash you take home. Your rate of return, or the cost for you to provide your product or service, must be positive. Profit is the fuel of your business.

**3/ Purpose:** This is about doing what matters most to you. Your business should tie back to your purpose by answering the questions, "What's in it for me personally?" and "What's in it for my community?" To get closer to your purpose, ask yourself how and upon whom your business makes an impact.

When I think of passion, it leads me to the big red burning heart with desires and dreams. It is something that can make us so vulnerable and yet can be profound within us. I mix multiple ingredients in the passion jar, which includes:

- One full soup spoon of "core values."
- Multiple drops of "core competencies."
- Sprinkles of "many stories" to create the brand stories.

Blending all of these ingredients to an expected outcome has led to the creation of the "vision." What are all these ingredients made up of?

**Core Values**
Are core values really just a cliche? Many business owners and their employees struggle to truly believe in these values. It's understandable if you haven't experienced firsthand the power of having a set of core values. If you haven't been stung by a bee, you won't know how much it hurts. Likewise, if you've never had raw honey, you won't know how deep its sweetness is. Some may even say that core values are just a ploy to keep employees with a company. From where I stand, however, core values have been tremendously helpful. In August 2018, I was

trying to grow a six-employee company to multiple companies with over thirty employees in nine months. I thought I had what it took to build an empire.

But then, in September 2018, I was told that I had to leave the company and that was when I realized why—my vision was too big, I was too ambitious. I had invested and loaned her a large amount and I valued providing the very best service to customers and giving back to my community. My business partner, in contrast, wanted a simpler life and a simple and small service company—if she made money at the end of the year, she was happy with a Chanel purse. She disagreed with all of my giving back and contributing both time and money to the community.

My core values were clearly at odds with hers, so I agreed to step out of the business. This mistake of not being true to my core values cost me a lot of money and even put me in a lawsuit—an expensive lesson, to be sure.

But later, in January 2019, I had the chance to learn more about non-negotiable values when I was invited to a class by one of my partners. We worked out a set of core values together and though they've been revised and have evolved over time, they have always remained focused on "doing the right thing" and having fun. Core values create a consistent culture that allows employees to stick together, as well as benefiting customers, vendors, and the community. So, can you still say core values are a cliche? To find out, you'll have to experience the sweetness of raw honey for yourself—it may take failing several times to truly get it.

### Core Competitions

Don't Wait, Give Yourself Permission Many years ago, one of my friends specialized in beauty. She was the best nail specialist I knew, and started at a nail salon when she was sixteen. At twenty-four, she owned her first nail salon. Despite the struggles of having very few customers, as the previous owner had opened a store nearby in an attempt to compete with her, she managed to revitalize her store within less than a year and had to turn away customers from time to time. Unsatisfied with being a nail specialist, she went on to study and specialize in lashes. She sold her nail salon after five years and started her own franchising business with three lash stores. She traveled to many different countries in Asia, such as Japan, Taiwan, Vietnam, and Korea, to look for manufacturers to create healthy and chemical-free glues and lashes.

During this time, she encountered challenges with the formulas of the products due to her lack of knowledge as a chemist. In response to this, she decided to study microblading for eyebrows and lips, an area in which she showed an incredible amount of talent. After three years of rigorous practice, she became a master in microblading and traveled to Norway and numerous other countries to attend various beautician conventions. Throughout the U.S., she underwent training sessions and worked with other beauty spas and salons.

At the time, I was content with my corporate job and thought that her career path required a ton of practice. However, I slowly realized the sheer amount of effort she was investing in herself through courses, travel, and other means. I waxed philosophical and asked her why she couldn't just stay in one place, owning many beauty salons and making a lot of money. Her response was that everyone has slight strengths and weaknesses; what she was doing was taking different techniques and tying them all together to create an optimal product. Furthermore, she knew it was not easy to find a master willing to share what they knew, and she wanted to become someone who could "teach people how to fish." It took me more than five years to fully understand what she meant, but finally, I gave myself permission to do the same.

At the end of 2018, when I restarted my CPA practice, I invested more than sixty percent of my time in gaining more knowledge on how to make small businesses profitable. I have all the skill sets to help a business to be in full financial compliance, yet I still don't have the full understanding of how to grow a business. I started by taking classes with Goldman Sachs 10KSB (10,000 small businesses), Harvard, Northwestern University, Global OKR (objectives and key results), and attended many networking and business conferences, like Profit First. In 2020, I hired myself a personal business coach. At the same time, I started to read many books on self-development and business strategies. While I spent most of my work time studying, my new revived practice tripled its revenue and continued to grow healthily in its fifth year.

**Vision.**

Back in 2012, while I was auditing various companies on a daily basis, I found myself questioning what I knew and my own complacency as an auditor. I left my secure job and started my own CPA firm, without any real vision of my own. I followed the paths of my competitors, wanting more customers, employees, and, of course, more money. But over time I realized that the vision should go beyond that, it should be about creating a real impact and change in the market. To gain clarity, I read Simon Sinek's book, *Start With Why,* and gained more insight into the WHYs behind my business.

Despite the struggles of going out on my own, becoming my own boss with the freedom to have my own schedule was part of my vision. Four years later, on a trip to Shanghai, I met a gentleman with a plastic tray manufacturing plant. Apple was one of his customers. His equipment was imported from Germany and, despite cheaper machines being available elsewhere, he had chosen quality for the durability and reputation of his products.

The move had earned him a leg-up in the highly competitive market as his products had to meet global requirements for phone containers. This gentleman first arrived in China and worked as a plastic collector on the street. After ten years, his business worked with one of the largest companies in the world.

This makes me question my capabilities in growing a company in the U.S. He and his business became a source of inspiration for me to restart the consulting practice and this time I set an intention to become a consulting practice for companies all over the world.

My mindset has helped my business to gain several international customers in just two years. Each of the components within the passion jar is the foundation of success. The grander the vision the company has, the more like-minded customers it can attract. Exceptional skills in the core competencies will help the company to charge a premium price. All of these will drive up the company's profit.

More profit will help to fulfill the purpose, and the further the company progresses towards its goals, the more fuel is added to the fire of passion. These are essential components of a successful business, not something to be added later as an afterthought.

To build a flourishing business, you need to take a holistic approach that harmoniously integrates passion, profit, and purpose. By aligning the 3Ps, you'll create a sustainable, prosperous, and equitable business so you can have more freedom and choice in your life.

## Wendy Nguyen

From the outside, Wendy Nguyen, CPA, had much success, a loving family, and successful businesses. But she wanted to do more—to make a difference in the world and give back. For two decades, she has pursued projects and consulted clients, guided by her mission to benefit others. During the pandemic, she wrote *Forbes* articles. One of the most read articles was "The most important thing you need to build a flourishing business." With fifteen staff members and her business partners, Wendy was able to retain over one thousand jobs and provided her clients with access to over $20 million in 2020 and 2021. She encountered many hardships and ideas which she pursued with entrepreneurial enthusiasm, even connecting with experts in government and the private sector. Wendy Nguyen, a philanthropist advocating for education, a board member of various national organizations, speaker at global finance conferences, an author, considered herself as a "Business Therapist." Early in 2023, she published her first book, *How to Get Paid Doing What You Love*. She interviewed entrepreneurs who followed their passion and built a business they truly enjoyed. It is available here: https://mybook.link/book/B0BWNW1Q54

**Contact Wendy Nguyen:**

- www.linkedin.com/in/wendynguyenofficial
- @wendynguyenprofitwhisper
- www.Facebook.com/wendynguyenofficial

# The Essence and Energy of Food

## By Olelo pa'a Ogawa

Food is medicine and it is sacred. It can provide healing to your body, mind, and spirit in a profound way. There was a time when our culture revolved around our sacred food preparation, and we were better for it. Our healthcare system is outrageously costly and obsolete; we don't have enough doctors, the health care providers are not getting adequate reimbursement for their services, we have a chronically ill society dependent on medication, and it is not health care at all, it is illness management. It is time for you to take charge of your health and well-being.

My name, Olelo pa'a, was given to me by the late Dr. Ihaleakala Hew Len. He meditated, and said my name means "the very spark of existence." Some of my other Hawaiian friends say it means I speak and share a powerful message. Now is the time for me to share my important message (in Hawaiian, it's called mana'o), in hopes you will join me in bringing back the sacredness of food preparation through mindfulness, appreciation, and inspiration. The truest way towards health and balance is through the same processes we need most to thrive: eating, drinking water, and breathing. What if we could incorporate all three through the process of food preparation? What if we could also incorporate love, mindfulness, and inspiration, and have this through our food preparation? This has been my special journey through my life, and this is what I want to share with you.

I have been cooking professionally for more than forty-five years, and I am still excited and passionate about food, our farmers, and everyone I prepare food for. In the last twenty-five years, I have also been learning to work with life force energy. It began when I was a chef consultant at a new hospital in our community. I was excited to work there because they had a department that offered a natural healing modality called Healing Touch, for the purpose of bringing energetic balance to the entire being. When the head of the department introduced me to this work, I started to feel life force energy for the first time. I was so inspired, I decided to take Healing Touch training, while I continued working as a chef consultant. A handful of us volunteered to work with patients, first by practicing on each other. I saw the results of this work on myself, on the other volunteers, and on the patients we treated. After I had become a certified Healing Touch practitioner, I went to see a patient who was in severe pain from a bad biking accident. I introduced myself and asked if she wanted Healing Touch. She firmly said not to touch her because she was in so much pain. "No problem," I said, "I will not touch you. I will only put my hands about three inches above your body." This she allowed, so I was able to do the energy work on her. I asked, "How much pain are you in? If ten is the highest pain level, and one is the lowest, how much is your pain?" She said, "My pain level is twenty! So don't touch me!"

I smiled tenderly and began to guide her through a relaxation meditation, then began to do the work on her. After about fifteen minutes her phone rang, she answered it, and started talking with her friend. "Oh my God!" she cried out, "I don't feel pain! Whatever she is doing is working!" She was one of many individuals I worked on, but the biggest validation was when I experienced healing on myself. There are no such things as accidents or coincidences. Before my time with the hospital, I was working as a restaurant manager at Mauna Lani Resort. I was badly stressed as a single parent, and very depressed. My son was only nine years old, and I was thinking about ending my life. I spoke to some close friends, and admitted I had thoughts of committing suicide. They told me that I should go to the doctor for help.

I called the doctor's office, but he was booked with many appointments that day. The nurse said, "Can you tell me what seems to be the problem?" "I'm afraid I want to end my life," I told her. She calmly asked me to hold on for a few minutes, then she came back on the line and said, "Can you come in two hours?" I went to the appointment and was grateful they made time for me. The doctor said, "I know you don't like taking medication, but please consider taking this anti-depression medication for a week or two. You will start feeling better." I took the prescription to the pharmacy in the grocery store nearby. The attendant said it would be ready in about twenty minutes.

Still dazed and depressed, I got a shopping cart and wandered up and down the aisles. On one aisle I saw someone I knew. She smiled and said, "I love your energy." I thought to myself, you must be kidding. I don't look good, I don't feel good, and I don't believe what you just said. But I smiled, and walked to another aisle, and someone else spoke to me. "My son said you are the best manager that he has ever worked for, so thank you!" I asked myself, "What is going on?"

Then I started down another aisle. An older lady friend said, "Hi, how are you doing?" "I want to kill myself!" I exclaimed. "Don't do that, don't do that!" she shouted. I still remember her fearful eyes. "I lost my twin brother last year because he committed suicide. I want to invite you and your son to my home for dinner tonight." I told her that I was going to be fine and not to worry, but she insisted. What did I get out of this experience in the store? I did not know then, but later I realized that these were angels on Earth; they were God-sent, and they helped shift my life in those few moments. I picked up my prescription, and with it was two pages listing the side effects. I looked down those two long pages and, despite my fear and the doctor's advice, decided not to take the medication. I went home, and when my nine-year-old son came home from school, I told him that I wanted to end my life. "Don't do that, Mom," he said, "because I will be sad and angry." That woke me up. I hadn't even thought about my son's feelings. I was so consumed with my pain that I did not consider how my son would feel. I held him close, thinking this depression was one of the most painful things I had ever experienced, but I would not let it hurt him. We accepted my friend's invitation to dinner that night and the journey back to my natural state of health had started.

The following weekend I had been invited to be a guest chef in Honolulu, to do a cooking demonstration for about two hundred people. At that time, it was rare to see women chefs in Hawai'i, and the whole thing added even more to my stress level. I shared my concerns with a friend on O'ahu. She suggested that my son and I come stay with her on the North Shore, in front of a famous surf spot called Sunset Beach. Our time there was healing—and it was just the beginning. When I came back, I learned about a training that was going to take place on Hawai'i Island called Self I-Dentity through Ho'oponopono. I signed up for it. Going through this process helped me remove thoughts of depression, fear, resentment, and sadness.

I loved working with food, but I did not like the long hours of work as a private chef. Restaurant management was stressful, and traveling for work took me away from my son. As I kept meditating and doing the Ho'oponopono process called cleaning (getting rid of toxic thoughts), inspiration would come in. I would have more clarity, joy, peace, and more. I had clients tell me the food I prepared would bring tears to their eyes. They'd ask what I put into the dishes.

Well, it is the mana (life force) that I learned how to access through Ho'oponopono. One time I did a cooking demonstration and talk at a Hawaiian Charter School and the Kumu hula (master hula teacher) said to me, "Your teaching and cooking is like doing a Hula." A parent came up to me a few months after that event and said, "I used to just go through the routine of cooking for my family, but I did not enjoy cooking. Now I have changed the way I cook, and I have an appreciation for mindful food preparation. *Mahalo* Olelo pa'a!" Twenty-five years later, I continue to practice this work in my daily life. From moment to moment, especially as I prepare food, I work on dispelling all hurtful thoughts.

And, after working so long with food in this way, the food itself and the land it comes from have messages for me to share with you, as well. The purpose of this book is to share the inspiration that is coming through me moment to moment. The Divine Source is telling me to share this message with the world. It is not about following a recipe; it is about bringing back the sacredness of food preparation.

Please join me in a healing journey towards remembering and restoring food as medicine. This, as my name says, is the powerful message I am inspired to speak and share. This may be the very spark of existence, the essence and energy of food.

## Olelo pa'a Ogawa

Olelo pa'a Ogawa, "The Energy Chef of Hawai'i," is an award-winning private chef. As one of the first female chefs in Hawai'i to emerge in the eighties, she has over forty-five years of international experience in the food and hospitality industry. She is proud to count some of *Forbes* magazine's "Richest People List" as her clients.

In her present work as an energy holistic life coach and business consultant, Olelo shares her expertise and passion for food in tandem with healing energy to facilitate wellness within individuals seeking clarity and direction in navigating an ever-changing world.

She exemplifies the practice of harnessing the energy within to improve the quality of one's life for optimal spiritual, physical, and mental well-being.

Olelo facilitates self-discovery in her clients to define their own energy, to act from the heart with intention, and to effect change. Olelo pa'a recently signed on to be a show host for the *Win Win Women Network*.

She works similarly with businesses to elevate and transform leadership to cultivate engagement, wellness, and productivity in the workplace. Olelo leads from the heart and inspires others to do the same in living healthy, joyful, and fulfilling lives.

These days, Olelo pa'a utilizes her gifts and talents by offering holistic coaching and business consultation, and has recently begun work as an inspirational writer and speaker.

Olelo pa'a is based on Hawai'i Island. You can connect with Olelo pa'a Ogawa on Instagram, Facebook and LinkedIn, or at www.glowhawaii.com.

**Contact Olelo pa'a Ogawa:**

@olelopaa_

www.linkedin.com/in/olelo-pa-a-ogawa

www.facebook.com/olelopaa.ogawa

www.glowhawaii.com

# Miracles Happen When You Follow Your Heart

## By Denisa Riha Palečková

"You were born to be a healer, a teacher and an educator, to help people in the areas of their lives where they feel most vulnerable." I'm in the first minute of a reading with Sonia Choquette, the world's leading psychic reader. Her words give me chills. Sonia knows absolutely nothing about me; to her, I'm just a voice on the telephone and a name.

"You have done this for many, many lifetimes. You worked as a midwife, a shaman. You lived on the fringes of society and you had to conceal your work. It was dangerous," she continues, and I have goosebumps because I sense the truth in her words. "In this life, the time has come for you to show your work. It is time for you to be in the public eye, to be seen and respected."

I swallow and think back to my beginnings, my first seminars and my first massages. I was twenty-five years old, but I looked fifteen. I had completed two years of training in bodywork and sexuality. I had studied sociology at Charles University in Prague and began working as a tantric masseuse at a leading Prague business club. At that time, I was still living with my mother and I felt that she didn't want to know about such things. At home, I told her that I worked at the front desk. I had no idea then that bringing topics that were not "talked about" into the light would be the DNA of my mission. Or that I would be able to sensitively, easily, and naturally talk about what others would prefer to keep hidden even from themselves. Parts of our lives that we would rather push away, such as feelings of loneliness and uncertainty and of not being good enough, drama, and alienation in our relationships. Thanks to my profession, people who look happy and successful have revealed to me what their lives are really like.

At that time, in 2001, I didn't realize that in my country, Czechia, pioneering experience with tantric massage would be an important building block for my future profession. It would be a profession, where I would be seen and heard, on Czech Television, on Czech Radio, at high schools, ground schools and universities, and on numerous stages, such as TEDx Prague. I would be talking about problems with sexuality, about shame, about vaginal mapping, and many other topics that leave people breathless because someone is finally speaking to their soul. Finally, someone is putting a name to what they know from their lives but has made them feel oddly alone and strange. But the main topic, above this all, would be love and relationships, to others and oneself. Through in-person and, later, online courses, I would help people be happy in their relationships. I would help save thousands of marriages and families, even those that marriage counselors and sexologists had written off as hopeless.

At the beginning of the new millennium, I still had no idea that I would do all of this. Even though I had come a long way, I still had a lot of work and healing to do on myself. Relationships in my family were painful. My mother was twice divorced. Both of my grandmothers were divorced. They perfectly followed the current statistics in today's modern countries: 50% of marriages break apart within three to five years after marriage.

With this family history, it's no wonder that I had a tremendous need to learn more in the area of relationships and intimacy. I have completed courses and training in many countries in Europe, Asia and Africa, as well as in the United States and Canada. Early on, as a student from a post-communist country, I didn't have much money, so I worked my way through some of the seminars by cleaning toilets or cutting vegetables in the kitchen. Most people take it as the norm that a relationship "cools off after a few years". They come to terms with the idea that sex will never again be as good as it used to be, if it was ever good at all. They also accept that they live side-by-side as if they were just two coworkers and caregivers. And I see that much of what makes people feel lonely and troubled remains unnamed.

The most common issues, I encountered, are:

- There's no longer a spark between us.
- We are alienated from each other.
- I can't tell him how I feel. He just argues or walks away.
- She's always blaming me for something. I don't know what I'm supposed to do.
- I don't know how to deal with her emotions. That woman must be crazy. She could act more normal.
- Everything changed after childbirth. I stopped wanting sex. My partner pressures me, but I just don't have the strength for it.
- I don't like the way he touches me.
- She doesn't turn me on.
- How am I supposed to have sex with her when I can't get an erection?

- I'm tired after a whole day with the children. I can't even think about sex.

These issues come up far more frequently than you would think. And most people feel alone with these topics, even though they're not. When our sexuality and relationships are healthy, we have a sense of happiness, ease, contentment, and personal strength. Conversely, when there is strife in our relationship or when our family falls apart, most of what we have built in our lives suddenly doesn't make sense anymore. Let's look at how it happened for Hana and Martin, a beautiful and successful couple at first glance, with two healthy children and a thriving business. Nice people. If you had seen them, you would have said, "They've really got it together! What a wonderful life they have! Such great kids! Such an amazing relationship!" But they were on the verge of separating. They came to a retreat for a couple's seminar in a last ditch attempt to save their marriage. I observed them during the course and, though I didn't know much about their story, I felt the situation between them. I felt their love for each other. And the pain that was driving them apart. I could perceive their lack of mutual understanding. How he perceived her attempts to improve their relationship as criticism, and he didn't know what to do.

She was fastidious. She loved her husband and she liked things to be perfect. She thus needed constant improvement in the relationship and in their business. He didn't understand her words. He took them as criticism. What he heard in her words was, "You are impossible. You can't do anything right. You're not good enough. You've messed this up, too." But that's not what she said or meant. He was rather hearing echoes from his childhood. Like many of us, he was repeating his parents' critical words to himself. He was also a perfectionist and his wife's words hurt him greatly. He felt, "I'm trying so hard! I'm doing everything I can for her. And it's still not enough?!" And because he didn't know which way to turn, he decided it wasn't worth it anymore.

I had a brief conversation with them as she sat sadly and tensely on a bench. I sat down next to her. Her husband came to us a moment later. I gave them my view. I described the dynamic that I saw between them and how I felt how much they loved each other but just didn't understand each other. I suggested to him that sometimes, she wasn't saying what he thought she was saying. I advised her to speak more about what her husband did well and less about what needed to be improved. Because he would understand her "advice" as his failure to make her happy. In essence, they loved each other in their hearts, but they didn't understand each other in their words. I then saw them again at other courses during the year. She attended a course for women and, a year later, they were together at our Core Touch training. It was there that the pieces of their story came together. Martin came to me with a gift: "Thank you for saving our relationship. When you came to talk to us, we were about to leave the course. At that moment, I had decided that it was over. That we had to get divorced. I was convinced that there was no way back," he said with tears in his eyes. "When I saw you sitting with her and I sat down with you, I took it as a sign, and your words touched me deeply." Now we were both crying. "Thanks for helping to bring love back between us. We live a completely different life now. I love my wife. I've changed a lot of things. My wife has changed, too. We have a beautiful life together now." I am moved again and again by such stories. Hana and Martin are one of many.

I look back with gratitude at how many women and men I have helped to change their lives and save their marriages. People who have overcome obstacles in their sexuality and gained loving self-acceptance and self-realization. There are legions of them. Tens of thousands. Millions of women and men around the world who argue and worry every day, feel unloved and rejected, and suffer from a lack of fulfilling intimacy. Usually only because they haven't learned otherwise. Because they were not taught by their parents or at school how to approach their bodies and sexuality with love and respect. Or how to recognize and communicate their needs and boundaries. I see before me a huge field of work, namely bringing high-quality and meaningful education about sexuality and relationships into schools and other platforms. And I want to do this not only in my small country, but around the world. I imagine a global network of radiant human hearts and souls. Women and men living in joy and love, satisfied with themselves and grateful for each other.

I know that when we have contentment in our souls and relationships, we make wise decisions. We have no need to fight. We then enjoy peace, joy and collaboration in our relationships with our partners, our coworkers, our children and our parents... and even with other countries. Because when we are content in our souls and relationships, when we can be kind to ourselves and feel fulfilled, we then have no need to hurt anyone. "Go write a book. Publish it with Hay House," Sonia tells me in our conversation. Hay House? Me? Really?! But I teach mainly in the Czech Republic. "Yes, it is time for you to take your teaching to the world," she continues. I am pleasantly surprised and my heart glows with joy. Because that resonates so much with my soul.

Denisa Riha Palečková

As a leading Czech relationship and intimacy expert, best-selling author and public speaker, Denisa Riha Palečková provides a whole new perspective on sexuality and methods of using it for health, happiness, and personal development. She has been a speaker at TEDx, as well as an expert guest on Czech Television, Czech Radio, Jack Canfield's Success TV and many other media outlets.

Since 2002, Denisa has helped tens of thousands of people lead more joyful and fulfilled lives. She teaches people how to live a life of love and passion in a long-term relationship. She is the founder of the School of Happy Relationships, Core Touch, holistic sensual massage training and the Arkaya massage studio. Denisa also introduced vaginal mapping and scar tissue healing to the Czech Republic and is the creator of numerous online programs for women, men, and couples.

She serves women and men who are ready for change in their lives. Her clients experience huge life transformations. Denisa helps them to have happier, more fulfilling personal lives, relationships, and intimacy. To find their power, feel life's endless possibilities and open their hearts to live truly meaningful lives.

Denisa is a sought-after expert. Her articles and interviews appear in a wide range of media and publications like ELLE, Harper's Bazaar, Playboy, and Forbes.

In addition to being an in-demand love and intimacy expert, Denisa is a happy wife and mom. She and her husband, Pavel, run her company together and are raising two amazing boys, Pedro and Oliver.

Her mission:

Less divorce, less broken families, and more happiness in peoples' lives since they will be following their hearts and desires without hesitation.

**Contact Denisa Riha Palečková:**

English:

- @denisapaleckova_official
- www.facebook.com/DenisaPaleckovaOfficial
- www.youtube.com/DenisaRihaPaleckovaENG

Czech:

- @denisa.riha.paleckova
- www.facebook.com/denisa.riha.paleckova
- www.youtube.com/denisarihapaleckova
- www.denisapaleckova.com

Do you want to improve the quality of your relationship or be better prepared for your next one? I have prepared three easy steps for you as a gift. The Three Secrets to More Fulfilling Relationships video series is available for download on my website at denisapaleckova.com / download it here:

www.denisapaleckova.cz/en/3-secrets-to-more-fulfilling-relationships

# Creating Results That Stick!

## By Tara Pilling

Do you feel stuck? Perhaps you're sick and tired of being sick and tired, feeling like there has to be something more to life? Or, maybe you feel like it doesn't matter what you do. You start something new, you might even get some good results from it but over time, things just go back to the way they were, or maybe they get even worse. If this is you, you are not alone. Many can relate, myself included! "It's not working your way. I can show you a way that works every time," I clearly recall the first time I heard my mentor Bob Proctor say these words. And, it turns out, he was right!

I don't believe in coincidences; you are most likely reading this book and these words for a reason. I call it divine timing. And it's true; I can show you a way that works every time with every person. There's just one catch; you have to want better results and a better life. What if I told you that I have a science-based recipe that dates back to a lineage over 150 years, and with practices and principles that date back thousands of years to the Bible, the Bhagavad Gita, and the Koran that get results that stick? Would you say "Yes!" if I offered to guide you through a system that creates massive transformation and prosperity in every area of your life? Would you be interested in learning more? Well, if you said yes, welcome! You are definitely in the right place at the right time. Read to the end and I will map out this "recipe" for you and show you how to get started in creating the life and results that you desire. The starting point of all achievement is *desire.* Desire is the effort of the unexpressed possibility within. The idea is seeking expression–it's cooking inside–it wants to be expressed! I want to share a little about my journey and how I learnt about this recipe before we go any further.

As Les Brown says, you have to be "hungry". Looking back over my life, I was exactly that. I was hungry for mentorship, for guidance, and knowledge. I'd been on this path of personal development and healing since before my mom's tragic passing in a house fire on Christmas of 1995. I was twenty-one years young and I was devastated, lost, and confused. I took custody of my younger brothers while planning her funeral and within months, I was also having to address a serious health scare that kicked my ass and almost took me out. Stress can do horrible things when left unchecked. Not to mention a devastating loss around a relationship that turned abusive and only added to my broken heart. I was young, there was no support and it felt like the whole world was on my shoulders. I felt like giving up during that time and for the years to follow, I often contemplated suicide, a thought I'd known well as a young child and teenager. I was the last person mom had talked to on the phone. She was drunk, she had broken her sobriety and I had told her to call me back tomorrow when she was sober. This had been something my mom told me to say to my dad whenever he was drunk, which he was most of the time. Mentally, I was a mess and my coping mechanisms weren't doing me any favors. My mind wasn't well and going out drinking with friends wasn't doing me any good. I was desperate and praying for a miracle as I really didn't want to live.

It's unbelievable looking back at how I was able to make it through those dark days, my dark night of the soul. At the time I was working at the hospital in Occupational and Physical Therapy on the therapeutic ward. I was encouraged to work to take my mind off things and I barely had enough money to buy groceries, what with the newly-added responsibility of my brothers. We even visited the food bank a couple times. Going back to the food bank was difficult for me as it reminded me of when we were kids. My mom went to the food bank a lot during my childhood. All this was playing on my mind as I was sitting at my desk on the ward. I clearly remember my eye being caught by a picture on the bulletin board. A picture of a stork with a half-eaten frog in its mouth, the arms of the frog around the stork's neck holding on for dear life, and above the image it read, "NEVER GIVE UP!" The power of a picture!

I'd gone through all those incredibly tough years of not giving up and that picture, for some reason, kept me going and gave me faith when I didn't have any of my own. I was surviving and getting by, thankfully, as it would have been so easy to give up. I am grateful to this day to my brother Richard for saying: "Tara, we need you." These words were profound in that moment and I carried them with me as a reminder anytime I felt like giving up. There was always something within me that kept me going, a desire to get better; better understanding, awareness, and find the support I needed in order to show up for myself and others. I knew my parents did the best they could with what they had, the inner healing work gave me the ability to stop blaming them for my life. Both my parents struggled with addiction and mental health.

So, of course I struggled with the same challenges. I would never have admitted it at the time but I did struggle and probably did most of my life, just like my siblings too.

Overtime, I studied and practiced with some of the best in health, healing, nutrition, yoga, meditation, personal development, and human potential. Basically from 1996 onwards, I seeked out the best help I could find to help me heal, feel better, and to help me find purpose. You name the world-renowned teacher, event, or course and you can bet that I was there, drinking it all up! I spent a very impacting year in 2015 with Robin Sharm, best known for *The Monk Who Sold His Farrari* and *5AM Club*. As my confidence grew, so did my desire. During the spring of 2016 until the fall of 2017, I dedicated my time to studying and traveling around the world with Tony Robbins and completing Mastery University and Leadership University. All of this was just incredible; I was living the dream and finally felt like I was getting somewhere. I'd also been in a Buddhist mentorship with another world-renowned teacher Michael Stone (Shoken) and had a daily commitment to my yoga, meditation, and Buddhist studies. I felt like there was a light at the end of the tunnel.

My life looked perfect. However, I always felt like something was missing. I didn't know what it was but I always felt like my emotions were based on what was going on outside of me. I still went through big ups and downs and I often lacked confidence. I didn't feel good enough and my business at that time was costing me more than what I was making. I knew I was capable of so much, I just didn't understand what was getting in my way. There are no coincidences. After a conversation on the flight home from Fiji with Tony Robbins, a colleague whom I was doing some energy medicine on mentioned Bob Proctor. She'd asked me if I'd ever studied with him, I said no. I commented to her that I remembered seeing him in *The Secret* when it came out many years previously. She said, "You should reach out to him."

And, of course this led me to a profound conversation a few weeks later with the late Bob Proctor who became my mentor till his passing in Feb. 2022. His words, "It's not working your way I can show you a way that works," You know when you hear something so profound that you feel it in your heart and soul? I had found the missing piece! Bob taught me how to think, really think, and he showed me how to upgrade the way I was programmed. He taught me how to understand my mind and universal law for the first time in my life!

If you are reading these words, I believe you are here for a reason. Perhaps this is an answer to your prayers; your paradigm shift! I bet there's something within you too that knows you're capable of doing so much more!

*You are programmed genetically and environmentally. Your paradigms are part of your mental subconscious program and the way you are programmed has almost exclusive control over everything you think, say, and do. Your results are a reflection of the way you were programmed. Change your paradigms and you will change your life!*

Here is the science-based recipe that works when you follow its twelve key steps:

1/ Get clear on what you want. You must get on the frequency of your dreams.
2/ Close the knowing-doing gap. Action is key! Knowing is not enough.
3/ You have infinite potential. The more you increase your awareness and understanding of your mind, the more potential you can access.
4/ An image of the mind brings order. You think in picture. Where there is no order, there is disorder and confusion. A deep understanding around your conscious and subconscious mind are key in getting the results you desire.
5/ You have six higher mental faculties, God-given gifts. Unfortunately, you've been programmed to operate out of your lower mental faculties, your senses (hearing, sight, taste, touch and smell). You have to strengthen your "gifts". React vs Respond.
6/ Your self-image sets the boundaries for what you can and can not do. Your current self-image is reflected in your results. Environment is but a looking glass. Your environment is a reflection of your self-image and what is going on within. Your goal is really a self-image upgrade.
7/ Get uncomfortable, do the thing that scares you. If you are going to reach those big goals and dreams, you are going to have to go through the four stages of the terror barrier: bondage, reason, terror barrier, freedom. Unfortunately, you've been programmed to stay stuck in comfort and complacency. The terror barrier is the difference between those that reach success and those that continue to fail.
8/ You will have to get praxis on what you desire and your goals. Believe. With belief, all things are possible. Your beliefs dictate your behaviors.
9/ Your attitude will make or break you. Attitude is the compilation of your thoughts, feelings, and actions. A great attitude equals great results. A bad attitude equals bad results.
10/ You must see yourself as the most valuable person in your life, not your partner or kid or friend, but you. You can only lead and serve others when you are leading by example. Real leaders know when to follow and know when to lead.

11/ You must leave others with the impression of increase. This is the number one key to success in anything you do!
12/ You must magnify your mind–mastermind. Working with the mastermind principles and magnifying your mind is a game-changer and will create phenomenal results!!

The next step is to reach out. I have included a gift for you here–a thirty-minute free mentorship call to support you in taking action toward your goals and dreams. Message me personally at tara@diamondmindconsulting.ca and use the CODE: GCEDiamond.
I look forward to meeting with you.

## Tara Pilling

Tara believes that everyone has acres of diamonds in their mind waiting to be discovered and shined up! A diamond in its rough state is unrecognizable, and a diamond is formed under intense heat and pressure.

Take a long, careful look at what you are presently doing. Napoleon Hill said that we should not go searching for opportunities but reach out and embrace it right where we are. Never forget that you are, at this moment, standing right in the middle of your own "acres of diamonds."

Tara is a peak performance mindset consultant and inner circle leader with Bob Proctor and Proctor and Gallagher Global Inc. She is also a law of attraction and prosperity guide, internationally best-selling author and speaker, holistic and energy-based practitioner, yoga and meditation teacher, and Ayurveda coach. Tara had spent over thirty years as a student and practitioner with some of the best teachers in health, healing, yoga, meditation, ayurveda, human potential, and prosperity, both researching and studying.

The tragic loss of her mother in a house fire when she was twenty-one years young was the catalyst, leaving her to support her younger siblings and at a place of unbearable grief and loss; depressed, suicidal, and with a heavy health diagnosis that came a few months later.

Holistic health and healing, personal development, yoga, and meditation gave her the skills and tools to heal her mind and body. Bob Proctor's mentorship and material gave her the ability to transform and change every area of her life radically!

Tara has supported hundreds of business men and women and individuals to access more significant potential and prosperity. Tara is an internationally recognized consultant with Bob Proctor, leading others toward the life and results they desire in their personal and professional lives.

With passion and purpose, Tara is continuing to lead Bob's legacy Tara leads online individual and group-based mentorship in Thinking Into Results and various courses based on understanding the mind, universal laws, and prosperity principles, combining clairvoyance and many years of training and practice as a holistic energy medicine practitioner and yoga and meditation teacher.

**Contact Tara Piling:**

- www.diamondmindconsulting.ca
- tara@diamondmindconsulting.ca
- www.facebook.com/diamondmindconsulting
- @tarapillingdiamondmind
- www.linkedin.com/in/tara-pilling-diamond-mind-consulting
- www.calendly.com/diamondmindconsulting/resultsthatstick

# "Universe, Be Really, Really Good To Me!"

## By Shannon Powell

I fell in love with music long before I fell for the Art of Feng Shui, and the lyrics that really hit home for me in my late teens and early twenties were sung by a woman that I looked up to. She had weathered the storm—gone through incredible adversity—and by sheer grit landed on the top of the charts and in everyone's hearts all over the world. I even performed one of her songs during a lip-sync band competition in college, with a couple of frat guys behind me playing air guitars and drums. My costume was pure Tina Turner vibes—mini dress, fishnet hose, and high heels (and of course, big eighties' hair). I was also touting those long legs.

Pretty sure I thought I had it all figured out back then as I flipped my hair and danced on stage while lip-syncing Tina's words, professing people better be good to her. Little did I know that life presents challenges for even the lip-syncing college sophomore trying to feel like a rock 'n' roll goddess. I had yet to learn the secrets of Tao and Chi, connecting man and the universe harmoniously through energy paths. These mysteries would be revealed to me in time. Many years later, I was married and had two beautiful children, yet our family didn't seem complete. After every infertility procedure I could muster, we realized I was not going to have another baby.

My husband Jim had been adopted into a loving family as an infant, and we decided that would be our family's goal—to adopt a baby boy. When Justen Mylles was placed in our arms, every worry flew from our minds; he was healthy and strong and happy, instantly pampered and loved by his two older sisters, and adored by everyone around him. Things were great until around his first birthday, when he began banging his head on the ground and screaming daily. After an alarming doctor appointment, we discovered his one-year-old body was filled with the testosterone level of a sixteen-year-old boy. He was diagnosed with CAH—congenital adrenal hyperplasia—a lifelong issue that commands his cortisone be regulated daily.

Without consistently correct doses his condition could be life-threatening. I began searching for answers. Why did this happen to our sweet boy, and why hadn't we caught it earlier? A few weeks later, while at the bookstore, I heard Tina's deep robust voice singing that song I had lip-synced so long ago in college—like a call to the universe—can't you just be good to me? Her voice rang out over the store's sound system. Soon after, I found myself surrounded by a section of books that changed my life, about how to use the Art of Feng Shui to achieve harmony, balance, and success. I became a Feng Shui practitioner. We moved closer to where our daughters were going to school, and not very long after we were hit with another blow.

Justen was showing signs of other medical issues, and the doctors wanted him to have an MRI immediately. It was scheduled right away. I will never forget the feeling I had when they told us the news that our two-year-old son had a brain tumor. We went to visit Mayo Clinic for a second opinion. At Mayo, they confirmed the diagnosis—a biopsy of the tumor was to be performed, and they agreed with Primary Children's Hospital in Salt Lake City that the place where Justen's tumor formed in his brain made it inoperable. It was imperative to know whether the tumor was cancerous. We scheduled Justen's biopsy surgery, placing this delicate procedure in the hands of a renowned pediatric neurosurgeon.

Soon after, we found ourselves surrounded by friends and family supporting us, and others blessing us with their prayers from every corner of the globe. As a newly certified Feng Shui practitioner, I decided it was time to pull out the house plans of our recently purchased home and do a deep dive into the bagua areas. (The bagua is a map or symbol in Feng Shui, divided into nine sections that represent specific areas of life, i.e., career, wealth, relationships, that is superimposed upon the home.) That's when I realized the main staircase was in the health area. A staircase in the center of the home drains the energy out of the home.

Our 1970s staircase was white metal, too, and each stair was open between the treads—open risers, meaning the chi, or energy, was falling between each step, losing its vitality as it traveled down to the basement floor. A metal staircase is not auspicious (not good) for the health area either. The health area is ruled by the earth element. In Feng Shui, metal exhausts earth. To cure the metal, I introduced a fire element by adding a coat of red paint under each stair (fire melts metal), and I hung crystals on the ceiling above the stairs to help the energy rise instead of falling between the risers down into the basement. Before Justen Mylles' brain surgery each family member wrote down their intentions and said them aloud, that his brain tumor would be benign and all would be well. We placed these intentions in the health area of our home, and in his room. Years later, I learned from

Feng Shui master Dame Marie Diamond that the home represents a third of our luck. Our will and intentions create another thirty-three percent of our personal overall success, and heavenly luck (the luck we are born with) completes the remaining balance. I believe this was the case for our family. Our home was finally in proper Feng Shui order, along with the written intentions, and the prayers of those around the globe for his well-being.

I feel this added to his heavenly luck. And it was all placed in God's hands. When the news from the biopsy returned, it was sheer joy that the tumor was not cancerous. From that time forward our family began the serious pursuit of written intentions in every area of the Feng Shui bagua of our home.

When Marissa was fourteen, she decided to paint her bedroom. Before it was painted, she asked if she could write her intentions on the wall. I agreed, this was a fabulous idea (one we now use to infuse success in each area of the homes we decorate, stage, and flip!). Her list included what I would assume a fourteen-year-old girl would say: become a famous singer someday, play volleyball in college, become an interior decorator, marry a tall, dark, and handsome guy, and the surprising part of the list for me, create a charity for adopted children. That one really caught me off guard.

I teared up a bit then, and still do, every time I attend the events sponsored by the foundation that she and her tall, dark, and handsome husband, Kyle Van Noy (two-time Super Bowl champion) created the first year he was drafted into the National Football League by the Detroit Lions in 2014. The Van Noy Valor Foundation has helped thousands of adopted and foster children and their families.

Nicol, two years younger, wrote her intentions on the career area of her bedroom wall before painting that year also. Her list included: volleyball, singing, modeling, and fashion designer. Two summers later she was in LA pursuing a record deal with her sister. She signed with an agency and modeled throughout her teens. She was 4A MVP for the state of Utah for volleyball in her senior year.

At high school graduation, her principal confessed how much he enjoyed watching her smack the ball down on the opposing team's court. By the age of twenty-one she was crowned Miss Utah USA 2015, sashaying down the runway at Miss USA. Her written intentions and power of will led her on fascinating adventures that landed her at FIDM—Fashion

Institute of Design and Merchandising—in Los Angeles, California, which, after graduation, segued easily into a buying role at a large e-commerce company. From there, her talents with design and fashion helped put the three in Three Golden Cranes. Three Golden Cranes has created a system of balance, written intention, and empowerment that brings homes to life as we decorate, stage, and flip them.

At Three Golden Cranes, we have a step-by-step process to a balanced and harmonious home, armed with the intention to accelerate your success in the nine areas of life. Each home tells its own story according to what direction it faces, and where the front door is located. We have been so happy to realize that everyone is in the market for a balanced and harmonious living space as we have decorated homes from the East Coast to the West.

*The Wall Street Journal* featured Marissa and her husband, Kyle Van Noy, following their journey of flipping homes along his career path as a star linebacker in the National Football League. Since their marriage in 2014, they have moved to different teams Kyle has played on. As they've moved, Marissa has decorated and flipped their homes, with her mother and sister's help, choosing the design elements which complement the areas of the Feng Shui bagua—except for one home, in which they collaborated their skills with a talented designer.

Eventually, it became clear that this was more than just a passion. Our collective life works gave us the tools to create a business together, and in 2021 we decided to form Three Golden Cranes, blending the powerful aspects of Feng Shui and interior design. The crane is symbolic of longevity and good fortune in Feng Shui.

Their homes began selling in the $450,000.00 market and have grown to sales to the tune of the 3.3-million-dollar range. Three Golden Cranes' harmonious designs appeal to everyone, from singles to young families, retirees, as well as multi-million-dollar sports professionals. The secret to a Three Golden Cranes home is its potential to amplify your wealth, health, love, fame, and all other aspects of life. It's the ultimate in luxury living, designed for optimum synergy.

Justen Mylles is now nineteen years old and living out his dreams in Southern California, studying Broadcast Journalism and Documentaries at Dodge College of Film, and Media Arts at Chapman University. And yes, in case you are wondering, his dorm room has been Feng Shui-ed!

## Shannon Powell - Three Golden Cranes

Three Golden Cranes is a passion project turned business. It began when a mother and her two daughters realized the powerful aspects of Feng Shui and how balancing energy affects the home, when combined with interior design. Three Golden Cranes was officially formed in 2021, but they have worked together for years decorating beautiful spaces. The trio consists of- Marissa Van Noy, Miss Utah USA 2013, graduate of Westminster College in Salt Lake City, Utah; her sister, Nicol Powell, Miss Utah USA 2015, graduate of FIDM/Fashion Institute of Design and Merchandising in Los Angeles, California; and their mother, Shannon Powell, graduate of Brigham Young University and Feng Shui practitioner. They have a unique approach to their designs which includes decorating, staging, and flipping luxury homes while incorporating Feng Shui principles to create harmonious and balanced spaces—luxury living designed for optimum synergy. The secret to a Three Golden Cranes home is its potential to amplify your wealth, health, love, fame, and all other aspects of life. A recent article in *The Wall Street Journal* featured a home designed by Three Golden Cranes in the New England area.

**Contact Shannon Powell:**

- Threegoldencranes@gmail.com
- www.threegoldencranes.com
- @threegoldencranes

# Lean Into the Whisper

## By Jessica Quimby

I'd hear a little voice, get a feeling, or experience a familiar knowing from time to time that would whisper, "You have something to give and it's impactful." I wondered if I was in the middle of a conversation. Was I in a conversation with myself, about myself? I landed on "Yes." I was in the middle of a conversation with myself about myself.

Over time, I started to make a connection with the voice. I didn't brush it off as much. And then Covid appeared. I could simmer instead of boil. The forward motion of everyday life became a gentle rocking, slow enough for me to listen even more closely. And, tuning in also came with a desire to learn again. My children were in college and I embraced that it was time to become a student again myself. This openness to learning and newfound quiet brought the teachings of Feng Shui and dowsing to the surface of my life.

Little is understood about these ancient practices. So, here's a simple explanation. Each object and space has its own unique vibration. Whether it's an apple, a golf ball, or even a home. And these vibrations can be negative or positive. The more negative the vibration of an object or space, the more negativity that it attracts. The more positive the vibration, the more positivity it attracts. This is the Law of Attraction at work. A home or business with a -30 vibration will attract more challenges. On the flip side, a home or business with a vibration of +10 or higher is positioned to attract positivity. The ultimate goal is to dissolve any negative energy currents and create an environment with a positive vibration. When I learned how to increase the vibration of spaces using feng shui and dowsing, the whisper began to come into focus.

Once I realized I could change the energy of my surroundings for the better, it dawned on me that I was connected to a vast place. I guessed it was a place. And at the same time, it felt like no place. All I really knew was that I was connected and that I belonged. And whatever it was that I was a part of, I could affect the energy of it through these ancient practices.

It seemed so out-of-the-box for my life thus far. And yes, I had impostor syndrome. How did I have the ability to do this? I have three kids, a dog and a husband. I work in corporate America and I have a house in the suburbs. But the whisper that was telling me I had something impactful to give was about to be validated; I could suddenly alter and enhance the energy of my environment and in places beyond what I could see.

*This transformation taught me that I could convert an unsupportive environment into a supportive one by increasing its vibration.*

I started removing energetic blockages and curing negative energy in my surroundings to improve my health, to disrupt old patterns, and to bring new opportunities my way. I mean look—I'm a co-author of this book!

**A Little Story**

One of my first poignant memories has to do with experiencing high-vibration spaces. When I was ten years old, I traveled to Europe with my parents. One of the experiences that left an imprint on me is how my mother insisted we visit what felt like every church that we drove by. It became a family joke that we drove around several European countries visiting countless cities and villages and along the way we stopped at every church in our path. When at home, we didn't even go to church. Maybe we attended church on the occasional Christmas Eve.

Looking back, what was meaningful to me about that adventure is how welcomed we were as Reebok and track-suit-wearing Americans, wandering into those churches, both large and small. The doors were unlocked. It was quiet inside. Our presence didn't ever create any resistance. Sometimes we saw other people and sometimes we had the church all to ourselves. No matter if we visited a church in Switzerland, France or Germany, I felt welcomed. I felt like I belonged. I know now the energy of those churches was very high and that's why we were experiencing these positive feelings.

Those feelings never left me and at the time, I knew that those feelings could be recreated. Just not for a while, until I learned how. It was meditation, Feng Shui, and dowsing that brought me back to that experience. These practices waged a connection with the special feelings of peace, unconditional belonging and support that I associated with those impromptu church visits which wrapped me in a warm, high-vibration, energetic blanket.

The time had come and it was right on time. I had learned how to engineer high-vibration spaces just like those churches. The whisper had told me so.

**Closely Guarded Secrets**

All three ancient practices of meditation, Feng Shui, and dowsing are rooted in tapping into energy and enhancing it for the better. Some of these practices have been closely guarded secrets for thousands of years and have recently become unearthed. Thousands of years ago, the mystic schools in Egypt, the Chinese, and the Druids used and taught these practices to enhance their lives, keep governments in power and create abundance. Unfortunately, due to closely guarded power centers and a lack of documentation, a great deal of information went underground.

**Harnessing the Invisible**

Through these ancient energetic practices, I realized I could do the unexplainable. I discovered how powerful it is to be focused, to be intentional and to make far-reaching connections. In a way, I became my own "superhero." I could harness the energy and create support for anyone in any environment. We're all impacted by the vibration of our environment and it's constantly shifting. It's not uncommon for someone to move into a new home with a low or negative vibration and begin to experience new challenges. This includes money issues, employment issues or health issues. Or, perhaps the clutter is uncontrollable or destructive patterns can't be shaken off. It's not unusual to experience more frustration, troubling relations with family members or unexplained accidents.

I'll give you an example. A few years back, I had a scary fall on my front steps while taking my dog out. Despite my caution and knowledge of the ice on the steps, I took a hard tumble and injured my shin. At the time, I had lived in my home for over a decade and took the dog out countless times while experiencing wintry weather. After looking into the Feng Shui of that part of my home, I realized there was a negative current running through the exact spot where I had fallen.

That current had just appeared, so I hadn't had a chance to cure it yet. As you can imagine, I've since cured those energetic patterns and no one in our home has suffered from an accident since. In a broader sense, maybe you're wondering what your life's purpose is and whether for some reason there's a block on discovering it. When there's a resistance that, no matter how much effort you expend, you can't seem to overcome, this can mean the vibration of your environment is low and is attracting exactly what it is you don't want. The good news is that we don't have to live or work in low-vibration surroundings. It's actually the opposite. There are solutions. By using Feng Shui and dowsing, you can change the course. By applying these practices, your environment can support you. It's possible to shift the energy to bring more healing, joy, abundance–and to even encourage creativity and support better relationships. The opportunities for improvement and healing are endless. It's simply a matter of tapping into them. Said another way, the fix is to increase your home's or office's vibration to attract solutions, support and peace.

There's also no geographical limits on where this can be done–I can tune into any space or location from wherever I am. Think of it as a Zoom call where you don't even have to click on the link to join!

### What To Do

I encourage anyone who is curious about the energy level of their home or business to reach out to discover what it is. Having the awareness of whether your environment is supportive or not is an important first step in improving or enhancing your situation.

By knowing this information and then taking steps to cure the negative energetic influences, I've helped people who have suffered while living in homes with negative energy levels as low as -30 and lower.

And when the energy is increased to a supportive level of 10 or higher, I've witnessed changes that seemed to happen overnight. One of my clients experienced an overnight surge in social media following for their business and has been able to monetize it in a more meaningful way. I've also seen family relations improve, increased prosperity, and creative streaks take off. I've seen children become better students and bullying stopped. I've witnessed relationships become more harmonious and large gifts of money come out of nowhere.

### Here's The Kicker

Harnessing the invisible energetic patterns of your environment is the work of a Feng Shui and dowsing practitioner. Once you've overcome the uniqueness of these practices, these solutions become a no-brainer. You might even wonder, "Why haven't we been taught this before?"

Here's the thing: it's similar to my experiences of impromptu church visits and leaning into the whisper. If this chapter resonates with you, then it's arriving in your purview right on time. You're ready to experience some good vibes, so lean into them and take the universe up on it.

## Jessica Quimby

Jessica Quimby is a speaker, author, and the founder of The Art of High Vibe Living, LLC.

She is a Diamond Certified Dowser who also utilizes the principles of Feng Shui to increase the vibration of people's spaces within their home and their business.

She's helped many near and far to harness the support of their environment that's available for them to tap into.

She invites you to visit her website at artofhighvibeliving.com or follow her on Instagram @the.art.of.high.vibe.living to learn more.

**Contact Jessica Quimby:**

- www.artofhighvibeliving.com
- @the.art.of.high.vibe.living

# A Pathway to Inner Peace

## By Kathleen Rafter

I couldn't believe what I was reading! My intuition told me to request a copy of a security report from our son's middle school. As I read it, I found that I was being accused of doing something that was absolutely not true! I had always tried to maintain a first-class reputation, but now that appeared to be falling apart at the seams. A school security guard was falsely accusing me of lunging toward my son to choke him during a conference meeting at the school one day. My husband and I have an adopted son from Russia who is now a wonderful, well-adjusted young man of twenty-two, but for many years, we had far-reaching challenges with him that affected every aspect of our lives.

My husband and I had tried to deal with his behavior on our own, but the situation was fast becoming personal now, affecting me directly. I knew that we had to find a solution to help our son control his behavior, and to help us, as parents, maintain our sanity. I'd been meditating since I was a teenager and had learned, through a program called the Silva Method, how to concentrate during meditation in order to create what I wanted to manifest. I had become quite good at it, but it was becoming very clear to me that I really needed to expand upon this, to learn how to influence this boy's behavior. I had to do it quickly, too, before things really got out of hand.

My husband and I tried to get help from so-called behavioral experts, but they weren't familiar with our son's behavior and they weren't much help at all, despite the high fees that they were charging. I had been a student of the great Indian saint Paramahansa Yogananda for several years, and I learned from him that the answer to any question that I may have was always available to me. I just needed to know how to ask for it and to be receptive to it when the answer did come. I trusted that I would receive the answers that I needed to turn this situation around before it was too late. My husband and I have engineering backgrounds and so were familiar with taking a desired endpoint and then using reverse-engineering to determine all the necessary steps that would be needed to complete the project.

So, we reverse-engineered our desired outcome; outlined all the necessary steps; and put together a plan of action. What was our desired outcome here? It was for our son to normalize his behavior so that all of us could relax, be at peace, and enjoy life. We also wanted him to be able to realize his full potential, without letting any adverse behavior get in the way. What was our intention? It was to bring this situation about as quickly, efficiently, and effectively as possible. So, we began. Every morning, I spent time in meditation, asking what action steps I needed to take for that day. We were obliged to retain certain experts and I prayed that we would find the best ones to work with.

Many of the people I contacted refused to even meet with us, but I continued to stumble forward. For the most part, we were able to attract people who were very helpful. Some of them were local professionals and others were teachers that I studied with from afar, online. During meditation, I would also spend time visualizing our son behaving in a positive way. I saw him controlling his impulsive and non-compliant behavior. I discovered that what I was doing was called: 'Holding a Seat' for someone, and that the patron saint of mothers, St. Monica, had held a seat for her son, St Augustine, for thirty years. With determination, I was willing to hold a seat for our son, for as long as it would take for him to change his behavior.

The most important lesson that I learned through all of this though was that change must first occur at the energetic level, before the effects can be noticed at a physical level. I discovered that my thoughts and emotions carried powerful energy that really affected the people around me, especially those close to me, like my husband and son. The most surprising thing that I came across, though, was that I could influence this boy's behavior through making some simple changes in our environment! I thought to myself, "Could it really be that easy to influence someone else's behavior?" I discovered that it was not only possible but that it was also a very powerful thing to do.

My research led me to the work of my mentor, Marie Diamond, who is a global transformational teacher and Feng Shui master. I heard Marie say that you could influence someone's behavior, using Feng Shui, by placing a photo of them in a particular direction in your home. I immediately placed one of this young man's school photos in this direction, and I eagerly awaited to see what would happen. A change in his behavior came about almost instantly, as he was much more cooperative. The best thing about it though was that he didn't even know that I was trying to influence him.

It was sneaky, but effective. I then discovered that there were more things that I could change in our environment such as: the layout of his bed and desk in his bedroom; the layout of our living room; even where we all sat at the dining table. I couldn't believe the welcomed change in him. I realized, though, that he was becoming very oppositional whenever I asked him to do something (or to stop doing something). He was more open to suggestions if I spoke to him mentally or telepathically.

I was amazed at the improvement in his behavior after I started to communicate with him, without even saying a word. I learned how to mentally take little actions when I was with him, like sweeping the negative energy off his back that he was carrying home with him from school, or after playing with other kids. I would also, in my mind, pretend that I was connecting my heart to his with a horizontal, pink-colored infinity symbol. He had no idea what I was doing, but I knew that he could sense that something different was happening. He seemed to like the change, too.

He was becoming much easier to deal with and I found that I was even enjoying our time together! It seemed that right after I included one successful energetic hack into my routine, I'd run across another one to try, and they all seemed to work perfectly together. If I noticed that our son was misbehaving, I would insist that he write a sentence affirming the opposite, desired behavior twenty times, to offset the negative one. For instance, if he was treating me rudely, I would have him write: "I am always treating mom with respect." I tied this affirmation-writing to something that he considered a treat, so that if he didn't write the affirmation, he wouldn't get the treat.

All these things had a domino effect. One positive change led to another, and they all nicely dovetailed together. The experts saw the change in him too, and wondered what we were doing. Even though they didn't fully understand what we were up to, they were very supportive of it and encouraged us to continue. Another useful tool that we found was EFT, or Emotional Freedom Techniques, sometimes called tapping. At a very low point, I was desperate and asked our son if he would be willing to try something new that was maybe a little bit weird, but very simple and easy. I explained that it might make him feel better, after trying it.

Luckily, he agreed and this became our turning point. Using EFT allowed him to regulate his emotions, especially his anger and his frustration. He had been thinking that things would never change for him, and that life would be a continuous struggle. Practicing EFT also allowed him to take actions that he never believed he could take. I was so amazed with these results, that I became a certified EFT practitioner, so that I could help others, too, to overcome their negative emotions and self-imposed limitations. Once things settled down, I began to look at what occurred and how we had made it all happen. I felt deeply grateful that things were improving, and I felt like celebrating!

I saw that we had been desperate and that we had had a definite purpose: to change our son's behavior, for his benefit and for ours. We had a powerful intention to bring that change about. We let go of our negative beliefs and the negative beliefs of the others around us, like our family members, along with the experts.

Most importantly though, we took action, and as we did, we experienced one success after another. I used all the energetic tools that I came across to empower us. Some were things that I had already been practicing like meditation and the use of affirmations. Others were new, such as: creating changes in our environment, using Feng Shui; tapping; and communicating with our son telepathically.

These steps worked beautifully for all three of us. Following them allowed each one of us to create individual inner peace along with a peaceful home, and this sense of peace continues, to this day. I realized that there were many people who were living chaotic lives who needed this information.

I had designed a pathway to inner peace, and now I needed to share it with others. After realizing this, I started a spiritual life coaching practice, and I now help people one-on-one and in group settings, to implement these simple, proven steps to help create inner peace in their lives, and in the lives of their loved ones.

I have helped hundreds of clients to develop a sense of inner peace for themselves and others by following this simple plan. The steps are easy to follow, but as with most things, what is easy to do is often easy not to do, so it helps to have an experienced coach, guiding you along the way.

So, if you're tired of living in chaos, exhausted from dealing with the struggle and juggle of your everyday life, apply for a free Discovery Session. I'll help you to start along your own pathway of inner peace!

Apply for a FREE Discovery Session here:
www.kathleenrafter.com/discovery-sessions

## Kathleen Rafter

For over twenty years, Kathleen has helped hundreds of clients and others to create a life of inner peace. She helps them to align their hearts and minds, to realize and act upon their true purpose in life.

She has been meditating for forty-five years and has studied with only the best including: Paramahansa Yogananda, Marie Diamond, and John Assaraf. She has also studied with successful organizations such as: the Silva Method; EFT Universe; and the Proctor Gallagher Institute.

More importantly though, she has applied what she has learned to create a life of inner peace and abundance. She is a certified life coach through her mentor, Marie Diamond, and a certified EFT practitioner, through EFT Universe.

Kathleen works with her clients online during one-on-one and group sessions, masterclasses, challenges, and online courses. She regularly posts to her blog and has a strong presence on Instagram, Facebook, and YouTube.

She helps her clients and followers create a sense of inner peace and abundance not only for themselves, but for their families, too. Kathleen's purpose is to create Enlightened Healing for the world, to heal 100 million people worldwide.

For her, this begins with helping people to create inner peace and abundance, one heart, one mind, and one soul at a time.

**Contact Kathleen Rafter:**


- www.kathleenrafter.com
- kathy@kathleenrafter.com
- @rafterkathleen
- www.facebook.com/kathleenmrafter
- www.facebook.com/rafterkathleen
- www.youtube.com/@kathleenrafter
- www.linkedin.com/in/kathleenrafter

# A Path to Healing Chronic Diseases Using Food as Medicine

## By Kyung Rhee

My mom always had a way of harnessing the power of Mother Nature to heal us of our illnesses. One of my earliest memories of experiencing herbal medicine was when my mom accidentally let the mound of dried herbs burn too long on the pressure point on my index finger, to remedy a flu I had. I can still remember the earthy smell of the herbs filling up the entire room that the four of us grew up in. I still have a faint scar there to this day, thirty-four years later. It was very common for my mom to steam my face over a large bowl of hot herbal tonics, or make me drink some, whenever I wasn't feeling great or had indigestion. Fast-forward twenty-nine years, I am living in Manhattan, running an extremely successful business in finance, earning many awards, recognition, invitations to prestigious circles, and what I thought was the American dream that our family moved to America for.

But over the course of two years, after my first daughter Sophia was born, my health began deteriorating. I had mysterious symptoms that the best doctors of New York City couldn't seem to explain. I visited many hospitals, doctors, specialists, and experts. I took X-rays, MRIs, biopsies, hundreds of blood tests, to no conclusion. They misdiagnosed me with so many different illnesses and suggested different pills to mask the symptoms, but no answers to cure the root of the problem. How could they fix the problem if they couldn't find it? It started with aches and pains in my muscles, joints and nerves. I couldn't walk for more than five minutes without shooting pains that would go up my feet and legs as if tiny knives were stabbing me from the inside out. Sitting in one position at my desk for more than two minutes became very painful, as if sharp needles were going into my spine, poking and prodding me. I was eventually diagnosed with osteoarthritis and severe sciatic nerve disorder.

There were days and days where I would get sudden spells of vertigo and not be able to sit or stand up. These would last three to five days at a time. I recall Sophia climbing onto my bed and asking, "Mommy, are you better now? Can you play with me?" to which my reply was, "No, I'm so sorry, baby, Mommy still feels dizzy". I had two miscarriages the following year. This was a major blow to my confidence and my emotional stability. I couldn't understand or process the grief from the miscarriages. It was such a lonely and isolating experience. I felt nobody could understand my deep pain and sadness. My first pregnancy came so easy. The entire pregnancy and birth went so smoothly that I had taken it all for granted.

Now, I felt like my world was tumbling down fast, falling apart at the seams, with nobody to help me. The world that I had spent years building, investing my blood, sweat, and tears in, was all crumbling in front of my eyes. This was the lowest point of my life. I had experienced hardships before but I always pushed through because I had my health on my side. But this time was different; I didn't have my health, and without my health I couldn't do anything, not even take care of my little baby girl. In a desperate attempt to get some reprieve from the dark sadness that was my current life, I left for the Mediterranean Sea on a four-week summer vacation with my family.

Before my flight, I visited my acupuncture and herbal medicine doctor whom I had seen from time to time during desperate moments for short-term remedies. This time, I needed something to get through the next four weeks, including the airplane and car rides, without any bouts of vertigo. My acupuncturist was an eighty-year-old man that looked like he was fifty; tight, youthful skin, energy that would make a twenty-year-old envious, and light shining from his eyes as if the sun was beaming out of them.

He gave me a Ziploc bag of little round balls that looked like peppercorns. He told me to take a tablespoon twice a day to keep the vertigo at bay. I was skeptical, but felt I had nothing to lose and desperately wanted to get through this summer vacation without vertigo so I could rest and recharge. This man was a miracle sent down from the heavens, I just didn't know it yet. I also had no idea at that time that he and I would later formulate my current herbal supplements, Revive, to share with the whole world.

By this point I had stopped drinking, went to sleep by 9 p.m., practiced gentle yoga whenever possible, and rested as much as I could. I honestly didn't have energy to do much else. The energy I had was very limited and usually not enough for me to get through even half the day.

Over the four weeks, I spent the days sampling all of the fresh seafood and vegetables from the shores of the Greek islands and Sicily. The first week, I felt no difference in energy. I still didn't sleep well, tossing and turning the whole night and waking up groggy, depleted, moody and irritable. I still had the aches and pains, no energy, among many other symptoms. Luckily, there were no visits from the vertigo fairy. By the time I reached Sicily I suddenly had more energy, the pains slowly faded, and I was strolling through the cobblestone streets holding Sophia's hand.

I was laughing and dancing and enjoying my life. My husband flew back to New York midway through the vacation. Sophia and I stayed behind with some friends. After four weeks, I returned to New York full of energy and life, carrying a sleeping three-year-old Sophia in my arms, carry-on bags on each shoulder that weighed about twenty pounds each, plus Sophia's bag. I walked the mile from the plane to the entry point at JFK in flip-flops.

As I was walking, I asked myself, "How am I doing this? I could barely push the stroller before I left. A bag this heavy would be breaking my arms off by now. Am I really carrying all this stuff AND Sophia and really walking all this way without any shooting pains?" I couldn't explain it. It seemed so mysterious to me that I couldn't make sense of it in my mind.

Three days later after returning to Manhattan, my pains started slowly returning and within a week, I was back to feeling depleted, irritable, shooting pains everywhere, tossing and turning all night, not able to sleep, and crying in despair. But then, by divine intervention, a lightbulb came on in my mind. It suddenly occurred to me, "IT MUST BE THE FOOD!" I had tried everything else with no results. The only thing that had changed while in Europe was the food!

With this newfound information, I excitedly began researching everything that I could find about food in America. How food was farmed, how it was made in factories, what happened to the nutrients and minerals during the process, what were the effects of modern-day farming, what happened when you replaced traditional methods of farming, harvesting, and cooking with modern day factory and machine methods.

I studied ancient cooking methods of various cultures across the world, read studies on healthy living regions that never seemed to get ill. I spent hours and hours sifting through medical journals, independent health studies, and research, and whatever else I could find to piece together the massive puzzle in my head that was holistic nutrition and herbal medicine.

Through painstaking research, lots of trial and error experimentation on myself and my own family, digging up lost memories of my farm-to-table upbringing, and long tedious hours of nutrition and herbal medicine classes, I was finally able to piece together and make sense of what happened to me, how I became ill, why I had all of those symptoms, why my body wasn't able to hold onto my failed pregnancies, why people couldn't seem to lose weight despite spending hours in the gym, and so many other burning questions the modern world couldn't seem to answer.

Now armed with this precious knowledge, I decided to start healing other women and children suffering from chronic diseases like fatty liver, lifelong acne, obesity, mood disorders, depression, anxiety, sleep disorders, asthma, sinusitis, long-term toxic viral infections, bacterial infections, fibroids, infertility, osteoarthritis, scoliosis, premature aging, endometriosis, PCOS, and so much more! I was even able to fix my own daughter's crooked teeth through natural food supplementation; no braces, no dentist visits.

What many of my clients fail to realize is that these diseases didn't just happen overnight. They were a slow progression over many years, one cell at a time, turning into failed functions of our body's systems. With every bite, every food and lifestyle decision we make, we decide the outcome of that day's worth of cellular regeneration. Through my classes and consultations, I teach them the steps they need to take in order to bring their bodies and minds back to health. I arm them with the information so that not only will they cure their disease, they will prevent it from coming back.

These methods have been proven over and over again through my clients as they see miraculous results when years of pills, doctors, and other interventions have failed. One client told me that I was able to explain to her in one hour the reasons for her disease as well as how to fix it, when months of doctors' visits couldn't give her an answer. Thousands of dollars in medication only made her worse. Another client spent nearly eight years trying everything the doctors suggested, including a painful surgery which only made things worse and intensified the pain she was experiencing.

I was able to minimize her symptoms in a matter of four days and completely eliminate them in two weeks. One of the biggest surprises my clients get is when I tell them to stop the intense exercising. Calories burned do not equal a healthy body and, more importantly do not equal a healthy you. My deepest belief is that mind, body, and soul are all connected. If your body isn't happy neither can your mind and soul be, and the opposite is also true.

My goal is to help my clients balance all three. Your body has an amazing ability to heal itself if you just give it the tools and opportunity to do so. I empower my clients to allow their bodies this opportunity and support them in their process of doing so.

For me, it is my great honor to be part of a global movement helping people end their suffering by healing naturally through the power of Mother Nature and what she makes available to us all. Through my website, classes, consultations, and monthly newsletters, I can share this knowledge. I love that I get to choose who I work with and which clients I get to invest my energy into. The greatest and most satisfying moments in my career are when a client cries tears of joy because they finally have their life back after years of chronic disease and suffering. It is my mission in life that I can make this kind of difference for those who seek it and for those who truly want it. Through this, we will heal the planet, one person at a time.

## Kyung Rhee

Kyung Rhee is a functional nutrition and herbal medicine therapist rooted in holistic practices. She helps her clients heal from chronic illnesses through her knowledge and experience in traditional Chinese medicine, Ayurveda, and food as medicine.

Her life started from humble beginnings as the youngest of four children born in South Korea during an economic depression after the Korean war.

Out of necessity, her mother grew most of their food in the open fields behind their home and they lived off the land. Her mother used wild herbal plants found in the field to treat illnesses for her family.

Through this kind of living, Kyung observed and learned the ways fresh organic food and herbal plants functioned to keep their family healthy and free from illness.

She learned traditional methods of farming and harvesting various crops, which would later play a vital role in her understanding of food as medicine.

At the age of eight, she emigrated to America with her family. She later married her British-Indian husband, which led her to deep-dive into the various roles that Ayurvedic cooking played in nutrition and holistic health.

Her journey through motherhood with her two children, as well as the painful and intense journey of her own chronic illnesses, eventually leading to her own healing and reclaiming of her life, has added immense wisdom to how she applies treatments to her own clients.

Kyung loves to split her time between life at home in New York and traveling the world to observe and gain wisdom from the various cultures and how they have sustained a healthy and happy life naturally without medical or food intervention.

She enjoys her thriving career helping her clients reclaim their life by healing through holistic nutrition and herbal medicine therapy.

**Contact Kyung Rhee:**

www.RainbowWellness.org

@RainbowHealthWellness

www.facebook.com/KyungRheeOfficial

# Life Is Short, Might as Well Travel First Class!

## By Anne Rigaud-Walker

I wake up with a jolt. My heart is pounding. I'm scared, so scared. I don't understand what's going on. I take a glance at the clock: it's 4AM. I must have had a nightmare to be in such a state of shock. In fact, this was not a nightmare. My life is the nightmare. Which explains why I always wake up violently at 4AM. Every night, I just sleep a few hours, enough to be able to survive the next day, and when that level is reached, I wake up in turmoil. My night is over, I've barely had the minimum amount of sleep necessary to survive. I have no more tears from crying too much so I lie in bed wondering how I'm going to find the strength to get up when the alarm goes off and get my five-year-old son ready for school. So, I wait for three long hours. I feel lifeless. I am lifeless. The clock finally reads 7AM and I hear my son playing in his room waiting for me, hopefully not knowing what his mother is going through. But how can I take care of another human being when I can't even take care of myself anymore? I am just desperate and sad. Deeply sad.

How did my life fall apart? How did I go from meeting with a financial advisor who proudly told me that my income put me in the coveted tier of the less than 1% of the world's wealthiest people, to finding myself with almost nothing and feeling so much despair? I had everything going for me. More than fifteen years at one of the biggest companies in the world: Yahoo! Fifteen years that seemed like an eternity. A life of hard work, stress and daily adrenaline shots, but also a life of fun, fantastic parties, tickets to the hottest concerts and events, and the list goes on. Glitz and glamor! And money, lots of money, especially when you are a top talent, which I was. I worked with fantastic people. I had amazing colleagues and most importantly, I had the honor of leading the most wonderful and talented team. We were great, we were the best, even our customers said so and gave us the award for world's industry best "customer service". Excellence was our fuel. My personal life mirrored my professional life.

I had a beautiful, adorable baby boy, I had been married for fifteen years to the most wonderful man and lived in a beautiful architect-designed loft. Life was great. But eventually I got tired of the downside of working in advertising. Long hours, great pressure, and most of all, I felt increasingly empty inside. What was the point of it all? What was my purpose? Had I waited to have a baby at thirty-eight years old only to have him grow up without me around? Things had to change. So, I decided to leave Yahoo to pursue a more meaningful career. I found the perfect combination of my love for the corporate world, personal development and meaning: I decided to become an executive coach. Going back to school to learn so many new things was very rewarding, but I had no idea how it would transform my life. Learning also started to make me feel less numb. My feelings and emotions had become so numb during all those intense years at Yahoo. I felt I was starting to wake up little by little. This is how it started.

I started to feel that the "never complain, never explain" communication pattern in my marriage had created a big gap between my husband and I, and that moving to a new city to build our dream home might not have been such a good idea. Indeed, it wasn't. We encountered so many difficulties, so many delays on the job site, so many dishonest craftsmen, huge losses of money, and so many difficult problems on so many various aspects that our marriage did not survive.

That was the death knell of those fifteen years together. And from that point on, my life fell apart. On every level. Our marriage – we put an end to a twenty-four-year relationship. My family – fiercely condemning our decision to separate. My health –deteriorating on many levels. My job – falling apart because my mental state would not allow me to work. My house – at a standstill, as the construction work was bringing me nothing but trouble. I had hit rock bottom. I spent months in survival mode.

Why was every aspect of my life falling apart at the same time? It was too much to handle, so I tried everything I could think of, from a different organization in my life to psychotherapy, without much success. I was able to understand most of my patterns, but conventional therapy wasn't helping. And one day, there it was. That ad on the web. It promoted a life-changing method. It sounded like yet another false advertisement.

It sounded too good to be true. But my desire for change was such that I decided to give it a try. I decided to try Rapid Transformational Therapy, an award-winning modality created by Marisa Peer that heals physical, emotional and psychological pain. Sometimes it takes courage to be happy. But it paid off, it paid off in ways I could never have imagined. One of those unanticipated ways was that after I bounced back and recovered, I decided to train to become an RTT hypnotherapist myself. And there was the metamorphosis!

After having changed my personal life, it was about to change my professional life as well. It did work. It allowed me to go from surviving to thriving. Today, I am a successful entrepreneur who changes people's lives by freeing them from what blocks and hurts them. In order to change, it is essential to understand the following: "Until you make the unconscious conscious, it will run your life and you will call it fate," as Carl Jung said. Working from the subconscious is the–only–way to change.

And the only way to access the subconscious is through hypnosis, because your mind works with the right brain waves (alpha) at that time. When thinking, the conscious mind works at 4,000 bits per second. Meanwhile, the subconscious mind works at five billion bits per second. That subconscious mind is the boss. It controls more than 90% of our life, which means we cannot change anything using your conscious mind alone. We must enter the operating system and work from there to create the change we want.

That is why studies show that hypnotherapy creates a 93% healing rate after only six sessions, while psychotherapy reports a 38% healing rate after six hundred sessions! Throughout your life, you acquire behaviors and emotions from your past experiences, they create a blueprint which first becomes your personality, then your identity. How do I reverse this phenomenon, and how do I work with my clients? I am committed to creating a real and lasting transformation in people, in a short period of time.

That's the other beauty of working with the subconscious mind: you can achieve amazing transformations in just a few months, with lasting results. After hundreds of sessions with my clients, I created custom programs for quick and permanent healing. The common part of these programs is to master the subconscious mind by eliminating self-sabotaging patterns (which over the years have become your identity), build self-esteem and self-confidence, and then work on what you want to achieve and build the life you want to live.

As you peel back the layers of the onion, you access your true identity, deconstruct the problems that life has put on your path and create your dream life. Of course, this won't prevent you from having other problems, but you will be strong and equipped enough to deal with whatever life throws at you. You will have great coping skills. My method not only includes RTT but also the very best of effective transformation modalities.

All of this, combined with my passion and dedication to changing people's lives, creates results that I desperately needed when my life was in pieces. So, who are my clients? I work with individuals and businesses with one goal in mind: excellence and efficiency. It has been said that we attract clients who identify with us.

Not surprisingly, I have worked with many women and men whose lives have hit rock bottom, as mine had. Many of my clients were depressed, had lost their jobs, gone through a divorce or separation, a mid-life crisis, or led lives that no longer made sense. And many of them had something in common: just like my new partner, they had encountered narcissists in their lives. About a year after we met, I realized his life had been full of them, and that they had created most of his problems and traumas.

Who are narcissists? So common and ordinary, yet sadistic and perverse.... To learn more, here is an article I wrote on the subject:
https://arwcoach.fr/en/deal-with-narcissists/

I had never met that type of harmful individual before my clients told me their story; it was a pure shock, and I am so grateful to be able to free them from toxic relationships. In addition to that, I also work on less problematic or completely different topics such as finding one's life purpose, finding love, overcoming repetitive patterns in relationships, helping teenagers resolve their issues, helping women get pregnant when medicine is not successful, getting rid of stress and anxiety, eating disorders, immune diseases, addictions, depression, lack of confidence, guilt, phobias, etc.

Each day I am in awe with the results my clients achieve, all over the world. In 2022, I helped families to have a baby, a man become free from thirty years of narcolepsy, a teenager to overcome anorexia, women and men to exit toxic relationships, others to thrive in the business, and so much more. They all had one crucial thing in common: they were willing to stop letting their past rule their present and future lives.

The other prerequisite for success is that you must really want to change. You have to be willing to invest in yourself and do the work. This is a key point, because I meet all kinds of victims who complain about their lives. They are very unhappy but not (yet) ready to change even if they feel miserable. When people are ready and walk into my office or when we meet online, I give them an unlimited amount of care, compassion, and positive energy. As I said before, I tailor a program for each client. Energy is just as important as strategy, if not more.

When I look back on all these years, I can honestly say that I am very happy to be making an impact on people's lives. From the bottom of my heart, I wish to thank all those who have trusted me to work together.

For the past two years, I've worked mostly one-on-one, especially after the pandemic, because people wanted deeper support, whether on a personal or corporate level. In the future, I want to help people on a larger scale with global effective healing programs.

I look forward to making an even greater impact and to taking healing and transformation to a higher level, so stay tuned! Are you ready to travel first class?!

You can find more details and resources on my website in French and English: https://arwcoach.fr/en

## Anne Rigaud-Walker

Anne Rigaud-Walker is a certified Executive Coach, Hypnotherapist and RTT® hypnotherapist. She is passionate and committed to creating a real and lasting transformation in people, in a short period of time.

After spending twenty years in business - including more than fifteen years in the digital economy with Yahoo, in management - Anne has developed a passion for helping teams and individuals to reach their full potential by healing and transforming what they needed to change.

Concentrating on both personal fulfillment and performance was essential for Anne, so she decided to give her professional life a new direction by starting her own company in Executive Coaching and fast transformative therapies: ARWCoach.

Her method not only includes RTT, but also the very best of effective transformation modalities.

Combining her unique method with her passion and dedication to changing people's lives, Anne has helped hundreds of people.

She is an expert in helping clients manage life crises, gain self-confidence and get free from narcissistic abuse, but she also helps people overcome immune diseases, infertility, depression and workplace issues.

Anne also co-facilitates workshops for couples that will transform your relationship to reach a new level of love, healing, intimacy and commitment.

Anne has trained with the best international teachers and therapists including Marisa Peers, Dr Joe Dispenza, Paul McKenna, and she took classes at Esalen Institute and HEC Paris where she got certified in Coaching. She works in both English and French with clients worldwide.

Her goal for 2023 and beyond is to help people on a larger scale with effective healing programs globally.

**Contact Anne Rigaud-Walker:**


- In English: www.arwcoach.fr/en
- In French: www.arwcoach.fr
- anne@arwcoach.com
- www.linkedin.com/in/annerigaudwalker

# "Fake It till You Make It"
# The Art of Possibility

## By Sandra Roth

Looking out of my small bedroom, I could hear the pitter patter of rain streaming down the windowpane, causing small valleys of water that disappeared. As I looked out onto this bleak scene, I could see the graveled playground that doubled as a washing area for the flats opposite. Deep down, I knew that there was life beyond that playground and my gray environment.

As I searched the horizon, I knew there had to be more than this. There was something inside me that was just bursting to come out and make a change in my life, in my family's life, and in the world. How could I make a difference? My family were poor but kind and dedicated to supporting each other. My youngest brother had a disability which meant, as the only girl in the family, I had to help with caring for him and that had made me grow up fast.

That distant beautiful world, my ambition to make a difference. How was it going to happen? How was I going to journey beyond that gray playground to see the world and help and heal others to fulfill their potential, both emotionally and materially? I welcome you to my dream, your dream, and the dream for humanity to communicate, to connect, and be complete. Just like me at fifteen years old, you're probably wondering how to fulfill your dream, begin your journey and achieve your ambitions.

This is a short introduction to my journey, of finding my inner strength and ability to make a difference in other people's lives. Of learning to recognise and act when mentors, situations, and opportunities stepped into my path and being brave to take that first step.

Now, this is not a rags to riches story. Instead, it's the story of the possibility and ability that lies in every single one of us. It is about recognising the opportunities and ambitions that can be realized. It is about attracting the right mentors and guides into your life and really listening to them. It is about stepping out, unsure of whether there's firm ground below or even around you but knowing that God and the universe have got your back.

This is my journey to finding the real me. If my story resonates with you, I can help you find your real self too by:

1. Building personal and professional confidence
2. Acknowledging and promoting your existing strengths and skills
3. Improving individual, or organizational performance by working with the art of possibilities
4. Successfully collaborating with teams to build positive organizational cultures and enhance customer satisfaction.

So, where do you start? You start by reflecting on who you are and what gifts you have. It does not matter if it is only one thing–it might be your voice, your ability to think up ideas, to paint, to skateboard, or to draw on sidewalks and buildings that thousands of people are going to admire each day. It may be to communicate compassionately with people living on the streets or those with a disability. I've also had to release the fear of feeling that those special things, success, happiness, and wealth, were not for me. They are for me and they're also for you too. My young self did not know who I was or what I wanted. But as I have gone through life, I've found that opportunity presents itself in the form of people who happen across your life. In my earliest days, I was asked by my parish priest to sit on the board of a housing charity. I nearly refused thinking that I had nothing to offer, no real life experience.

However, he insisted on asking me every time he saw me and I finally said yes. I learnt so much from that experience, such as:

- How to speak in public
- How to prioritize information
- How to meet and talk with people with different life experiences and skills

The other people who sat on the board encouraged me by valuing the unique insights and experiences I shared that they had not had. This included me being a young woman living in a poor community. I realized that the people who they supported through the charity had their own gifts and talents. This validation of other peoples' gifts is something I was able to share, and I believe every one of us can see something special in others, even if you cannot see it in yourselves.

I was a young black woman. I was taught by my family, especially my dear mother, that being young, black, and a woman were positive attributes, even if these were not always seen as a positive by others. I would like to tell you that I fully embraced this positive perspective on who I was, but no. Being a woman felt like a burden. Women do not always feel confident at home or work unless they tick all the boxes, and this is true of my experience. One of my earliest memories was seeing Martin Luther King Jr. shot on the television and my father, who never cried, shedding a tear. Being a child meant that you could not always say what you wanted to in the company of adults.

However, my parents continued to paint that positive picture of me, even if I did not quite believe it at the time. So, the lesson for me is that positive reinforcement of you, either by you or others will eventually make a difference. It's as important to listen to positive messages as it is to dispel negative messages. I eventually learnt that when people said negative things about me, to just ignore it and to think back to the positive messages that had been instilled in me. I know you're thinking: "What do I do if I haven't had any positive messages installed in me?" To that, I would say to take on the mindset of someone that you admire and make their qualities your own. Yes, you will be faking it, but "Fake it 'til you make it" came from somewhere! It's all about telling yourself "I am enough, and I deserve to live my perfect life."

And so began the journey that helped me get an education and move into the world of health and social care with a focus working with people with mental health issues. In my first role, I was working with a young man the same age as me who had mental health issues. What I found sad was that he could see no way out of his situation and had been cut off by his friends and family. Yet, there was only a thin line between his life and mine. He wanted a home, to travel, and to have a job. Instead, people who he had grown up with would now cross the road when they saw him coming. We had lots of conversations about what he wanted in life and I helped him realize that he was capable of getting a home, getting a job, and having fun. He went on to achieve most of his goals and I went on to support hundreds of similar people find their real gifts and unique talents.

My success grew in my health and social care career as I advanced to deputy director. What a privilege to help organizations be creative, transform work teams to collaboratively work together, and to support the people they worked with to achieve their potential. I loved my role adopting a strength-based approach for individuals finding their true selves and working as a transformation and efficiency expert for improving services. Then, the unimaginable happened. My mother died suddenly and unexpectedly from cancer. The bottom had fallen out of my world and it was as if I had fallen down the rabbit hole. Unlike *Alice in Wonderland* however, this was a dark and murky place and I felt lost and depressed. It was a place I was not sure I could return from and at that time in my life, I did not feel I was in control. I managed to continue working but a void existed between me and the real world and I wasn't sure how I was going to return. On one of the days when I ventured out, I went into a bookshop and veered towards the health section. I was hoping to find something that would help shake myself free from my foggy existence and bring me back to health, and I did. The book had fallen off the shelf, almost as though it had tried to jump straight at me. When I picked it up, it had "Feng Shui" written on the cover, a topic I knew next to nothing about. I'm not sure how long I stood there, lost in thought and leaning up against that bookshelf reading the words in that book. But at that point, I knew that what I was reading was important and meaningful. I left the shop clinging on to my newly bought book, went home and continued reading it. That was the first day of my Feng Shui journey.

That journey brought me to Marie Diamond, who I consider to be one of the greatest Feng Shui Masters in the world. My journey with her deepened my knowledge of Feng Shui, Diamond Dowsing, and healing. I added these new skills to help heal people's environments. When a client complained about having continuous back and hip pains, I dowsed her environment and found she had significant energetic stress affecting her from two directions where she was sleeping. This not only immediately reduced her pain but also helped cure her husband's knee pains. This ability to help heal pain and peoples' environment is an area that I will continue to expand in the future. This extraordinary tradition was a gift to me and to many of the people whose lives and environments I have had the pleasure of improving.

During this time, my life has continued to improve, in health, wealth and happiness, and I have been able to coach with hundreds of individuals and transform many organizations. I am proud of my achievements in helping individuals to find their unique strengths and gifts to build a fulfilling and purposeful life. Helping organizations learn to collaborate with the gifts and talents of the team so that everyone can contribute is a great source of joy for me.

My ambition is to coach thousands of people and organizations to find their best true selves and to improve their environments through coaching, team building, Diamond Dowsing and Feng Shui. If you feel that this would be useful to you or your organization, email or message me at sandraroth259@gmail.com. I look forward to hearing from you.

## Sandra Roth

Sandra Roth is a transformational leader who has thirty years of experience at director level in health and social care. Sandra has board member experience with a UK national charity. Sandra is also a professional and organizational coach and a dowsing practitioner, taught by Marie Diamond.

Sandra transforms organizational culture and performance. Coaching individuals and organizations to find the hidden talents within. Sandra can dowse environments to realize and release individual and organizational trauma caused by energetic stress.

Sandra will help you find and deliver your unique vision, ambitions, and dreams. She will help identify your purpose to improve your life and your customers' experience.

Sandra identifies what is important to that person or organization by listening to and building on individual and organizational strengths in order to:

1. Find unique contribution and gifts
2. Develop the art of possibility
3. Develop leaders and improve customer satisfaction

Sandra's goal is to continue to help people to find the real gifts that are unrecognized within them, and then to develop and nurture those talents. She has done this successfully with hundreds of individuals and many organizations.

She celebrates achievements, leaving individuals and organizations feeling stronger, positive, and more focused.

Sandra's recognized track record of delivering success, passion, and enthusiasm through her coaching will transform your organization, making a difference in your life and the lives of those around you.

So, join her and you too can find the real you and transform your life and your organization.

**Contact Sandra Roth:**


- sandraroth259@gmail.com
- www.facebook.com/SandraHowardRoth
- @sandrahowardroth
- www.linkedin.com/in/sandrahowardroth

# Unbecome Everything the World Has Made You and Fully Embody the Miracle You Are

## By Katarina Runa

"It should have happened already! I should be happy by now," I whispered with tears in my eyes to my cat Ester, the only connection left to my picture of a happy life. Nothing made sense anymore, and I felt like all my efforts were in vain. My beautiful, sunny, spacious apartment where my husband and I were supposed to create a happy family was listed for sale and we were about to get divorced. Despite two diplomas from prestigious universities, working twelve hours a day in two jobs, trying to get my own business off the ground, I was sitting in a miniature apartment, unsure how I would pay this month's rent. I felt like a hamster in a running wheel—tired and stuck. Moreover, it was like being in quicksand—the more I tried to dig myself out, the more I toiled, the more stuck and unhappy I became. I just couldn't understand what went wrong and why. I've always tried so hard, worked incessantly, checked off every single box my parents, teachers, and society handed me on the list of "how to be happy." Best grades. University. Respected career. Marriage. Beautiful home.

However, despite doing everything "right," instead of feeling satisfaction, I was on the brink of despair, alone, deeply disappointed, deceived, sad, and most of all, angry at the whole world. I consider this moment to be my rock bottom. Did it hurt? You bet. But did I concede and accept that from now on, this should be my life? Not at all! I refused to believe that I was born for this. I was determined to find my way out. And I succeeded. Do you wonder what my life looks like right now? I'm living a life I did not even dare to dream of before. My second husband is the love of my life and even after ten years together, we still have a deep, loving, and passionate relationship.

We rise in love together. We are proud parents of three wonderful children—Dorothea, Jakub, and Magdalena. We spend most of the year on the divine exotic island of Bali. On top of all these blessings—I do what I love and it brought amazing success into my life! I am guiding my clients from all over the world through their journey of empowerment and self-discovery. I support them in finding the inner courage to change their lives from the ground up, to find the source of their true power and inner happiness, and to embrace and live their dreams. I have already reached hundreds of thousands of clients from forty-two countries and now I am about to bring my knowledge to an English-speaking audience as well. I managed to create a successful seven-figure business company in a short time, and it is still growing. Thanks to the amazing abundance flowing in my life, I keep fulfilling my dreams. I travel, explore beautiful places, support projects and charities I believe in, I grow my wonderful team that supports me in my vision and mission: to help millions of people find their way to a joyful, happy, and fulfilled life—by unbecoming who they are not and to fully embody the miracle we all were born as.

I started eleven years ago and to this day, I have helped tens of thousands of people to find the source of their true strength, deep happiness, and courage to change their lives from the ground up. But it's not only my students who benefit immensely; their success imprints on their loved ones as well. As the saying goes, "happy wife, happy life;" that works with "mom" or "partner" as well. But my goals do not end there. I dream of helping millions—that's why I have decided to offer my unique method to the English-speaking audience as well. Would you like to know how I managed to change my life? The first step was the decision to do whatever it took.

I knew that the instructions I received from people around me on "how to be happy" did not work for me. And, not even for them—after all, most of them were far from living the life of their dreams. I decided to find my own, authentic way to what "being happy" meant to me. That was the first real question I had to face. What does it actually mean to be happy on my own terms? What do I really desire? And so, I went looking for answers. I traveled around the world, visited sacred places and personal development centers—I also established one in Slovakia, my native country, and ran it for years.

Through therapies, courses, and training with the best domestic and international teachers, studying with the best mentors and learning from old spiritual teachings, I got to heal my soul and body. Through this experience, the answers appeared. I longed for a relationship in which I could be truly myself. I longed for a relationship where I didn't have to fit into the "proper wife" formula. I wanted a vocation that would make me happy and make me feel fulfilled every day, but at the same time, didn't require me to pay the price of no free time and the lack of a personal life. On the contrary; I wanted to have enough space for myself and everything I loved. I wanted to have an abundance that would allow me to not have to think about whether what I wanted was within my means. And above all, I wanted to live my gifts and my mission fully and authentically. Maybe you have similar desires and maybe you too are asking yourself the same questions I asked myself: What is standing in my way? What are the obstacles that are blocking me and will not allow me to fully experience what I dream of?

Based on my extensive studies, I understood what my biggest detriment was: The version of myself that I believed I needed to be in order to "become" lovable and acceptable. I believed that I had to mold myself according to the opinions of others, behave in a certain way, achieve something, fight against and even let go of some parts of me. All in order to deserve love, appreciation, and attention. All my life I have heard, perhaps just like you, who I should become, what I should do to please important people in my life—I had to have good grades, be an obedient daughter, go to dance class, graduate from a prestigious school, be a good wife, and a successful professional. And I really tried. But all these requirements I imposed on myself created layers of inauthenticity that over time buried the real me. I realized that what I really needed was to unbecome who I made myself believe I should be. And I should do that with compassion and kindness towards myself and others.

Moreover, I understood that every request I did not manage to fulfill, every betrayal or bad treatment I received from a family member, my partner, or even a friend, created a deep wound on my soul. And these wounds from the past directly affected my everyday life—how I perceived myself, what I believed relationships should look like. These wounds and layers were like a perpetual twisted chrysalis—with no butterflies in sight, it rather became a cell of my own infallible design, always keeping me in the dark, always unhappy. But step by step, I managed to tear the walls down and free myself. Based on my studies, my own experience, and my work with my students, I have created my very own, powerful METHOD OF DEWOUNDING and THE PROCESS OF UNBECOMING. We identify, address, and heal profound wounds, but also go back to even before the wounds formed.

It is a process that could be described in three steps:

1/ Find out, fully understand, and acknowledge who you really are. Dive deep into your desires and the unique way the Universe (Source, Fate, God, you name it) wants to express itself through you. This is very specific to you and no one else will have it the same. Build trust in yourself!

2/ Understand what parts of you are not authentic. What was created because of the hurts and struggles you have been through? Find out what you gave up and replaced with something more "acceptable and lovable."

3/ Do not only heal, but unbecome who you are not—everything you've experienced makes you who you are today. Become authentic. Allow yourself to fully step into who you were meant to be—the embodiment of wealth, well-being, and happiness you always dreamed about—in all areas of your life!

Most healing techniques focus only on the third step. They require us to change. However, change without understanding why "I Am the way I Am" is not lasting. It's like mowing down weeds without removing their roots. It looks great for a while, but your garden will soon get overrun. That's why the Dewounding method goes deep—to the very root of our limiting beliefs, afflictions, and pains. The treatment is gentle and kind.

Imagine, dear reader, what it would be like to identify, accept, but most importantly, break free from who you became in response to the pain or deprivation you have experienced. Imagine letting go of feelings of shame, guilt, or inadequacy, and embracing your deepest desires as expressions of your true self. What would it be like to finally create and live the life of your dreams? You might doubt, if it is even possible.

My own story, as well as the countless stories of my students, are proof that it is more than possible! Every day, I receive grateful messages about how they are opening up to deeper relationships, to more authentic self-acceptance, to wealth, and how they saved their family, marriage, or their sanity. How, day by day, they are succeeding in creating a life in harmony with who they really are.

Did I pique your interest? Do you feel that my Dewounding method is a path for you? Then head over to my website, www.katarinaruna.com, where you can learn more about me, as well as my programs. Introductory or intermediate courses are available.

You will also find a lot of free content there, because I know how important it is that we resonate with each other before you decide to set off on the journey with me. New blogs on self-improvement, relationships with men, and much more are added regularly. I wholeheartedly hope you will find in life not only what you desire, but also what you really need.

## Katarina Runa

Katarina Runa is a highly sought-after European transformational leader and mentor. In guiding others, she applies the same techniques that brought about the life she envisioned for herself.

Rather than focusing on transient behavioral change, Katarina helps her clients achieve lasting results by addressing the root causes of the unhappiness through her very own **Dewounding method**.

She expedites healing from within by guiding her clients to take over the reins of their lives. She has helped tens of thousands of women from more than forty-two countries to transform their minds and lives.

She appeared as an expert in several national TV channels, radio, and many major Slovak magazines and newspapers.

She is the founder of the first self-development center in Slovakia and a speaker at international conferences focused on personal development, appearing with famous names such as Neale Donald Walsch, Joe Dispenza, Eckhart Tolle.

Following her calling to help as many people as possible in finding their true selves, she established an annual, online, international conference: The Good Life Conference. It is a multi-day event focused on personal development and boasting some of the most respected speakers from

Europe and abroad, as well as practical workshops, exercises, and meditations.

She is the author of several successful online programs, such as the Path of a Woman, The Infinitely Rich Self, or the Key to Men's Soul.

Katarina's mentees, who enter her most coveted transformational programs, work under her guidance on blossoming into the people they dream to be for a whole year.

**Contact Katarina Runa:**

- SVK - www.facebook.com/runa.katarina
- EN - www.facebook.com/katarina.runa.int
- www.facebook.com/katarinka.runa
- SVK - @katarina.runa.durove & EN - @katarina.runa
- SVK - www.youtube.com/@KatarinaRuna
- EN - www.linkedin.com/in/katarina-runa-70281511
- SVK - www.tiktok.com/@katarinaruna.sk
- EN - www.tiktok.com/@katarina_runa

# Menopause To Marathons

## By Theresa Russell

There it was again. My hot flashes had come back. Their intensity was spiraling out of control. There seemed to be no end. I could feel the perspiration pop up on my body and the river of sweat wash over me, my bra and back wet, and my shirt sticking to me. I wanted to scream. A level of anxiety that I had never felt before engulfed me. It was May 2020. But the worst is yet to be told. I have suffered from night sweats off and on since I was thirty-six years old. In my late forties, my symptoms worsened. The hot flashes increased in intensity. By the time I turned fifty-three, the flashes had risen to about fifty by lunchtime. Finally, I was offered a low-level hormone replacement therapy pill. That was after years of complaints to the doctor, during which I received no help or insights into my symptoms. I was told I could only take the low-level HRT pill for two years, and then we would discuss the next step. That next step did not happen. During Covid, my gynecologist closed shop. My primary care physician retired. At the same time, my HRT pill could not be found anywhere. I had no advance notice. I felt like I had gone haywire, walking the tightrope over an abyss. Levels of anxiety that I had never felt before would come over me. What is happening to me? Why am I acting so overwhelmed and anxious? Why can't I think straight? Why do I feel like crying?

I had always believed in myself as being motivated, but I could not have imagined the transformation and self-confidence I experienced once I emerged from the dark side. How did I control my symptoms while living in isolation, in complete Covid lockdown, with no medical advice? Controlling your mindset is a lifelong job. First, you must have a clear identity, know who you are and hold on to that, no matter what. You must be prepared to find yourself alone, with no expert books or scientific advice to guide you. You must learn about your reactions to your problem areas and use that knowledge to transform yourself, not let your reactions determine and govern you. But you can only achieve that feat with practice, and not suddenly, when caught off-guard by symptoms. In our culture, menopausal symptoms are tied to medical definitions derived from specialized and inaccessible research institutions and medical schools, walled off, and closed to the lay public. This makes women who want to talk about their symptoms and find ways to integrate these experiences into their daily lives stick out like sore thumbs. Women feel awkward, forced, and unnatural with what is a natural process. That adds stress, anxiety, and fire to the painful and simmering tinder box. I want to share the life experiences that helped me change how I looked at the symptoms of menopause forever. By changing my mindset, I changed my health and well-being. I was shy and quiet from an early age. I grew up in a large family. I knew how to avoid conflict, even if that meant hiding underneath the bed to wait for the storm to pass. I used moments when I was alone to pray for peace and calmness. I was introspective.

I knew at an early age that I could control my thoughts and, therefore, my actions and outcomes. I felt like I was the responsible one, the conflict solver. I was very empathetic. When I was fourteen years old, I met someone I fell in love with. He gave me attention, and I felt he could become a part of my life. Two years later I became pregnant, and had Vanessa in the summer of eleventh grade. He left us before she was born. He came back and asked me to marry him. I decided to call off the wedding three days before. I concluded I had value, and his lies were not for me. I had spoken to God about my situation and I realized He wanted me to have my baby. I saw this as a gift. At the same time, I felt humiliated. No longer was I able to look at myself as the perfect one. That early time was hard. In high school, I would overhear classmates saying mean things about me because I was pregnant. However, to me, that isolation meant something else. I decided to change the bad into the good. I could change who I was. I would not let my environment define who I was, inside. I decided to have complete control over my life. Life was not about what had happened to me but the meaning I gave to what happened to me. How would I respond to what happened to me in the future? Sometimes, the most challenging things that we go through are the biggest blessings in our life. I resolved to have a heart of gratitude and always focus on the good. I made myself believe that nothing and nobody could define my life. Only I could. I was going to be the action-taker, to be determined and disciplined. When we moved to a different state for my senior year, I decided to make a clean slate. I would not feel trapped by the constraints of motherhood, unfinished education, and destitute finances. At my new school, I had very few friends; it was just me and my thoughts. But I took many actions. I put my hand up to run for senior class treasurer.

I did not get elected as an officer, however I was so proud of myself for stepping out of my comfort zone and resolved that I would continue doing that. My dad told me to always say "yes" and figure it out later. I was given the "I Dare You" award. I had made an appointment with the district superintendent to change high school policies and procedures that were repressive of students' religious freedom. I graduated seventeenth in my class. I was offered a full scholarship to be a dietician. I had to turn it down because the college was too far away, and I would not be able to see my daughter as much as I wanted. I worked odd jobs to support my daughter, laying carpet and vinyl, assistant trim carpenter, and at a factory. I met my husband when I was nineteen and working at an equipment company. I have always tried to live a life of gratitude and believe in the good qualities in people. Having an open mind led me to find the man of my dreams. I had faith in overcoming my inner struggles and decided to give life a chance. Having faith and the right mindset required that I be physically fit. Any relationship involves overcoming hurdles, and I made sure to be there for my husband and daughter. My path of personal growth required stamina and strength. I have been following a fitness protocol that included weightlifting and participating in half-marathons for over forty years. I have completed eighty-six half-marathons and one full marathon. My running journey could have been easier. It took courage and persistence. Due to minor issues, I never thought I could run a marathon. In 2022, having the physical edge plus the mindset that enables one was crucial in my victory over menopause. I decided it would be my year to lose my fear of a few things. I got the call in late August that there was a spot on a charity team. I could do the NYC Marathon if I said yes. I said "yes" without hesitation. I would worry about the "how" later. In November 2022, I completed the NYC Marathon. In September 2023, I signed up to run in Berlin, Germany. There are only limitations if you make them. In 2022, I revisited two races I said I would never do again.

I got lost on one, and they had to find me, and at the other, I was dehydrated and ended up in an ambulance. I revisited the race that had put me in the ambulance. This time I placed first in my age group. I had many fresh starts after I embarked on life when I was seventeen. I decided I could change who I was with God's help. I decided that nothing is predetermined. It is up to me to snap out of being sidetracked. It is up to me to refuse to become hopeless or to give up my power over the situation. What it boils down to is: "What do I want?" Mother Teresa said, "If you don't know what you want, work on yourself." I strive to be a little better today than I was yesterday. I strive always to be a light to others. I know my story is reflected in my actions, and I do not hide any part of myself. I take responsibility and control. There is not one piece of information that defines me or my life. I was put here on earth for an intended purpose. I was stuck in Covid lockdown with terrible hot flashes, my medication was terminated, and no physician was in sight. What were my options to fix myself? I had already been studying mid-life perimenopause, and menopause. I dug in deeper on everything and anything that I could find on the subject matter. I discovered that the brain could adapt to hormonal changes through neuroplasticity. The brain is part of our physical body; however, it can chart new pathways through willpower and discipline. By charting these new pathways, the brain can eventually restore hormonal balance. The mechanisms behind this mind–body connection are still being studied by science. However, the power of our mind over the body is undeniable.[1]

The power of lifestyle changes is more significant than women think! You can implement lifestyle changes with focus, self-love, and self-respect. And by implementing lifestyle changes, you can manage your symptoms. You must take the initiative and stand up for your health. Listen to your body, be mindful and adaptive, and raise your awareness using prayer or meditation. That will allow you to give the meaning to your symptoms that your symptoms ask you to give to them, and solutions will open up. Never be overwhelmed or give in to your symptoms! This approach has been proven by science. The discipline, willpower, and focus you apply in your self-care will restore hormonal balance. I took determined, simple, but decisive steps to calm myself when I felt anxious and overwhelmed. I can name only a few. Such lifestyle changes will help you lift your energy and well-being. They will build your mind and make you into a stronger person. I am doing deep breathing exercises. I added daily yoga to my routine, which helped me relax. I cut back on red wine and sugar. I put together a new night hygiene routine that included an Epsom salts bath that would help my body relax for a good night's sleep. I told my husband what was happening, and he did not know how to help me. We would be watching TV, and I would tell him to "pause," and I would walk out of the room for a few minutes.

I always returned, but I needed to be alone for a few minutes. Pausing to gather your thoughts is important so you don't snap back at someone. These are a few examples of things that helped me get to a better place. It has now been three years, and I am back to being my upbeat self. I have learned to control the feelings of being overwhelmed and anxious. Self-love has become even more important to me. Because of my journey, I decided to coach women who are struggling the way I

---

1 For more information on this topic, please see *The Menopause Relief Paradox*, Conclusion: Know Thyself! Stop Ignoring Your Better Half! by Dr. Maria Ian, Cave Sun Publishing, 2022.

did. There is a way to go through this so you, too, can return to a purposeful life. But for any of these changes to occur, we must speak about and know our symptoms.

You cannot be expected to be disciplined if you live in isolation and ignorance, or if your symptoms are treated dismissively, and you are angry with your environment. I invite you to join the movement, speak about it, and improve daily! It's time to make a difference.

## Theresa Russell

Theresa Russell is a menopause coach that works with individuals as well as groups. Theresa is on a mission to share her passion and knowledge to help other women find their clarity, their purpose, and know that life is not over—it has just begun. Offline, she lives with her husband in North Carolina, USA. She is an avid runner, and has completed eighty-six half-marathons and one marathon (NYC).

**Contact Theresa Russell:**

@skincareandsneakers

www.facebook.com/theresa.lesterrussell

www.facebook.com/groups/237600635034194

www.linkedin.com/in/theresa-russell-cpcu-aic-ais-1847b7101

# Paying It Forward With "Speakers Are Leaders"

## Harry Sardinas

### The Universe Always Has Your Back

My life needed a reset. I came to London hopeful and, frankly, a bit arrogant, with a chemical engineering degree and five years' webmaster experience from Spain—but no English. I had some money to keep me going for a while. I had time. I felt like I was on top of the world. I was young, vibrant, and charming. I was ultra-confident everyone would fall in love with me at first Cuban "teddy bear" sight: I was chubby, bald, and lovable. After a while, I felt a massive stamp across my forehead—it read FAILURE in big block letters. Rejected from working at McDonald's. Rejected from all jobs due to not speaking English. Rejected from all banks. I reluctantly had to accept work as a bartender and room service attendant in a Hilton hotel. Months of rejections made these jobs feel like a massive win.

### Be Charismatic

I was not sure how I was going to get paid without a bank account. My money was quickly running out. I said to myself, "I'll try this last bank and if they say NO—I am done." I went in and made a great connection with the banker who opened my bank account that day. My charm saved me from being a complete failure. I had no money; however, I had something which could translate into money—I was a masterful instant super-connector.

### Be The Best Version Of Yourself

Despite not speaking much English, going above and beyond providing customer service got me awarded with the 100% Mystery Shopper Award multiple times. I was born knowing the **language of love**—loving, helping, accepting, and making people feel at ease was easy for me.

***Lesson: When you've got nothing—smile and master the art of connections. The Universe is preparing you for the best by giving you the worst.***

### Always Add Value

While working in the Hilton hotel, I learned everything about renting rooms, and that gave me the idea for my first property management business. I quickly realized my clients needed English lessons, places to eat, jobs, and I gradually started offering them these services as an add-on to room rentals. I was adding massive value to my clients by making their lives easier and they were helping me create wealth. That business sold over five million dollars over a few years.

***Lesson: Find out what people need and give it to them.***

**Create An Ecosystem**

As a business owner, I quickly understood the power of listening and kindness, for creating a community of recurring buyers for whom I was solving the multiple problems I experienced when I came to London. My own pain inspired me to help others with landing services so they could easily integrate. It also taught me it was possible to offset client acquisition cost by offering multiple desirable products to the same client base. For that to occur, excellent customer service was essential for getting repeat buyers.

***Lesson: Build and nurture a community of recurring buyers.***

**Hire Exceptional People**

I started hiring the right property managers to help me with an ever-better service so as to increase the revenue per customer. That is how I met Lily Patrascu, who was at the time someone with great unexplored potential. I initially hired her to manage the English school I had. She gradually increased revenue for that business by adding multiple methods of payment collection, publishing a book about how to learn English quickly, teaching English, making sales, and a great advert on the high street which was bringing leads for the school and for the property business as well. She increased sales for the property business by a total of forty-one percent with the same number of properties, simply by being proactive, upgrading the brand of the company and the image of the properties via inexpensive refurbs, great customer service, improved marketing, and sales.

***Lesson: Hire extraordinary people; they'll do your job better and faster, they'll save your company a fortune in optimization, and they'll find the hidden money in your company.***

**Attract Clients By Publishing A Book**

One of the most impactful things I have ever done was to publish my first book, *Climbing Big Ben. How To Survive, Thrive And Succeed In London*. I wanted to help my clients succeed in London by getting their first job, starting and growing their business. I was providing accommodation for unemployed, newly arrived, non-English speaking tenants seeking work in London—a market nobody wanted. I knew everybody deserves a chance to thrive in London, plus I was once in their shoes. I also knew a lot of them were highly skilled in their home country and just needed someone to give them one opportunity to work. Lily and I started giving the book for free to targeted potential property clients and that led to clients quickly learning how to settle in London, and dramatically increased profits, credibility, authority, trust, and faster connections, and reduced work, from twenty viewings to rent a property down to one or two. I also wanted to get visibility and exposure to start my speaking career and help attract more clients for my property business.

**Speakers Are Leaders**

I had always dreamt of speaking on worldwide stages and yet, had no idea how to get there. My publisher invited me to speak about my book at the National Achievers Congress in 2016, where over two thousand people attended and the world's best influencers were speaking. Tony Robbins, Eddy The Eagle, and Kevin Green were headline speakers at that event. Years earlier, I was dreaming of speaking at a Tony Robbins event and I was now briefly talking about my book at the same event as him. I quickly understood the power of a book to catapult me and my business to the next level so I could fulfill my dream of helping millions of people free themselves from fears and empower themselves to achieve anything they wanted, including growing their business.

**The Workshop That Transformed Thousands Of People's Lives**

Lily helped me put my ideas together, redesigned my branding, helped me find my message, and published *Speakers Are Leaders*, a book that was based on a workshop I had created to empower Lily and the thousands of entrepreneurs I was meeting regularly to overcome the fear of speaking and to speak confidently about products and services offered, on worldwide stages and online. The **Speakers Are Leaders** workshop started out tiny; the very first one had forty-five people. The workshop was ultra-fun for me and for all participants, who became raving fans. They were eagerly leaving amazing reviews.

**Build A Global Brand**

Lily and I started empowering **global heart-centered entrepreneurs** worldwide. The brand name, **Speakers Are Leaders,** appealed to entrepreneurs who wanted to make a difference because they could feel we were heart-centered leaders who were keen to share their expertise to empower others. The Singapore event started out with only six people. We weren't deterred. We kept momentum going and noticed bigger and bigger numbers. Six people turned into seventy for the next event. Seventy turned into 250 people. Ten thousand people worldwide attended it in person and I never felt I was working. I was in flow when I was speaking on stage. I was **born to lead. Born to love. Born to empower.**

Lily and I continued leveraging the workshops and the books for lead generation. We were giving the books for free or selling them to desirable potential property clients, property investors, influencers, speaking promoters, and potential joint venture partners. Speaking on global stages resulted in global speaking opportunities, media features, radio interviews, features on the cover of *Business Fit Magazine*, free invites to luxury events, collaboration opportunities, and we started attracting multimillionaire business owners, leaders, and powerful influencers to us. Later on, I was invited to speak at the same event as famous speakers such as Les Brown and Raymond Aaron, thanks to being a published author with a luxury book.

Everyone wanted a piece of Lily and I; we were attracting **global heart-centered entrepreneurs** who desired our done-with-you business growth services: speaker training, guaranteed speaking gigs worldwide, organizing events in person, broadcasting and live streaming, book publishing, influencer marketing collaborations, paid social media marketing campaigns, creative customized business growth solutions, such as seeking investors for their business, influencer websites, e-commerce websites, event websites that sell, branding, guaranteed media features.

The **Speakers Are Leaders** workshop became a global brand with recurring workshops in the UK, Singapore, Mexico, Peru, and UAE, and invites in a further ten countries to empower entrepreneurs. I started helping heart-centered entrepreneurs become public speakers and turn their business into a global brand from the stage.

### Pay It Forward

As a non-native English speaker with a strong accent and recurring grammar mistakes, I was struggling to pitch myself to other speaker promoters so I decided to organize my own events. Every event would attract further speaking opportunities worldwide because I was focused on adding value to the speaker promoter, being fun and easy to work with, sending my marketing materials on time and in an organized manner, being generous, kind, loving. I was focused on giving first. I was willing to allow anyone I collaborated with to win first for a long time before I did. I had a strong desire to help more people so I started traveling worldwide, creating connections and building the Speakers Are Leaders brand globally.

**Become An Influencer To Multiply Your Impact Worldwide**

If you'd like a step-by-step plan to go from **zero to influencer,** here it is:

- Publish a book.
- Brand yourself and your business.
- Overcome the fear of speaking.
- Create a workshop/online course based on the teachings in the book.
- Get invited to speak at other people's events.
- Perfect your speaking through practice.
- Empower yourself to sell your high-ticket products effectively.
- Prepare your media kit.
- Prepare your virtual TV home studio.
- Offer your products to a global audience online or from the stage.
- Create a social media community.
- Build a database of potential clients.
- Hook your followers with fun, love, variety, certainty, and growth.

**Associate With Powerful Brands**

The luxury branding Lily designed for Speakers Are Leaders, and our easy-going fun nature, attracted high-profile heart-centered speakers to our events—Feng Shui Master Marie Diamond, marketer Armand Morin, YouTube influencer Master Sri Akarshana. As I grew my followers to 283,000 and expanded our social media reach to one million people, I became the business growth strategist for **Threedee.io**, a company needing to become pitch and investment ready.

**Threedee.io** creates digital cities for games, animated movies, and the metaverse faster than anything on the market, with a patented software. I noticed the immense power of the brand association with influencers speaking at our events as an amazing tool for being taken seriously, being heard by leaders, and opening the right doors for joint ventures. I managed to take the company to a valuation of $20m by leveraging my network to bring clients, creating their business model, the right pitch deck, branding and packaging the offers so they could become investment and pitch ready. The company got multiple buy-out offers, media features in magazines, and is still seeking investment. When you create a business that transforms the world, you attract everything you desire.

## Harry Sardinas

Harry Sardinas is a **Business Growth Accelerator Strategist** and **Empowerment, Leadership and Business Coach** living in London, **Influencer** with 283,000-plus followers, **Events Organizer**—connecting investors and entrepreneurs with opportunities.

Harry helps companies to turn their products into global brands from the stage and he mentors tech companies and businesses to **Get Pitch Ready and Investment Ready.**

He is the Founder of **Speakers Are Leaders**—public-speaking, branding, and marketing workshop. And also, Shareholder and COO of **Threedee.io** – 3D procedural modeling company that can build digital cities for metaverse, gaming, animated movies, NFT, real estate, quickly, easily, and user-friendly.

Harry is a High-Impact, High-Energy and Entertaining Speaker and the Author of ***Speakers Are Leaders*** **and** ***Climbing Big Ben***.

Harry can help you with getting connected to investment opportunities, startups, investors and joint venture partners; creating pitch decks and video promos to get funding; overcoming fear of speaking on stage or online; creating experiential online events, workshops, courses, coaching.

He can also easily set up your virtual live stream studio at home for your online speaking and coaching business; get booked to speak worldwide, and become a confident and charismatic speaker.

He is looking for entrepreneurs wanting to grow their brand and business through speaking on worldwide stages or online and gaming, metaverse, and animated movies companies. Some of Fun Facts: He is an amazing salsa dancer, occasional actor.

His Achievements are:

- To Be the King of Paying it forward
- Empowered over ten thousand people in five countries on worldwide stages to speak confidently and charismatically, and reached over one million people at online events; invited in twenty other countries to speak about the power of speaking to grow your business.
- Helped a tech company go from $250,000 valuation to $20m in one year.
- Invited to participate in the Commonwealth Celebrations in the presence of the Queen of England and the Royal Family.
- Organized hundreds of entrepreneur events worldwide.

**Contact Harry Sardinas:**

hello@speakersareleaders.com

www.speakersareleaders.com

www.facebook.com/harrysardinasofficial

www.youtube.com/@SpeakersAreLeadersMotivation

www.linkedin.com/in/harrysardinas

@harrysardinas

www.threedee.io

# Lessons Learned: Reflection On The Experiences That Shaped Me

## By Yvonne Schimmel

People who meet me now will not believe that I was, till a couple of years ago, a very insecure and introverted person. Growing up with a narcissistic dad (and later married to a narcissistic husband), minor sexual abuse, bullied at school, and being an empath and kind of psychic, were the cause of that. Nowadays they call me the Mayoress of London because I connect so many people together and organize a lot of events. A friend of mine said jokingly that I am the honey, attracting all the bees and connecting them together. What a difference to the person I used to be.

Growing up in my family, I always felt very lonely. I was the youngest and the only girl, with two older brothers. I felt I didn't fit in, I was different. It's not that there was no love, I knew my parents loved me; every evening, before bedtime, there would be cuddle time. Those moments were very precious to me. But for my brothers I felt I was their annoying sister. Of course, that was my impression of them, they are five and seven years older than me. And maybe I really was their annoying sister because I never felt a real connection with them when I was young, probably because of the age difference. Having a narcissistic dad had a great influence on the whole family. There was no space for me being me. My mum did her best but was also not equipped for standing up to my dad. Coming home from school, my mum always had tea and a biscuit ready; that was really welcoming and felt great. But when my dad was at home, most of the time it felt like we were tiptoeing around him. I do understand now where his behavior came from but that still is no excuse for passing his past on to his children. His word was law; we had to do as he wanted. I know he did his best raising us, the best he was capable of.

And of course, it was not always bad—we also had a lot of fun as a family together. My first husband was completely the opposite of my dad, but didn't make me happy in the end either. My second husband was a narcissist in disguise, the funny nice guy to the outside world, but back home, the narcissist. He made me even more insecure than I already was. In the last years of our marriage, I turned it into a challenge for improving myself, went to therapy, and started to realize that I needed to heal my inner child. But it took me until last year to finally find out what the issues were that needed to be healed. Sexual abuse came to the surface in a magic mushroom session. I had always tucked it away because I never saw it as abuse but later, I realized that even though the abuse was minor, it has been a big influence in my love life, always choosing the wrong man for the wrong reason, sex. Being bullied at school was another reason for my insecurity. The ages of six to twelve weren't my best or easiest school years. I had a love/hate relationship with the girl that bullied me. I realized at an older age that she had done it out of her own insecurity. When I was a therapist, one day she called me for help and I must be honest, a part of me wanted to turn her down. But I realized that wouldn't help us both so I booked her in for a consultation. It felt like a victory, me being able to stand above the past. Being an empath is not easy, especially at a young age when you have absolutely no idea what it is and what it does to you. And actually, even today it is still not easy to deal with because I always see the good in people, feel them, and want to help them. Unfortunately, people take advantage of that and you end up disillusioned, again.

You also pick up on emotion and you are not always aware that what you are feeling might not be your emotions, but those of other people who you have met that day, or even people who thought of you that day. I often pick up emotions from friends I am really strongly connected with. Bit by bit, I am learning to just acknowledge it and let it go, or when I feel I have to contact them I do so, or I wait for them to contact me. As an empath, you want to take the whole world on your shoulders, but that's not the way it should be. Every person has their own responsibility and their own karma to work out, as have I, myself. All these experiences turned me into the person I am nowadays. I can empathize with a lot of people because of all that happened for me. I never think that things happen *to* me, but always *for* me, to learn, to experience. And I also think that I attract my clients based on my own experiences; everything is energy.

I believe that people need to feel heard and know they are being acknowledged. In today's society there is hardly any space and time for this, not with the regular healthcare system and not with society in general. We live in survival mode nowadays, all with our own problems, and unfortunately most people are not really interested in someone else's well-being because of their own issues. What can I offer as a holistic therapist? I will give you a medical diagnostic measurement with my high-tech bodyscan (official medical device 2). It uses an electromagnetic field to do the measurement and treatment. It measures 650 parts of the body. You get a complete insight into your health, for instance, brain, heart, lungs, all other organs, low grade inflammation, digestive issues, micro-organisms, stress level, energy level, toxins, heavy metals, hormones, muscles, skeleton, nerves, lymph, food intolerance, deficiency of vitamins, minerals, fatty acids, etc. With this complete insight we can get to the root cause instead of just treating the symptoms. Next to that I will also look at the emotional side, not only what is going on in your life at this moment but also what happened in the past. We will look at how we can change your perspective on what occurred and continue from that point on. Nutrition will be an important aspect, too; what needs to be changed and what needs to be added. I recently connected with another med tech company and we can measure and treat people remotely with a new high-tech device. The only difference is that this machine works remotely. So, from the comfort of your own house, I can find out what your health issues are. I believe that telemedicine is the future.

I get fulfillment out of helping people, knowing that one conversation could change a person's life forever. When I first came to London, I had a talk with my roommate in the place I was staying temporarily. I told him he could do much better in life—better housing, better job, more money—just because he was worth it. Never settle for less. We kept in touch after I moved out and about one year later, he told me that I had changed his life for the better by having just that one conversation. My goal for the future is traveling all over the world and helping people who come across my path and need help. I did that for almost ten weeks when I was traveling through America in 2019 and it gave me so much fulfillment; that's what makes me happy, no money in the world can compete with that. And healing people is healing myself. My trip through America healed and changed me too. Before I left, I felt like a nobody, felt I didn't matter, who would be interested in me? Over there, I found out that I did matter, that people were interested in me. Stepping out of my comfort zone and going to America on my own was the best thing I ever could have done for myself. I challenge you all, step out of your comfort zone and become a better version of yourself! If you are interested in my work and would like to read some testimonials from my clients, please check out my website: www.healingworldwide.info. You can give me a free call from all over the world, also if you just want to have a chat with me when you can relate to my story. As my website says, "healing worldwide," I do work worldwide. I am also looking for people with a medical background who would love to start working with this amazing new high-tech remote bodyscan or with the supplements.

## Yvonne Schimmel

Yvonne is a health practitioner who is experienced in a wide field of health issues. For over the last ten years she has helped thousands of clients in different countries like the Netherlands, Germany, Spain, Mexico, and the UK.

She works with high-tech medical devices, also used in several clinics worldwide. These devices give a complete insight into your health. She's also a nutritionist and weight-loss coach, so she can give you excellent nutritional advice and help you to lose or gain weight.

She has written two books about health, too: *How to Get and Be Pregnant the Healthy Way*, and *Healthy Nutrition in a Nutshell*, sold on Amazon.

Yvonne has helped her clients with a diversity of health issues, like chronic fatigue, chronic pain, digestive issues, inexplicable issues, infertility, long Covid, and vaccine issues.

As of this year she works at the clinic of Felix Economakis, the UK's famous psychologist, well-known from several TV programs and podcasts. "Working as a team in his clinic with all kinds of practitioners, we have the best interest for our clients," Yvonne says.

Reiki and healing are two other things Yvonne does. After living in Mexico in 2022 and doing all kinds of healing sessions herself (kambo, ayahuasca, magic mushrooms, temazcal, rebirthing, hypnotherapy, breathing sessions), she empowered her reiki and healing capacities.

She has helped and healed a huge number of people in the last thirty years. Not only does she do treatments face-to-face but also distance healing sessions. She did her official education as an energetic therapist in the Netherlands.

Next to all this, Yvonne works with high-end supplements to complete your diet. Nowadays it's very difficult to get all your vitamins, minerals, fatty acids, and amino acids out of your nutrition. Unfortunately, you have to add them with high-quality supplements.

In the past, Yvonne has worked with the London charity Our Forgotten Neighbours to help them with their soup kitchen, and has raised thousands of pounds to help homeless people, to provide mental health care, food, and toiletries.

"When going door-to-door or standing on the street raising money, I often heard people say, 'No thank you, I am fine.' Yes, you are fine, but so many people are not fine. So please, next time you see a fundraiser, give something, even if it is just £1. Do something for people who are in need; one day it could be you."

Yvonne thinks that you are the creator of your own movie, your own life. Health, wealth, abundance, prosperity, people you meet up with, situations that occur, you create it yourself by your own mindset. That's why it is so important to become aware of how you experience life, your emotions, your thoughts. By changing that, you change your life. Yvonne can help you with becoming aware of all this with her intuitive coaching.

**Contact Yvonne Schimmel:**

- www.linkedin.com/in/yvonneschimmelofficial
- www.facebook.com/yvonneschimmelofficial
- @yvonneschimmel

# "Let This Life Be For Freedom" - Mooji

## By Snehal Shah

Namaste, beloved reader. You find me writing to you to share the deepest and ultimate discovery one can make in one's lifetime; you are consciousness itself. How this discovery unfolded for "me", the person called Snehal, is one each of you can relate to. It is universal, it has been told for eons, and my story is your story.

All my life I struggled with mind attacks, depression, low self-esteem and all that these would bring into reality and experience, due to external environment, social and cultural conditioning which led to mental anguish and victim mentality. Moving into young adulthood, the pursuit for career, status and wealth (that which was expected of me and which I believed would bring happiness, peace, joy, and security) led to a self-destructive workaholic lifestyle, keeping up the appearance, and manifesting even more internal anguish.

Nothing in the outer world could bring the tranquility that I sought internally. This vicious cycle came to an abrupt end, when the body and mind could no longer sustain the cycle. At the time, I was working for the United Nations War Crimes Tribunal for the Former Yugoslavia which was to be my last employer and February of 2011 was my last month. However, two months prior was the trigger! It all came to a crescendo on a cold, December evening in 2010, whilst I sat watching the thoughts and emotions bubbling up inside.

For the first time though, it was coming from a place of detachment. I had what some would call a life review flash in my mind's eye, of everything that had led me to this moment. All the decisions I had taken, all the ones I had not, all of the choices that played out and all the blame, shame, guilt I was carrying. In that moment, it was all reflected back to me in the macro world through the images and testimonies of the people who had experienced their own hell through a war. What was it all about? "This is what unconsciousness looks like on this planet" was the realization I came to ponder, whilst reviewing work files and images of war and its aftermath.

Even prior to working at the tribunal, in the years of working in a corporate environment and living superficially, all the dissatisfaction, anxiety, depression, loss of purpose, trying to fit in, get a better position, better everything, navigating through the negativity, and all the bickering and arguments at work and in my personal life had led to that one simple, yet strong contemplation. As the tears ran down my face, I felt a sudden rush to run, to run away and escape this reality, and just as my body flinched to move, another thought "Where can you run to, where you are not?"

This, dear reader, is what led me to take my first step into the unknown and become a conscious entrepreneur. After resigning from the Tribunal, I took the rest of 2011 off to explore consciousness. This time out from formal employment served as the retraining as an energetic therapist (something that I knew I had the gift for as a child, but ignored and suppressed), traveling to India, and opening up my first business; Sanctuary Holistic Treatments.

As the years came and went, more and more of my clients at the time started wanting to speak to me, not just lie on the table for treatments. Here, I found a voice coming through me, connecting the wisdom of the body to the perceptions of the mind. It was now 2014, and I felt called to pursue more credentials in cognitive therapy, behavioral science, and the mechanics behind reality creation.

I qualified as a master practitioner of NLP (Neuro Linguistic Programming), gained life coaching credentials in Amsterdam, and took another timeout in India for almost seven months. Part of this time I spent gaining a yoga teacher training qualification, sitting with mentors in south India, and then entering inside a Tibetan Buddhist center in North India for some deep spiritual contemplation and integration of all the aspects of the material and spiritual world I had been studying (intellectually) but was not yet able to embody.

When I got back home at the end of 2014, I experienced another spout of the most unexplainable depression and isolation I had ever experienced. I became a recluse and a hermit, closing down my holistic treatment practice, rounding off all my meditation classes and just locking myself into my apartment. I cannot really speak or recall what was happening, I just know now that some paradigms were shifting.

I was shedding the "person". I reached rock bottom of the affliction and addiction of the ego. 2015 to 2017 were an utter blur. I was just existing but to the outside world it may have looked like the effects of a business failure, personal burnout or breakdown and mental health issues. Yet, at the same time, I was experiencing revelation after revelation; I was awakening.

Least to say as an entrepreneur, I had not succeeded in creating a booming business, instead the raising of consciousness was occurring, and birthed the book *Conquer your Circumstances, the Art and Practice of Metaphysics*. The book allowed me to share the basics of what I had come to know as Truth and also was an opportunity to share the signature coaching methodology namely the 3't process.

It was also at this time that my business evolved to being called Satori Vison. The book can be purchased via www.Satori.Vision but please be advised, it's available in paper copy only. The time in the self-imposed reclusiveness also heightened the intuitive abilities and exploration of the energetic fields and quantum field of existence. That "time" was used to explore the timeless, what and who I am came into experiential wisdom, and deepening of the understanding that "I" am consciousness itself.

This transpired through deep contemplations and meditation, as well as adopting the witnessing conscious perspective. It was during this time that I came to discover the living Master Mooji, whom I credit for the writing and content of this chapter. A moment of full circle realization came when I heard him say on one of his videos the exact words "Where can you run to, where you are not?", the same words I had heard several years earlier, back before I even knew who Mooji was.

Between 2017 and 2019 I was coaching by instinct alone, and I found that my audience was changing and I wasn't making any sense to anybody. After a deep meditation at the end of 2019 (December again!), I was called to be more visible and approachable and was shown to be of service back in the "matrix", so to speak. I found myself enrolled into a Certified ICF coaching programme with iPec, gaining even more perspectives and abilities to communicate at all levels of consciousness.

This leads us straight into Covid times where more than ever, the absence of using our physical senses forced us as a collective to dig deep and re-evaluate our priorities. Here I gained even more hands-on coaching practice through Zoom hosting masterminds and group calls for the networks and communities I volunteer for, such as Mindvalley and Evercoach. This was also the time where the teachings of Mooji began to ripen within, where shedding of personhood took on its own priority. The laws of the universe had played out and I began to "see"'. This observation deepened also to watching the thoughts, emotions, and patterns emerging and playing in the psychological realm of others.

"I" watching became a dedicated practice for months. This ability served me well in coaching sessions and quickly I gained the reputation of being a very intuitive coach and mentor and being able to "read" people.

I leaned into this by offering wisdom sessions, which were not coaching sessions but rather intuitive channeling and mirroring to clients and to those who resonated more with the spiritual guidance and perspectives that were coming through me. For this, I have no credentials!

***"The question "Who am I?" is not really meant to get an answer, the question "Who am I?" is meant to dissolve the questioner" – Ramana Maharshi***

I now flow with ease and there is peace within that cannot be touched by any circumstance. I am able to quickly navigate through the mental and emotional systems for myself, and teach this to others. As an entrepreneur, I am attracting the right resonating clients, fulfilling my purpose of service in the raising of consciousness of the collective, and I am happy. I am free.

I still experience bouts of low energy from time to time as I pick these up in the collective field, plus the fact that I'm an empath means this is bound to happen, but the thing that has shifted and which much insight and heightened consciousness now reveals, is that I am aware this to be just a wave and frequency; I am not that.

This account is but a glimpse of how the awakening unfolded for me. For you, the circumstances may be different. The triggers will differ, for you, the attachments and afflictions will play out in a different way, but one thing remains the same; the suffering and the mind that causes the suffering, by sharing my experiences, I trust you will be able to navigate through your own evolution knowing and taking comfort that you are not alone.

That you are not your mind or your body or your emotions and that the reality that is created through the mind is relative, can be shifted and dissolved, that you can move past all conditioning. You are that which is aware of these taking place; you are awareness itself.

As a quantum coach and a mystic, I serve you in the raising of your consciousness, equipping you with the tools and knowledge of the universal laws. I can impart the wisdom of quantum mechanics in the manifestation process so that you too can come to realize this for yourself and find everlasting peace within. For those of you who wish to explore beyond the mechanics of manifestations, those who wish to manifest virtues in this dimension rather than material things, those of you who are awakened leaders, entrepreneurs, pioneers, teachers, coaches, parents, and mentors, I serve you in offering all the wisdom I can share on metaphysics and offer this as a year-based mentorship, through which you can shift your paradigms, as well as learn how to facilitate the process for others.

I thank you, reader, for purchasing this book, for manifesting this into your life. I wish you love, light, and peace beyond all understanding.
Yours eternally,
Snehal

Book an online meet up with me via www.Satori.Vision and let's start to explore the universe within together.

## Snehal Shah

Snehal Shah is a quantum coach, mystic, and author who specializes in helping people prevent, manage, or recover from mental, physical, emotional and/or spiritual burn-outs.

Her book is titled *Conquer your Circumstances - Mastering the Art and Practice of Metaphysics.*

As an expert in using metaphysical modalities, Snehal introduces, teaches, and facilitates a process of knowledge transfer, equipping people with tools and techniques to help them achieve their desired outcomes.

Her passion and purpose is in service to raise individual and global consciousness.

She is known for her peaceful, yet strong compassionate presence as well as her warm and welcoming leadership style.

Using her heightened intuitive gift and emotional sensitivity, Snehal is able to get down to the root cause of a problem.

She is then able to map out a flow of solutions to the areas of concern.

She has developed the "3 T" model in which she guides her students and clients through the metaphysical journey.

They benefit from her humor, light-heartedness, uplifting healing, and expert teachings which enable them to navigate through the sometimes difficult periods of their lives.

Through Snehal's support, clients and students become self-sufficient in balancing their own energies, activating their own empowerment and creativity, thereby becoming "Masters of their Fates, and Captains of their Souls".

**Contact Snehal Shah:**

- www.satori.vision
- @satori_vision
- www.facebook.com/satorivision888
- www.linkedin.com/in/snehalshahofficial

# A Feng Shui Awakening

## By Holly Andra Small

*"Sometimes one must touch the darkness to truly know the light"* - Galadriel

In 2015 I was a mostly normal person. I lived in a mostly normal world, in a mostly normal universe, where A was A and 2+2=4. Within a matter of months, however, my entire universe was turned upside down as I was sent through a whirlwind, wrenching, pit of chaos, projected into what would be the most transformative spiritual awakening of my life. As I wound my way through that pit, half-dead from my failing body and half-alive in a way I'd never before experienced, my path required me to acquire deep and ancient knowledge.

It required me to learn and master modalities and skills that often took a lifetime to do so, and to frequently visit the deepest, darkest parts hidden within myself to acknowledge and transmute what was there. It would prepare me for higher levels of my awakening that would come at a later stage–though none would be as difficult as that first one. It connected me with a beautiful, amazing community of fellow awakeners and also showed me where so many were getting stuck. It sent me on paths I'd never dreamed of going down, and while I didn't always know the way, I kept going. While I look back now and marvel at the transformative process I had to go through, there was a time I didn't know if I'd come out alive. But one day, a friend introduced me to a book on Feng Shui, and everything changed. A sleeping dragon was awakened.

In 2015, before my personal armageddon, my boyfriend (now husband), Evan, and I had decided to move from Dallas, TX to Kansas City, MO. We'd both left behind nearly everything that was our identity–our hard-earned careers, our social lives, our city, our solid income, our apartment that we adored, and our entire community. We were both starting over and it was off to a rocky beginning. Evan hated his first position here, and although I had a good position with my family's company, I had severely underestimated the triggers and emotional turmoil that come with working with family (lol). We were both an emotional and mental wreck. In addition to taking a hit financially and mentally, my health had started to decline. After being in Kansas City for some time it quickly went from "easy to ignore" to "my body is shutting down." Before I knew it, none of the radiance I used to have was left – I was gaunt, pale, skinny, and sick looking, and I felt even worse. I'd gone from a healthy size six to a double zero, my hair was falling out, I was having terrible pains and passing out, my skin was completely inflamed and cystic, my hands were locking up, and my extremities were numb. I felt nauseous, sick, and had hunger pangs no matter how much I ate, along with a host of other maladies. My body was literally failing and no one could tell me why. In addition to my health issues, I was having very disturbing experiences. All of the sudden feelings, sounds, sights, and situations that I could easily stomach before were becoming unbearable. I was having disturbing dreams and could hear snippets of conversations happening around me if I was in any kind of relaxed state. I could sense things that I couldn't see, and they made me very uncomfortable.

Before I knew it, everything had come out from under us. Our community and sense of stability was gone, our finances had plummeted, we were miserable in our jobs, and now my health–and seemingly my sanity–was unraveling. Then one day, everything changed. A friend casually showed me a book on Feng Shui, and when I looked at that book, something in me stirred, just like a memory that I couldn't quite place. I'd had no introduction to any kind of energy at that point, but something in me knew this was important. Shortly before the book introduction, I'd had a clear flash of insight regarding my health.

Something inside me had told me that it was me who held the answer, and me who held the power to fix it–not some doctor or some pill–and I knew this book was connected to that feeling. That night after returning home, I bought the book and as I poured through the pages, I felt a key opening a previously locked door. As I read, I felt more and more doors begin to open and rooms I didn't know were there suddenly lit up inside me. I had epiphany after epiphany, piecing together parts of me and the universe in a way I'd never imagined possible.

I immediately began to apply what I was learning about the universe and Feng Shui to my surroundings, and suddenly breadcrumb after breadcrumb started to appear in my life, leading me from this solution to that. I also had this sneaking feeling I'd done this before–and not just done it–I'd *mastered* it. It wasn't just this invisible force outside of me, it was in me too. After being led to a Chinese Medicine practitioner, the first time she placed acupuncture needles in me it felt like I was hooked up to a circuit board and a physical current was turned on. Shortly after I began having goosebumps in strange river patterns all over my arms and legs. I was now feeling energy flow through me at all times and physically feeling my own energy interact with the outside world. There was no denying what was happening–I was physically seeing and experiencing it. That realization led me on a never-ending journey of discovering everything that had been hidden from me about this ancient force that I knew, but didn't know. I sought out every esoteric source I could, read every book I could find, and took every class that came across my path. Feng Shui led me to deep spiritual teachers which led me to life-changing meditations. During a particularly impactful meditation, my physical body felt like it was in one of those spinning rides at an amusement park. I felt my body begin to spin and get sucked deep into a portal that took me deep into a void, into the womb of the universe. In that void I experienced who and what I really was–the entire universe in a body. That experience led me to other modalities, and the next, and the next, and so on. I was spending every spare moment in study and deep practice, and all the while the Feng Shui principles were dancing around me, sparkling and guiding the way.

It wasn't easy, and it wasn't always pretty. It was wrenching. I was filled with doubt, fear, anxiety and overthinking and it constantly propelled me into the deepest darkest parts of myself and the world around me. I encountered the dark side of the spiritual world often and it forced me to master *especially* those fears. It was often downright miserable in my body, but I was determined to claim it, and my life, back no matter what I found; to keep cleaning and mining tunnels within it to release what was there and allow the real me I had experienced in that womb of the universe to come through. I just kept following the dots put in front of me. Kept acknowledging and working on what I found with whatever tools I'd acquired to that point.

It felt like I was following those dots in a random chaotic fashion. But one day, I looked back and realized those dots hadn't been random at all–they had been forming a beautiful picture. Along the way, little by little, they were reshaping, restructuring my life, taking it from the brink of despair and death to the richest, most amazing life I could ever hope to have. It brought spiritual gifts and abilities I'd never imagined. It brought a deep understanding of the highest universal archetypes and taught me to plug and play with them in the physical world around me and taught me to help others to do the same. It completely changed my physical life. It solidified and deepened my relationship with my amazing husband, and brought a level of depth and understanding within our own family relationships that we'd never dreamed possible. It brought thriving finances, businesses held up by a stronger-than-ever family foundation, and it brought a deep profound relationship with my body as

I took charge and watched my health blossom. I was claiming back all of my physical and energetic body after realizing just how out of my body I'd been for so long. I gradually began to share my knowledge and work with loved ones and the amazing network of spiritual seekers I'd acquired over the years. As I deepened my work, I realized it wasn't just me; everyone was experiencing what I had in some way. If we're not connected to our bodies then we're not fully connected to life, and everyone was living life mostly out of their body. If they had secure and stable finances and businesses, they were cut off from their spirituality and relationships. If they had brought their spiritual gifts online then their physical world was struggling–often in health and finances.

It might be experienced as focusing on someone else's issues or needs instead of your own, or constantly keeping busy or distracted so as not to deal with the pain that might be in your own energetic or physical body. If you're spiritual, you may feel wonderful when you spend time in the "upper" dimensions (where your fun gifts and abilities come from) or in spiritual practice, but feel uneasy once you finish, or feel disconnected from "earthly" things like money or relationships. Once I anchored back in deeply, I could physically feel myself leave my body when something I perceived as negative happened–like receiving bad news–and I would literally feel myself go into a sort of daze until I pulled myself back in. I not only realized how much the average person is out of their body, but that we each have to do the work to clean that camp up and get back in there, because no true embodied spiritual, physical, and emotional growth can happen unless you're in your body. Until that is done, you can only ever have a half-life, constantly dodging from one trigger to the next, with minimal impact to the world and greater universe around you.

But you're not alone. There is a beautiful force looking to guide you on your journey–you just need to turn down the noise and chaos so you can hear it. My mission is to help you connect with that force to remember who you are–who you really are–so you can anchor back in your body, truly thrive in your life, and fully impact your loved ones and the world around you as we anchor in this great shift we're all experiencing. When I look back, sometimes I don't know how I did it. But I emerged from that pit a grounded, embodied, and powerful creator and so can you. If you've been in your spiritual practice for years but feel stuck, or if your "earthly" things are struggling, getting back in your body is the key to truly start changing your life–to allow a flow to carry you instead of constantly swimming upstream. And lastly, if you are in the middle of your own pit of chaos, just keep going, because the other side is so amazing.

## Holly Andra Small

Holly Andra Small is an energy architect and quantum creator. A certified Feng Shui practitioner, reiki master, clairvoyant, and business expert, she is the author and creator of *Feng Shui Awakening*, which uses the foundational tools of Feng Shui, along with other powerful modalities, to help reconnect you to your true identity and source, face your fears, and discover the powerful creator within you. She is on a mission to help the world step out of the matrix, get back in our bodies, and awaken the true gifts and magic within all of us. She's helped hundreds cultivate and deepen their abilities and to allow their life to transform into the beautiful journey it's meant to be. Having been the CEO and co-owner of two "normal" businesses, she gets "real" life and can help you to pair the "normal" world with your spiritual awakening and practice. She lives in Kansas City, MO, with her best friend and husband, Evan, and her amazing dog, Glock. She's created a video series for you to jumpstart your journey to reconnect to your environment, get back into your body, and begin to allow that flow to carry you to the amazing path that's waiting. Simply enter your email at FengShuiAwakening.com/jumpstart/ to get started.

**Contact Holly Andra Small:**

- www.Fengshuiawakening.com
- www.pinterest.com/FengShuiAwakening
- @FengShuiAwakening
- www.linkedin.com/in/hollyandra

# Problems Usually Solve Themselves If You Don't Disturb Them

## By Rabea Katharina Stenger

I was fifteen when I started throwing up. I was in ninth grade and had gotten chemistry homework: to research the effects that bulimia has on the body. I wasn't happy with my body. I thought I was too big, even if it was just in my head. I went down a spiral for two years, throwing up one to three times a day. It came to the point where I didn't want to live anymore. I knew something had to change. My mom started noticing what I was doing and, even though I lied to cover up my problem, she was my mom, she knew. One day she turned to me with tears in her eyes and said, "You know you´re going to die if you keep going like that, right?" And when I didn't reply she said: "Why don't I just give you a gun so you can shoot yourself? Then I won't have to watch this any longer." Despite the fact that she didn't really mean it, I never threw up again after that day. But I was still very unhappy, so one very important thing had to happen.

I sat down and turned to the universe. I said out loud and very clearly: "Okay, listen; I am here for a reason. You and I both know that. My life has a purpose, so if you don't want me to jump off a very high building, I want the following: I want the body of my dreams without having to do a single thing for it. I want to be able to eat what I want, when I want, where I want, and with who I want, otherwise you can find someone else for the job!" And what can I say? I got exactly what I asked for. Sometimes it's okay to demand something, to give the universe the opportunity to show you that it has your back. I had just witnessed the miracle of the power of the universe. And there would be many more.

To be honest, this wasn't even the first time I'd felt that connected to the universe. I had always had a certain confidence and I never really knew where it came from. Totally insecure otherwise, but a deep, magical confidence as if the universe was standing behind me. That's what it feels like to have the most powerful backup there is. Yes, I had always felt it, I had just never been conscious of it. I had always been confident in my purpose even if I didn´t know exactly what it was. Even if I still don't know what it is sometimes. It is always a feeling, and the next step always presents itself. This is living in the now and sensing what needs to be done right now. Not earlier, not later, but now.

Because linear time is just an illusion. Every single moment, past, present, and future, exists at the same time, so the only way to access it all is through the present moment, which is in fact not limited but all-including. If you want, you may now reverse the programming of time for you. Feel how the illusion of linear time feels to you. Take a deep breath, sink deeply into your heart, and speak the following out loud or to yourself: "I now connect with linear time and everything it stands for. I align all this consciousness vertically and I send the divine mercy and the divine order into all this consciousness. I now revert all this consciousness and reverse its programming."

How does it feel now? Feel the tailwind that time gives you now, it's silent, weightless, nothing moves. It's fluffy, draws outwards. Before, it was cramped; now, it's wide. One of my tools is the divine order. When you send the divine order into something, it automatically aligns with it. The feeling of incredible calm starts to spread. It is being in peace with everything that is. And all the consciousness changes immediately to being aligned with absolute love, forever. It's like letting the air out of a balloon, letting the air out of the illusion, realizing that there was nothing behind it, and it disappears. It's a very powerful tool and can cause massive changes on the outside.

My job here as a lighthouse, as a consciousness optimizer and healer, is to transform, through my being and my words, everyone and everything that comes near me, for when something isn't ready it will stay far away from me. When the time is right many people will see my light and remember their own, remember that we come from the same source. It will go very fast; time quality is changing and there becomes less and less to say and do. One day I asked the universe: "What is my mission?" And the answer I got was: "Simply do nothing; allow everything to just happen. The illusion of having to actively do something to achieve something on the outside is widely spread. But for you, it's time to see through it and dive into your true creation. For true creation happens out of being and not doing."

One day I did a painting, it took me about thirty-five minutes. The canvas was forty inches by forty inches, so relatively big. After I was done, I stepped back to look at it. It was almost like I had just woken up and I couldn't really explain how the paint had gotten on that canvas. I actually never signed it because I never had the feeling that I painted it. I had provided my body to a higher energy that expressed itself through me. By the way, I do the same when I clean my apartment. I simply provide my body and the apartment cleans itself. This is what I meant by "true creation." It doesn't mean doing nothing, it means being in tune with a higher frequency so that all the actions that need to be done in order for you to achieve what you desire will do themselves through you. For you don't know how to reach your destination, but it knows how to reach you, when you allow it to.

For no higher power will force itself on you. They can only help you when you actively allow them to. A very big part of that step is your vision. A vision is the purpose you put behind everything you do. It fulfills you inside and shines through your eyes when you look at the world, it shines through everything you do, everything you say, and everything you are.

This is my vision:
"I consciously decide to be a canal of the spiritual world in the name of love and light. It may flow and shine into me, inside me and through me, for my highest well-being and for the highest well-being of all. I step aside and let true love take over. I am in partnership with the universe. I am empowered. I am free. I am mystic. I am attentive. I co-create with the universe. I am in tune with my true being. Great things, brilliant things, come into existence through me. I open up myself to the unknown. My future is going to be better than what I can dream now. Only the best will come true with joy and ease."

What's yours? Take time to write down your own vision and connect with the energy of it. If you're ready, put your hand over your heart, take a deep breath and speak the following out loud or to yourself: "I align my vision vertically and send the divine mercy and the divine order into all this consciousness. I anchor my vision deeply into my consciousness forever. I integrate my vision into everything I do, everything I say, and everything I am."

Take a moment to feel into those words; what changed? Now, if you are ready, add the following: "I connect now with my focus. I turn it from the outside fully to the inside. I forbid all energies and beings that don't answer to true love to approach me and to set foot into my surrounding field. May it be so. Thank you."

Take another deep breath, and feel inside you. How does it feel now? I want you to thank you for being here, being in this moment with me. I want you to know that everything is perfect just the way it is. Don't bemoan yourself, for you are magnificent, unique, and beautiful. You exist only once in this world, so enjoy it. Live every moment to the fullest. Enjoy your life entirely. Become aware of what it's really about—it's about your intention. There's nothing you have to do. Let go of everything. Let go of all views of the world. Let go of all conceptions of what has to be. Let it go, because it doesn't serve you anymore. It has had its day. Let go of what wants to go and welcome the stunning new miracles into your life. There's so much waiting for you, grand things will happen, so don't hold on to anything. You are experiencing yourself, in all your depth, to all your extent, in all your facets, in all your light.

I have recently had a dream with a vision for the future. It was for all lighthouses to come together and connect to each other, no matter where in this world we are. The vision was to become a "healing crowd." I like the expression, it feels very homey and comfortable, as if that's what we were meant to be all along.

Together, we can shine brighter than we ever did before. Together, we can see behind what's happening to see what needs to be done at this moment. Together, we can change the world, from the inside out. In the background, seemingly quite unspectacular, but far more meaningful than any spectacle.

## Rabea Katharina Stenger

Rabea is a consciousness optimizer and healer. She has training and experience in access consciousness, reiki, numerology, family constellation, Feng Shui and consciousness research. She has touched hundreds of people's lives in many different ways on their path to themselves, to become conscious of what they really are: A bright, wonderful, magical, peaceful, unique, powerful divine being.

She uses her powerful tools to clear and heal any consciousness. She does business optimization and real estate optimization, clearing the energy and consciousness of a business or a building and its property, and aligning it with the highest.

Rabea wants to touch as many souls as possible on their way to seeing through all illusions and returning to the essence of their true being.

Her passion is painting, writing to herself what wants to flow through her, playing the piano, and simply being.

Her vision is for all lighthouses in this world to come together and connect to be part of a healing crowd.

"Together, we can change the world. We can change the future by seeing behind what's happening to see what needs to be done."

"We are here to find out that everything is love. Shine your light into everything you believe isn´t love and you will realize that it is a part of it after all. The question of what should and shouldn't be doesn´t present itself because if it is, it should be."

**Contact Rabea Katharina Stenger:**

www.rabea-katharina-stenger.de

www.facebook.com/rabea.k.stenger

@rabea.katharina

# Charted

## By Christopher Stilson

Have you ever had an experience where you felt as if you knew what you wanted to do in life, but God has other plans for you? Well, you charted it so it is not God's fault but we feel the need to blame someone. I sure have and now I would not change it for the world. Take a seat, relax, and get to know my story on how I found out I did this to myself. I was born psychic but the earliest I can recall communicating with spirit is the age of four. My mother was in an abusive marriage and had me young. My "father" had my mother pinned down on the couch and was screaming in her face. The amount of anger and the deep color of red that filled his complexion are what scared me the most. I, being four years old, ran behind the love seat crying. Head in my knees, and tears rolling down my face I heard a voice. "Christopher."

I look up to see a beautiful, thin caucasian woman with dark brown eyes, dark brown hair, a cute little pointed nose, and high cheekbones. She was sitting down looking at me at eye level. I did not feel any fear, in fact I felt calmness and a sense of love. "Your life is about to change, just listen to me," she said with a beautiful smile that showed all her perfect teeth except for one which had a slight discolor and a little chip in it. I quickly looked away but when I went to look back, she was gone. She was right. My mother had the man arrested and she divorced him. We were poor and my mother worked very hard but instead of feeding herself, she would pick through the food while she was cooking it and gave all the rest to my siblings and I. Later she met a wonderful man. His name is Patrick Stilson. They teamed up and went from renting a little apartment that needed a lot of work, to a home that fit well for our perfect family. They got married and he became a wonderful father and one of my biggest heroes. Ever since that day that woman came out of nowhere and left as quickly as she'd showed up, I would hear her voice.

Having a wonderful father now was not the only change in my life. I started seeing other people around that no one else did. I started "knowing" things before other people–what they would ask or do. I would know who was calling before mom would answer the phone. Everyone else would look at me as if I had ten heads. By the end of elementary school, I soon realized no one around me was sharing the same experiences. I didn't want anything to do with it so I started to do my best to block it out. My last year of middle school I came across the word "schizophrenic" and thought for sure that was what it was. I even started suffering from anxiety and depression. More than half the time, I felt as if I ate a ton of rocks that were constantly moving around my stomach until I would throw up. I would have what felt like nine to ten panic attacks a day. One day in the middle of my freshman year of high school, I was having yet another panic attack sitting in my room. Crying out loud I said: "I wish this anxiety would just go away!"

I then got a reply by the voice that would never leave, which always felt as if it was coming from a distance but yet still right next to me. It said: "Christopher, if you would just listen to me I can help you." At this point I would do anything so I decided to go along with it. "If you can help me, from now on I'll listen to you. If you can't, LEAVE ME ALONE!" I replied back to her thinking I was just going crazy. The voice answered back, quickly explaining to me that I am a psychic medium and I am here to help others through life. The reason for the panic attacks was due to spirits using my body which made me feel as though I was malfunctioning. For example, if a soul passed away from a sickness, my body would feel as if it was shutting down. If a soul had problems with communication or passed away from something related to their throat, mine would start feeling like it was closing. As the conversation went on, I found out this voice that has always been with me was my spirit guide. Her name is Anna.

Anna and I went through some time to learn how to channel and allow spirit to communicate without going into another attack. Of course, I had to ask her the question if I was truly just psychic or schizophrenic. She explained to me the difference, which made me feel better. With her help, I've not had a panic attack since and feel so much better about who I am. I had so many ideas about what I wanted to do in life. At one point I wanted to be an actor. I tried in high school but my head was always filled with matters not of this physical realm, but from the other side. As such, I always had a hard time remembering my lines. Anna said to me one night as I was laying in bed, racking my brain as to how I was going to be successful in acting: "You will be on stage but not how you think." This only confused me more and just made me think that my life was not going to be the one I'd been planning for myself. We all go through hard times once in a while. Depression had hit me like a ton of brick and I felt like I couldn't deal with anything. I wanted it all to end.

Anna chimed in, explaining to me that I was going to help shine the light on the world, teach, love, and connect with so many people, and that I can not just give up because that is not how my life was written out. "What in the hell do you mean by that?" I asked as I began to get irritated with what I felt was pure nonsense. She explained to me about our charts on the other side in which each soul has chosen a path to learn from. This was how I was going to do my readings.

Readings? Me? In front of people, telling them information about their lives and connecting with their loved ones to relay messages? I don't think so; that certainly wasn't part of any of my life goals. After high school, I worked at a place called Masco. This wasn't what I wanted to do for the rest of my life either. Two years in, I decided to go along with what Anna was still continuing to push me to do. I started doing readings after work a few days a week.

In my third year at the end of October, there was a mandatory meeting which was odd since they normally have them on the first Wednesday of the month. I sat down and started to daydream until I heard the words "voluntary lay-off."

They wanted a certain number of people to agree to be laid-off for two months, then come back to the same pay and same position. The two months off were November and December. Of course, I asked Anna if this is something I should do. She said yes. I was chosen and I took the two months to do readings. Word spread and more people were coming in to see me. I built up my clientele enough that I never went back after those two months were up. Before coming to the physical world, we create a layout of our lives.

This layout, or what I like to call our charts, is actually known as the Akashic Records. Planned in detail, they reveal what we want our lives to be like with our chosen spirit guide by our side. At this point, you're probably questioning why the hell would you have written all of this? Well, Anna explained it to me like this. We as souls choose to come into the physical world to learn what we want to learn for ourselves and for God.

God, of course, is all knowing but he learns even more through us because we have him running through our spiritual DNA. In other words, we're like little fax machines with everything that we learn getting faxed back to him. As we go through our life experiences, so does he.

We have free will and we may sometimes feel as though we're "off the path" but in reality, whatever it is our soul charted, we will continue to learn, no matter how long it takes. Think of it this way–life is a school and before coming here, you have to pick out classes that you need to take and learn from. I laugh about it now. In the past, I would never have seen myself doing readings as a psychic medium. Now, I have helped thousands of people. Running a full-time business for the last six years, I've helped people that were grieving and those who have felt lost in life. I've also created a little web series with my local news station WETM called *Twin Tiers Medium*. The web series were little clips on different subjects that helped to draw in people and help them understand the spiritual side of life. I like to say that I am a spark of light, here to help light others. I'm still on stage and will continue to teach people about my studies and the lessons I've been taught both in the physical world and from the other side. I have so many ideas for other projects that would allow me to reach out to millions of people.

As I continue to grow as a psychic medium, I also want to connect with others as an influencer, spiritual teacher, motivational speaker, and I would love to write more books. I want to share my life and have my knowledge written down on paper, to last forever and be passed down. I want to be the light that continues to light this world and help heal the world one soul at a time. God loves you, and so do I.

## Christopher Stilson

Christopher Stilson is a psychic medium from a small town in upstate New York called Elmira. He is also known as the Twin Tiers Medium. He was born psychic but the earliest he can recall communicating with spirits is when he was only four years old.

At the end of elementary school, he soon realized that no one was sharing the same experiences as him, so he decided to try his best and block it out. This led him suffering from anxiety and depression. In the beginning of high school, he was having another panic attack when, out loud, he asked for the anxiety to go away.

A familiar voice answered back: "If you would just listen to me, I can help you." He agreed to accept whatever advice he was given. He found out from that conversation that he was a psychic medium and that the familiar voice that had followed him throughout his life was his spirit guide Anna.

Now, he and Anna have come together and have helped hundreds to thousands connect with their loved ones on the other side and to read their life charts in order to help them move forward and feel more confident on their own, wonderful life path.

He does this all with his God-given gift and information he has gathered in his own studies and from what he also receives from the other side; our true home.

To get more information on Christopher or his services, please visit his website at www.ChristopherStilson.com

**Contact Christopher Stilson:**

- www.ChristopherStilson.com
- www.facebook.com/TheStilsons
- @PsychicChristopherStilson

# Treeconomy: Why Trees Are Important For Your Health, Your Wealth, And Your Well-being

## By Tom Thompson

Lenny's earliest memory was playing in the grass with his siblings and his friends. The sun was beating down, the air was fresh, and the days seemed to last forever. They would run around in nature, climb the trees, and sometimes leave their marks on them. These were his fondest memories. Then one day, Lenny felt a short, sharp, stabbing pain and everything went dark. His next memory was him emerging from a small cell into a cage. There was cold, hard concrete on the floor and the walls, with metal railings around some of the sides and the roof. There were people staring and pointing at him. Some were smiling and laughing. Some were watching him in awe.

Lenny had arrived at London Zoo. It was the 1970s. Lenny was a lion. Lenny was not his real name. It was his English name that was given to him because his "lion" name was difficult to pronounce. He did not settle in well. He was bored and lacked stimulation. He paced up and down his small, stark enclosure becoming listless, unmotivated, and uninspired. His muscular, highly toned physique started to deteriorate, and his hair was falling out due to stress.

Unbeknown to him, Lenny was part of a captive breeding programme and after some months, he was introduced to his partner and expected to perform and produce the goods. To be honest, he wasn't feeling it. Breeding was the last thing on his mind and his sperm count was significantly suboptimal. This keeper was a fairly smart guy. He said, "Something's not right, you know." He was not sure what though. I only said that he was *fairly* smart. London Zoo eventually decided to create a more natural living environment for Lenny and his new lion friends. They tried to mimic his natural environment as much as possible to make them feel more at home. This included larger enclosures with more grassland and some trees to play in and climb up.

Eventually all zoos realized the error of their ways. This marked the transition to the modern-day safari parks. It did not completely mimic the natural environment because the lions were still kept separate from the antelope and zebra, but it still made a big difference. It helped with the animals' stress levels, their health and well-being, and their breeding. You might be sitting there thinking: "Yeah, we know, this is obvious! You can't take animals out of their natural environment, put them in an artificial environment, and expect them to be happy, healthy, and perform at their best." You might have reached that conclusion whilst you are sitting in your office, your house, or your car. We have become trapped in our little work prisons, driving there in our small mobile prisons, and returning home to our house prisons, all disconnecting us from the outside world.

So how have we as a species become so detached from a natural environment? Living in a man-made environment; all concrete steel and glass with artificial light and areas devoid of trees and vegetation and wildlife. It's not natural and we wonder why our health and well-being are deteriorating. You might think that you have adapted to it or even that you enjoy it. I know I felt that way especially when I was younger. Excited by the bright lights and the big cities. However, it isn't an environment that we are suited to. It's stressful and it has detrimental effects on our health and well-being.

We are all busy being busy, and not being present. Rushing around chasing our tails, anxious about the future, and worrying about things that have happened in the past. We are having more and more stress-related conditions, we are suffering a mental health epidemic, and enduring many medical conditions contributed to by living in stressful, polluted, man-made environments. How is it that we know that this is damaging for animals, and yet we are happy to subject ourselves to these conditions? The United Nations (UN) predicts that by 2050, 64.1% of the developing world and 85.9% of the developed world will be urbanized. It is not just our urbanization that has caused this. There are other factors that have contributed, including lack of exercise, increased work and financial pressures, and a faster pace of life. The loss of nature is a contributing factor. Restoring it will help to mitigate these symptoms.

I became acutely aware about the power of trees and woodlands to heal in the 1990s. I was partying very hard. We would start on Friday night and by Sunday, we would usually end up at a lake, still partying. I had been partying too hard for too long and it all got too much. I didn't want to be around people at that moment. I walked off into the woods to be alone and to find some peace. In the woodland there were sounds, smells and movement all around me, stimulating my senses. From the noise of the birds and the insects to the movement of the leaves and trees in the wind, from the smell of the flowers to the feeling of the vegetation as I brushed past it. Yet this all calmed me and helped me to deal with my feelings of being overwhelmed. It returned me back to some sort of normality, at least until the next Friday when it would all begin again. It took me years to realize what was actually going on. I had long since ceased partying and had been working with and studying trees for many years. Initially this was in forestry and more latterly in arboriculture or urban forestry. This refers to trees and green infrastructure in urban areas. The Japanese have been studying this for years, initially with Shinrin Yoko. This term emerged in Japan in the 1980s but the practice had been going on long before that. It is the practice of being present and relaxed in nature and paying attention to your surroundings.

This was more recently expanded to scientific studies of test subjects as they were monitored whilst they experienced forest-bathing. It turns out that it reduces blood pressure and cortisol levels, thereby reducing stress. This is partially explained by the tranquil environment but also a chemical reaction to the pheromones and other chemicals given off by trees. We had no idea. If only there had been an indicator that woodland was relaxing? Possibly the fact that you may be one of the millions of us that every year go to the forest to relax! Where better to be present than in nature?

My studies of arboriculture had informed me how important trees were for our health, our wealth, and our well-being. They reduce the impact of environmental events such as floods and urban heat islands, reduce CO2, absorb pollution, as well as increase biodiversity, all of which have both a direct and indirect impact on you. They also reduce heating bills in winter, reduce cooling bills in summer, and even increase house prices. They also improve our physical health and mental well-being. This results in you having fewer sick days or having to take less time off work in order to take your children to medical appointments such as asthma clinics. I go into more details of all the benefits of trees in my book *Treeconomy*.

Dr Catherine Wolfe in Seattle is one of the leading global researchers on the health and well-being benefits of trees. One discovery that she found was the link between how treed an environment people live in during pregnancy is and the birth weight of their babies. I know how important birth weight was to relatives, as this was one of the first things that they announce to everyone they speak to. "It's healthy, it's a boy/girl, and it weighed so many pounds."

I did not know how important it was though. A premature baby will almost always require significant medical attention when they are first born. It's more than that though; a premature baby will have ongoing health problems throughout their life as a result of their premature birth. Generally, the lower the birth weight, the greater their ongoing health issues. Maybe you lost sight of the need for nature in your life. This may have occurred gradually as you progressively become more caught up in the modern world. You would have had a wake-up call a few years ago, back when we had the lockdown! Maybe you were not one of those breaking out of lockdown to sit in parks and woodlands, defying the government guidance. Maybe you were. At the very least, you would have become more aware of the natural environment around you, your need for it, and your craving for it.

You would have been making the most of that one hour a day of exercise that you were allowed and noticing things that you had been previously oblivious to or taken for granted. The mature tree near your house that you never noticed or the sound of birdsong from the bush that you were not previously aware of. It gave us all time to rest, reset, and re-evaluate. Sadly, many of us have now reverted back to our old ways. Maybe you are someone who looks to material things to find happiness. If not, then you will certainly know someone who does. This is not the answer. We have more things now in terms of technology, leisure, fashion, and entertainment and yet we have more unhappiness and dissatisfaction than at any other point in history. More anger, sadness, and depression than ever before. This is at least in part due to detachment from nature. We can't buy happiness.

The next generation are preconditioned to this. Our current "screenagers" are so plugged into the phones and other mobile devices. So busy filming events to share with others, rather than actually experiencing them. And yet we find ourselves almost apologizing for putting in open green space as if it is an afterthought. Always almost begrudgingly put into our developments and then squeezed out as the financial constraints take their toll on the projects. I find clients who tell me that they love trees and then proceed to tell me that they want to build all over them. It is possible to build around trees carefully. This can be achieved with no-dig construction techniques and the use of piled foundations. We can incorporate all sorts of innovative solutions and yet, all too often trees are removed out of fear before starting the planning process or applying for insurance. There needs to be less tree surgery and more tree consultancy as we look to improve our urban forests. We endeavor to do that with all of our projects, trying to retain trees where possible and encouraging new planting where it is not. We always now provide our clients with an economic and intrinsic valuation of their trees to make them aware of their tree resources and help them move to a more sustainable management regime. Trees are not the only solution, but they have to be part of any solution. Making the environment cleaner, healthier, and more liveable. Then our next generation can grow up playing in the grass with the sun beating down, with fresh air, and days that seem to last forever. Running around in nature and climbing trees. All the while feeling healthier, happier, and more energized because the urban forest has improved their health, their wealth, and their well-being.

## Tom Thompson

Tom is a tree consultant and director of his own company Arbor Cultural Ltd. He has over twenty years' experience in the tree care industry. In the past, he has planted over one million trees but now he is more focused on managing established trees in urban areas. His company focuses on providing tree reports to enable clients to obtain planning permission, house purchase completion, and to address their insurance or duty of care requirements.

As well as dealing with planning and insurance matters, he is also an expert witness, qualified in tree risk assessment and valuation and committed to embracing new developments in technology in arboriculture (urban forestry).

He was an early adopter of building information modeling (BIM), digital practice, and augmented reality to represent trees and green infrastructure in the design, planning, and construction processes as well as into the ongoing management of projects. This enables him to represent trees in 3D and 4D models over time. Tom started up the Digital Arb group.

He also embraces new technology, including sonic tomography, Resi drills, and chlorophyll fluorescence testing. He has training in England, Wales, Germany, Sweden, and Canada, and has three degrees in related fields.

He is a professional member of the Arboricultural Association (AA) and an International Society of Arboriculture (ISA), Certified Arborist, as well as being chairman of the Consulting Arborist Society (CAS).

He promotes trees through his work and also in his talks and presentations and will be publishing his book *Treeconomy* later this year. He supports various tree-related charities. He is transitioning his business to cover all aspects of green infrastructure. He has a dark, dry, and ironic sense of humor that does not always come across, especially in the written word.

You can connect with him on Linked In, Tom Thompson Tree Consultant, Facebook, Tommo Thompson or Arbor Cultural or through his personal website, TomThompson.co.uk.

**Contact Tom Thompson:**

- www.tomthompson.co.uk
- www.linkedin.com/in/tom-thompson-tree-consultant
- www.facebook.com/tommotopia
- www.facebook.com/Arbor.Cultural
- @ArborCultural
- @arbor_cultural
- @VoiceoftheTrees

# My Journey Of Becoming A Multi-Talented And Multi-Passionate Global Entrepreneur And Coach

## By Lu Wang

### Vision and Mission

I am a multitalented and global-minded entrepreneur. In addition to having over a decade of experience conducting educational and psychological research, I have a deep understanding of violin techniques and pedagogies, a passion for translating scientific research into everyday language that's accessible to a broad audience, and a knack for Chinese calligraphy. Causes that I care about include education, science and technology, arts and culture, and sustainability. My vision is to help late starters on violin transform their playing with ease and freedom, so that they can fulfill their musical dreams while enjoying the journey of getting there.

My mission for the next few months is to help late starters (i.e., adults aged between eighteen and forty years old) overcome psychological barriers, such as the belief that learning a musical instrument is only possible during childhood, and pick up an instrument. Through a 1:1 private coaching program, participants will develop the mindset that learning to play the violin is possible at any age, learn proper posture and foundational techniques to play with ease, and perform easy to intermediate-level violin repertoire with gusto within twelve months or less.

### Overcoming Adversity Along the Musical Journey

As a young child raised in a single-parent household, I did not have the opportunity to take private lessons, despite having shown an early fascination with musical instruments that included the violin and piano. My childhood and early teenage years were filled with eavesdropping on my downstairs neighbor's violin lessons, occasional consultations with kind-hearted violin teachers who agreed to offer occasional lessons at reduced costs, and curiosity-driven explorations on a factory-made violin.

Fast-forward to the age of eighteen where I, thanks to the generous four-year merit-based scholarship I received, formally started my violin journey under the tutelage of conservatory-trained concert violinists and by taking music history and theory classes offered by award-winning faculty at the University of Pennsylvania. After landing my first job as a college professor, I attended in-person and virtual workshops and retreats on violin pedagogies at the Juilliard School of Music, Jacob School of Music, and the University of Illinois. These learning experiences and personal encounters with world-renowned violin pedagogues expedited my violin mastery.

They uniquely positioned me to support the journey of late-starting violinists through individualized private coaching and by applying the core principles of experiential learning that are tailored to support working professionals and entrepreneurs who aspire to participate in gigs, join a community orchestra, or simply play for personal leisure to reach their goals.

**My 1:1 Private Coaching Package and Online Course Offering**

Throughout my childhood and early teens, I was indoctrinated with the beliefs that violin is an instrument that one can only effectively learn at a young age. These beliefs are ingrained in the minds of most teachers (conservatory-trained or not), many parents, and even the learners themselves. The limiting beliefs and social expectation that you cannot teach an old dog new tricks applies especially to human endeavors where fine motor control and prestige are at stake, such as violin learning. I feel personally called upon to debunk this social conditioning passed down from generations of frustrated late-starters who have not received age-appropriate guidance to counter these limiting beliefs, which in turn, hindered the actualization of their musical potentials.

I plan to counter these self-fulfilling prophecies by replacing limiting beliefs with empowering ones, and by connecting my own experience of mastering violin techniques at a semi-professional level, despite having started late. I offer 1:1 private coaching packages that enable participants to join with varied commitments of three-month, six-month, and twelve-month, depending on their learning goals. I anticipate scaling up three to five years from now with the creation of experiential learning online platforms that can make the learning experience accessible to more people simultaneously, and leverage the positive synergy of network effects entailed by an online community to steer late-starting violinists towards their learning goals.

The online course format makes it easy for busy career professionals to stay on track in the face of schedule complications. Because I will apply experiential learning principles when designing the online courses, this will enable learners to visualize their future successes, and it will provide an intuitive roadmap of how exactly the learners can accomplish their learning goals at the outset. I am confident that learners will be highly engaged during the program and internalize their constant wins well-beyond the conclusion of the program.

**Becoming Entrepreneurial**

My extended family elevates academic pursuits above anything else and disparages any tendencies of having a business mindset. This upbringing effectively steered me away from taking business and economics-related classes in college, even though I studied at a university where one of the leading business schools, Wharton, is housed. However, as an international student whose livelihood was dependent on the generosity of the merit-based scholarships received and a work-study program, I often found myself in situations where I needed to exercise my intuitive business acumen in order to make ends meet. For instance, as a calligrapher, I have monetized this skill to pay for private lessons in violin by selling my calligraphy artifacts to bookstore owners in Chinatown, Philadelphia.

I have also tutored Business Chinese to Wharton students and taught Chinese calligraphy to stressed-out business school students who sought out calligraphy practices as a way to relax. Finally, I have purchased brand new textbooks from various online stores at low prices, kept them in great condition, and then sold them at a profit instead of buying them at the used books section of the university's bookstore. These personal experiences transformed my view on the importance of a business mindset and exposed me to economic conditions and strategies that I have only come to fully appreciate since completing my formal studies.

After having worked in higher education for seven years, I decided to hone my skills in areas that are essential to a business leader and entrepreneur at the Quantic School of Business and Technology, a selective global online MBA / Executive MBA program (the acceptance rate is typically between 11% and 13%). Through Quantic's innovative and streamlined online education, I developed an in-depth understanding of the fields of finance, accounting, business analytics, corporate strategies, data-driven decision making, economics, marketing, and project management.

Beyond the comprehensive studies at the Quantic School of Business and Technology, I am also grateful for the mentorship of success coaches and entrepreneurs such as Marie Diamond, Vishen Lakhiani, and Marisa Murgatroyd, among others. I look forward to applying insights and practical wisdoms garnered from formal education and entrepreneurial endeavors to making a positive impact on people's lives and taking my business to the next level.

## Future Projects and Their Benefits

### *Project 1: Key concepts in blockchain technology, explained in plain terms and illustrated with graphical art (eBook) and blockchain in a Box (online course).*

As a multi-talented entrepreneur, I am interested in contributing to humanity in multiple ways. Tailoring existing violin pedagogy, which is predominantly child-centered, to age-appropriate teaching to help late-starters on violin overcome technical challenges of motor control, dexterity, and flexibility origins is one way I can contribute to the betterment of artistic expressions across the lifespan. There are two other areas that I have expertise in. Building on my research in career and business training, I am in the process of creating an e-book that helps demystify various jargons and concepts in the discourse of Blockchain technologies.

The e-book will be written in everyday language and illustrated with graphical art, so that a typical high schooler can easily understand it. This project is in alignment with my mission of making science accessible to a broad audience. The main objective of the e-book is to increase public awareness of the growing importance of Blockchain technologies and their diverse applications in multiple fields of human endeavors.

Following the publication of the e-book, I plan to create an online introductory course on the same topic. Because many individuals have invested in cryptocurrency without understanding the premise of Blockchain technologies, my mission in creating an online course is to expand on the coverage of the e-book and make foundational knowledge in Blockchain bite-sized, digestible, and interactive.

Online platforms and learning communities enable me to leverage the power of experiential learning to maximize students' engagement with the content. More importantly, through constant wins and by experiencing peak emotional states as learners successfully apply what they learn to make better investment decisions and solve practical problems in diverse fields, learners will generate unstoppable momentum over the course of their studies and move towards their learning objectives at light speed.

***Project 2: Attain mindfulness through the practice of Chinese calligraphy (1:1 private coaching packages and online courses).***

Today's world is teeming with uncertainties which is a major life stressor. Learning how to not only survive but thrive despite the daily stress, existential angst, and information overload, is both an art and science. Scientific research has shown that regular mediation practices induce mental states that reduce chronic stress and are essential to our well-being.

Practicing Chinese calligraphy is a powerful way of entering into a meditative flow state whilst producing gorgeous pieces of art that can be gifted or displayed as showpieces in your living room. It appears that you can have your cake and eat it too! As a precocious calligrapher, in the short span of seven years in my childhood (between seven and fourteen), I was a ten-time national and international calligraphy competitions winner.

The positive impact of practicing calligraphy is long-term and goes beyond artistic expression itself. Having worked with calligraphy aficionados and novices from various backgrounds, I pride myself for catering to the learning needs of diverse learners when I teach. While 1:1 coaching is very effective in teaching artistic practice, especially at the beginning stage, online courses can leverage the economy of scale so that more learners can gain access to the learning experience.

Online courses can also augment 1:1 private coaching by charting out a roadmap of the learning journey, providing a rich contextual background of the art form, and utilizing digital gadgets that help learners self-assess and monitor their progress.

Likewise, while solitary practice is an important component of the learning experience, a global learning community helps connect calligraphers around the world and enable them to exchange ideas, upgrade their skills, and attain spiritual enlightenment in a supportive environment.

Most importantly, the online format increases accessibility of the learning experience to individuals who would otherwise not be able to participate due to budget and/or geographical constraints.

## Lu Wang

Lu Wang, BA, Ed. M., Ph.D., and EMBA candidate received her bachelor's degree from the University of Pennsylvania, master's degree from Harvard, and doctoral degree from the University of Georgia. She is expected to graduate from the Quantic School of Business and Technology with an executive MBA degree in July 2023. In addition, she is currently pursuing a second bachelor's degree in music technology, building on her prior training and experiences in music history, theory, violin pedagogy, and computer programming.

Lu Wang has ten+ years of training in psychological and educational research, data analysis, instructional design, and delivering editorial and peer-review services. In her six years of working experience at higher education institutions, she produced sixteen+ research publications (www.scholar.google.com/citations?user=zfUNpIsAAAAJ&hl=en&authuser=1), worked on an Institute of Education Sciences (IES)-funded three-year project that investigated the development of spatial skills in young children in relation to their number sense and math achievement, taught 720+ students in-person and online, coached fifty+ individuals one-on-one, and conducted 180+ peer reviews.

Although many of her clients are affiliated with higher education institutions, her entrepreneurial spirit has also led her to collaborate with corporate business leaders and entrepreneurs, and receive guidance from globally renowned personal transformation leaders, authors, and entrepreneurs such as Marie Diamond, Vishen Lakhiani, and Marisa Murgatroyd. Beyond her expertise in research, online education, and coaching, Lu Wang is passionate about music education (and in particular, violin pedagogy), making scientific research accessible to a broad audience (e.g., conducting translational research, demystifying scientific concepts through blogging and podcasting, writing trade books on the topics of mind, brain, and education), and inspiring the world to appreciate Chinese Calligraphy, an ancient artform, as a pathway to spiritual enlightenment through her private coaching and online course offering.

Lu is indebted to the Juilliard School of Music, the Jacob School of Music, and the University of Michigan for inculcating in her a deep understanding of scientifically researched and clinically validated systems of violin pedagogy that have benefited generations of violin virtuosi. Lu is also grateful for having studied privately under the directions of Ghislaine Fleischmann, Neil Weintrob, Gert Kumi, and Nathan Cole, among others.

Her endeavors to popularize scientific research has taken her to produce the following podcast (www.researchpod.org/education-training/tackling-maths-anxiety) that is based on her widely cited peer-reviewed journal article that was published in Educational Psychology Review, a flagship journal in the field.

Lu started her Calligraphy lessons at the age of seven and showed a knack in Chinese calligraphy six months into the lessons. Between the age of seven and fourteen, Lu was a ten-time first prize winner in national and international Chinese calligraphy competitions.

She also participated in calligraphy cultural exchanges with calligraphers from Japan, Hong Kong, and South Korea. As one of the three winners of two international calligraphy competitions, she was invited to visit Japan and Hong Kong to attend award ceremonies and to participate in Calligraphy exchanges with local calligraphers in her youth.

**Contact Lu Wang:**


- hgse.lu.wang@gmail.com
- www.linkedin.com/in/lwang1
- www.scholar.google.com/citations?user=zfUNpIsAAAAJ

# How To Find Your Strength In Your Own Journey

## By Patricia Whyte

Have you ever had a dream that was incredibly real and realized it was showing you something very important? I had an experience like that last night. I dreamed about my life in the future. It showed the results of my life if I had not found the strength to change it. I am sharing this experience about finding strength to change my life, allowing me to grow and prosper in my power, so that you can find your strength for your own journey. The strength I found ultimately led me out of an unbalanced and emotionally absent marriage in Australia and supported me to move back to my hometown in South Carolina, and continues to support me to be a Global Conscious Success, Abundance, and Feng Shui Coach, because my purpose is to enlighten 200,000 and more people. It all started with a book in the airport gift store.

This book brought me the light of hope and then dropped me back into the valley of my life with a road map. You see, sometimes it takes someone else's story to pull us out of our own, like this story. The resonance of their experience touches ours, whether known or unknown, and helps us see what we have kept hidden even from ourselves because it's not easy to look inside ourselves and even harder to look at the face of fear and pain. The book I chose at the airport gift store did that for me. Little did I know when I chose the book my niece shared with me that I would have a lightning-bolt epiphany. In this book, I read about the author's experience on the bathroom floor, crying many nights and praying to God for help in the middle of the night while her husband was sleeping. I was completely hooked as I had done the same; crying continuously for help in the middle of the night while my husband slept. I had never admitted this to anyone but God. The author's circumstances and location were completely different, but the emotion and the action were exactly the same.

As I read her life story I started to cry. I was looking into the face, better yet the eyes, of pain—albeit it was not the writer's eyes, it was my own eyes. I cried uncontrollably as she continued her story; as I read of the unfolding of her life, mine was unfolding in front of me. I was invisible to everyone as I experienced this huge lightning-bolt transformation, 40,000 feet in the air over the Pacific Ocean. What was my fear and pain that I was experiencing as I read this book? The fear of the unknown in my life. Like, what was life going to be like when I arrived back in Australia with my husband of eight years? Was it going to be the same painful living experience of him losing his temper, yelling and throwing things at the drop of a hat every day and at any time of the day, whether I was sleeping or awake? And was I to live like this for the rest of my life, as I was taught by family, Church and society; till death do us part? But also, the fear of what I was going to do when he went into these fits of anger.

Because up until that point, when this happened, I became a statue and couldn't move; nor could I speak. I guess I thought that I would be invisible if I stood still long enough and didn't say anything. For whatever reason, this book from the airport gave me the strength I needed; it was like an insertion of light to look each of my questions squarely in the eye. I saw clearly, as if I were on top of a mountain. I could see every path that could be taken as well as the path that I was to take to find my way through. I could see all the obstacles, I saw the light, and I felt my strength. It all comes down to choice. What is your choice? It is that simple. I looked into that light and said, "I want to live a life of happiness, please help me." It was just that simple. And that light of the Universe responded with support beyond anything I could have imagined. That week, when I arrived back at my home in Australia, I looked for a support group. Somewhere, I found the strength to vocally as well as physically stand, and I asked my husband to join me.

He said no. He actually said no! So, I went by myself... once a month... September, October and November. Each time I came home from the support group meeting he had double the amount of anger, and it increased each month to the point that I was overcome by tears and shut myself into my room in fear of my own safety.

For that reason, I quit going to the support group. A month after that experience, in December—the week of Christmas—I made an appointment with a therapist for Boxing Day, the soonest she had open. Again, from somewhere I found the strength to vocally and physically stand and ask my husband to join me. Again, he said no. He actually said no! So, I went without him and I went once a week.

My therapist was preparing me for every moment, including when I left him after the vacation. A year before, we had scheduled a vacation together for the end of January; at the last minute, my husband decided not to go and instead to go to Sydney. I decided to continue on with our plan and go on vacation in Victoria without him. Again, I found the strength to vocally and physically stand and tell him that I was going ahead without him. You can see all the strength it took me to continue to choose me. I didn't do this out of selfishness, but rather to support myself.

Deep within us is where strength comes from; it is in a place so deep that we overlook it. You ask, where is this place? It is in the center of your heart! The only way to access it is to open your heart, by feeling what you are feeling every second. This could be mistaken for selfishness by the outside world. I say that because this was what was expressed to me at various points and turns in my journey. Pay no mind to this and keep your focus. Remember, when you change your internal being the outside world is going to protest.

I have learned to do a check-in with myself even now, and I ask myself these three simple questions when someone asks me to do something or when I am making a decision:
1/ Does this feel or look good to me?
2/ Is this what I desire or want?
3/ Will this give me happiness?

If a request or idea does not meet all three questions, I respond with, "No, thank you," and sometimes that takes time—to feel what you feel inside and to then speak it out loud. Take the time you need. You can say, "Let me think about it," or, "Let me meditate on this," or, "Let me pray about this," and if the person puts any pressure on you then that is an indication that it is an unbalanced request. As I have come to learn, supporting myself first is the most important thing I can do in order to be healthy, and in order to then help others. No matter what the people in our lives say or do, this is imperative to all our lives. Things went very fast after I made the decision to leave.

I confronted my fears, pain, became visible, and found my voice within. I used those three questions every step I took, and on some days, it was a large number of times. The real work started after leaving, with the help of so many. You see, I knew that if I didn't seek help to change my beliefs, my habits, and my thinking, I would go back into that relationship, or another relationship of the same type. Two weeks after leaving, the first step was given to me at a weekend workshop, and it was to create a daily script. I wrote my script every night before I went to sleep, for years; I do it even now.

Daily scripting is what attracted my lawyer, who helped me legally separate my life from that of my husband in three months. It helped me move physically back to SC, and it attracted the monetary ability to travel the world for almost three months. I promise you, it was miraculously easy to attract this, and at the same time a leap of faith, like walking off a cliff. The Universe supported me the whole way and it will support you too. It starts with one step, and the strength to take that one step. The second step I was given was goal setting, which is another Law of Attraction exercise. Goal setting is what rooted me into SC and started my coaching business, attracting and buying my home.

When I was taught goal setting, I remember thinking and even saying out loud, "Oh my goodness, I can actually write what I want in my life." It was truly an epiphany, a new way of completely seeing and living. It took a load off my shoulders, helped me clear my mind and see further into the future, and to the path right now.

Both the daily scripting and goal setting are the foundation of my company, Matrx Coaching, established in 2012. These two exercises are what attracted me to Diamond Feng Shui and, years later, Diamond Dowsing, which then attracted the opportunity of being mentored personally by Marie Diamond as one of her Certified Diamond Life Coaches, transforming lives globally.

This was an amazing opportunity to help others and the healing continued even deeper for me. Diamond Feng Shui and Diamond Dowsing changed and healed the energy of my home, allowing me to heal the roots of my life, because our homes root us in our existence. If our home has energy leaks then those energy leaks are represented in us.

So, when we heal our home, we in turn heal ourselves. I am grateful for all the experiences in my marriage because they led me to know my strength and stand in my power and be a Global Conscious Entrepreneur. I am grateful to offer healing, success, and abundance to help you do the same, so that you too can find your strength for your journey, just as I have.

If you want greater strength for your journey, come talk with me; you are welcome to email me on my website: www.PatriciaWhyte.com. As a gift to you I am offering the opportunity of a complementary thirty-minute session. Thank you for your interest in finding your strength.

## Patricia Whyte

Patricia Whyte is an international success, abundance, and Feng Shui coach, supporting the global community with her online coaching. She is certified in Diamond Feng Shui, Diamond Dowsing, and Diamond Life Coaching personally, through the globally renowned movie star and Feng Shui Master, Marie Diamond, as well as supporting Marie in her purpose by being one of her Diamond Life Coaches.

Over twelve years, Patricia Whyte has coached individually over 250 clients, helping them write goals, move beds and desks, energetically clear their spaces, and achieve amazing results.

They come from Spain, Canada, Australia, France, India, Slovakia, Korea, Hawaii, California, Massachusetts, New Jersey, New York, Texas, Colorado, Chicago, Florida, North Carolina, and South Carolina, with professions ranging from doctors, property developers, lawyers, accountants, housewives, entrepreneurs, jewelers, professors, artists, hygienists, and teachers. All achieved the success they hired Patricia for.

Patricia's longest-standing client is now the executive partner in a firm; they hired Patricia in 2012 as her client was an entry level business person making $50K, and now make $200K-plus as the executive partner.

Patricia has volunteered locally, coaching over seventy-five homeless women and children.

She and her business, Matrx Coaching, were awarded the 2019 Best of West Columbia Training Center and, in 2013, West Metro Chamber of Commerce Volunteer of the Year.

Patricia holds a Bachelor of Science Degree in Business from the University of South Carolina, and a Homeopathy Degree (DIHom) from the British Institute of Homeopathy.

She is a published co-author of *Million Dollar Strategies*, and published author of *5 Matrx Tips to Success & Abundance*, *3 Matrx Tips for Resilience, Energy & Focus*, *5 Easy Steps To Great Feng Shui*.

Patricia also wrote a weekly column in the *Lexington Chronicle* for five years, with a readership of 9,000 in the Lexington County area, and reaching into the state of South Carolina. She was in the movie *Ouija House,* released by Sony Pictures in 2018.

**Contact Patricia Whyte:**

- @patriciawhytefengshui
- www.facebook.com/patriciawhyteFengShui
- www.linkedin.com/in/patriciawhytefengshui
- www.youtube.com/@patriciawhytefengshui
- www.youtube.com/@matrxcoachingsuccess
- www.patriciawhyte.com
- www.matrxcoaching.com

# A Transformation To Radiant Beauty

## By Michelle Williams

I stood in the center of what felt like everything in the entire world. People, energy, images, thoughts, and lights were swirling around me, but there was a clear space of about six feet directly around me, almost like a protective layer keeping everything else at a comfortable distance. I was six years old and could see the energy swirling around, it was different shades of gray. No color, no excitement, just gloom, stress, and chaos. I wanted nothing to do with it, it was terrifying. My chest was heavy with fear but at the same time, I felt protected. This was an experience that came to me during a deep connection with divine energy through a breathwork session.

Before the session, I set the intention to be shown what steps I needed to take to align with my authentic self and divine path. As I brought life force energy into my body with each breath, I could see this experience very clearly and I knew what I was seeing was me at six years old, even though I have no conscious memory of it.

As the experience continued, I asked for clarity about what I was seeing. The experience started to shift forward in time and I grew older as I stood in the middle of that chaos. It became clear that the energy I was seeing were the fears of everyone around me in a cloud of heavy dense energy. That protective layer got smaller as I continued to grow older and the energies eventually consumed me.

That little girl shifted into a lifeless gray form. I could see that my mind was full. I was busy and in fear, just like everyone else. Everything that I was seeing made perfect sense. The energies of everything around me had consumed every aspect of my energy, body, and mind causing an emotionless life of struggle. I didn't feel safe anymore, I only knew fear. Memories started to surface that showed me what fear truly was. Until we become aware of the energies around and within us, it is difficult to identify what choices we are making out of fear. Until I was in my early thirties, I lived my life in fear. That's what I was taught.

Everyone around me judged each other, tried to control all aspects of life and they were all unhappy. I thought this is what life was and we had to struggle, hustle, and live with pain. Little did I know, I was conditioned to believe that I was just fitting in with everyone else and it was normal to live this way. I grew up in a loving, united family. There was always food on the table, shoes on our feet, and enough money to get by. Our more distant family got together on holidays and when someone in the family needed help, we were there. I went through life doing what I was told, regardless if it "felt" right. I didn't know I had a choice (unconscious fear).

As I moved through life, I was doing everything I was "supposed" to do in my career. I moved up the ladder in my organization quickly and was in middle management for my company before I was thirty. By this time, I had two Master's degrees and was working extremely long weeks, and managing over 110 employees. For my professional growth, I knew the right people and was invited to the right gatherings.

Many people in my situation would have been enjoying every minute and taking advantage of the opportunities. But instead, I began to hide. I felt a deep resistance to continuing to build this life. The societal beliefs that I had absorbed and learned from others were keeping me stuck in a life that I no longer wanted to be a part of.

I felt trapped and that I had no way out. When I was in my late twenties, I started to experience major resistance with my career. I had difficult relationships with co-workers and felt diminished in my knowledge and abilities. I lacked confidence and self-worth. I coped with alcohol every day and made many self-diminishing choices.

I was deep in the gray dense fear that consumed that 6-year-old girl. This resistance created a downward spiral in life that kept getting worse. I was missing work and had a hard time controlling my temper. I felt a deep sense of emptiness and sadness every time I went to work. When I realized I still had thirty-plus more years of this agony, I knew I physically wouldn't survive.

I had to do something, but all I knew was struggle (unconscious fear). The memories of this time in my life continued to pass by with each breath during the session. I saw the sexist boss, the narcissistic boyfriends, the untrustworthy friends, the illnesses, the alcohol, the bad choices. I saw past lives, ancestral, genetic, and earth energies. Everything was swirling around me and penetrating my energy field with chaos and fear. I could see that all this energy was building up layer by layer within me causing me to become angry at life. I asked to move forward.

A white light came in from above and consumed my energy field. Everything I was experiencing stopped. I was dominated by a deep sense of calm, peace, and unconditional love. The energetic swirl began to reverse, the white light turned golden and absorbed all the gray. The cloud around me began to get brighter and shifted into the light. The inner peace got stronger with each breath and gratitude began to embellish me.

As the energies began to release, that dark dense energy that I morphed into as that child started to shift and transform. It started to grow taller and brighter. The human form came back, showing her femininity, and long beautiful brown hair wrapped around her body.

She was glowing with beauty and love radiated from her, creating comfort, joy, and a sense of freedom. The chaos was gone, there was no fear, but a deep appreciation for life. The radiant feminine energy beamed with light. As the energies around her continued to shift, they grew into balls of light mixed with gray energies.

The view lifted higher and higher, and I could see all of these energies surrounding her as she opened her arms to provide comfort and healing. I could feel the sadness around her but the love she emitted overpowered everything else. She was a being of light bringing healing and peace to all around her. She was me.

As I came out of that session, I felt the love beaming from my heart. I immediately understood the symbolism within that experience. The life force energy with each breath showed me the clarity of my intention. My true authentic self is here and it's continuing to reveal itself layer by layer as a beautiful feminine energy within myself.

By surrendering to my life purpose and leaving that career, I was able to let the healing light shine through me and reach others. The white light transforming the energies that were consuming me were the healings I had done with practitioners and on myself. It was the divine energy coming from the "All That Is" that was healing and transforming me.

It created inner peace giving me the permission to be on my divine path as my authentic self to help others shine their light to the world. The energies surrounding me were a portrayal of everyone who is ready to bring happiness and peace into their lives by stepping onto their divine path with authenticity. I open my arms to help with this process.

As humans in this existence, we are here to learn how to live in true authenticity and abundance with all the energies around us. Without even knowing it, we go through life allowing the energies to come into our field and shift our reality into something we may not want. Until we become aware and have clarity of this process, we are living in the dark. We allow emotions, trauma, guilt, and shame to completely consume us. We allow the energies from the people in our lives, ancestors, the environment, past lives, soul contracts, group consciousness, and more to run our lives. The unconscious choice to allow this to occur is what creates our challenges, struggles, relationships, emotions, fears, and our human experience.

I share this personal experience to help you understand that making lasting changes in your life doesn't have to be difficult or scary. Every decision you have made in life has gotten you to where you are today, and you are exactly where you are supposed to be. You have not done anything wrong, you are not broken, and your life is not a mistake. You have just forgotten your birthright and purpose in this existence. It is okay! You can shift that energy into a place of forgiveness, trust, and compassion to allow forward movement, fulfillment, and a life of your dreams.

You are the creator of your experience, and you have a choice to create from love or from fear. You have the choice to step into the true authentic energy of you and live a life of abundance. You have the choice to let go of the fears within you and be freed from the burdens of others that you are carrying.

Life is a magical journey, and everyone is here for a unique purpose. I am here to be of service to others, but it took over thirty years to step out of fear and allow that purpose to come to light. Everything is in perfect divine order. The beautiful thing is, we have the choice to work with that divine order or against it, to live in pure joy or in struggle. Everything is a choice. Make the choices in life that feel good to you, that light you up, and bring excitement to your life.

I invite you to visit my website at www.IAMmichellewilliams.com/gcebook for more details on how I discovered my divine path, and for exclusive information to help you reconnect to your true authentic self, and bring the excitement back to your life. Every step forward on your divine path brings you closer to a life of abundance, joy, and peace. Breathe in life force energy, exhale fear.

## Michelle Williams

Michelle is an international spiritual healer, teacher, life transcendence coach, and two-time best-selling co-author based in Georgia, USA. She is passionate about helping others step into their power and authenticity to purposefully create inner peace, spiritual connection, and an excitement for life.

After spending half of her life in the information technology and project management field, she felt there was something more to life and explored her love of self-development.

She quickly discovered that she was highly intuitive, and her divine path is to be of service to others through healing, love, and trust.

Through teaching and modeling practical methods, concepts, and tools, Michelle helps those who are ready to truly create the life of their dreams become aligned with their divine timing, plan, and purpose by helping disentangle the past patterns that are holding them back.

She received divine guidance to learn many healing techniques, allowing her to create her signature Quantum Transcendence method.

This method allows for healing on many energetic levels, providing deep and lasting life and soul transcendence.

Michelle is continuing to grow herself and her healing abilities as she is called, which allows her practice to continuously expand based on the needs of clients and the collective.

Some techniques Michelle uses include; human design, spiritual response therapy (SRT), ThetaHealing®, Diamond Dowsing, breathwork, hypnotherapy, VoiceBio, and other energy healing systems.

While Michelle's passion is helping others, she is also the proud mom of an energetic yellow Labrador Retriever, and enjoys volunteering in her community, helping children cultivate their creativity.

**Contact Michelle Williams:**


- www.iammichellewilliams.com
- michelle@renewlifehealing.com
- www.facebook.com/iammichellewilliams2
- @iammichellewilliams2
- www.tiktok.com/@iammichellewilliams2
- www.youtube.com/@iammichellewilliams2
- www.linkedin.com/in/iammichellewilliams2

# The Law

## By Pearl Williams

"The law is the law is the law," is a phrase that one of my college professors would repeat almost every session. I enjoyed the way in which he stuck out his chest and seemed to go into a type of Romanesque character as he belted out his favorite saying. From what I recall, he was an adjunct professor at Houston Community College, and an attorney as well. I was a twenty-year-old single mom of three. My last child was born in April of 1994, and I began classes the following August. I initially sought to become a nurse, until I saw the degree plan and was not feeling all of that math. I course-corrected and began to look for an associates degree with the least amount of math classes possible, and therein lies the beginning of my criminal justice career path.

I loved everything about my criminal justice journey, learning about the various aspects of the law, coupled with the case studies that proved to be both fascinating and, at times, horrifying. Everything I was taught in the criminal justice courses began to shape the way in which I viewed the world. I obtained my associates degree in the summer of 1997 and immediately set out to transfer to the University of Houston's Downtown campus to earn a bachelor's degree. I noticed a culture shift right away. For some reason, it appeared to me that everyone spoke proper English but me. I felt out of place and wondered how this institution could be so different from the community college that I was so accustomed to. Although these idiosyncrasies were not going to deter me, they were minor happenings that I observed. I began to notice while in this higher education system how the Criminal Justice System is not so just after all. Having various law enforcement officials as fellow cohorts became the norm. We were all in the same boat, individually vying for goals of completing assignments, taking written exams, and participating in classroom discussions.

There were two major incidents that stood out to me. The first was when the Rodney King incident happened and my White (law enforcement) counterparts were having a conversation. I recall one of them saying, "That's a big ole boy!" I interjected, "That's a big ole man!" I never went back to that class; besides, it was early in the semester. The second incident did not involve law enforcement. This was a business writing class and the assignment was intended to be an icebreaker. Everyone was to write down a fact about themselves that no one knew. Everyone's response would be placed in a container and picked randomly to be read out loud by the professor. One person wrote, "I don't really like minorities, I only tolerate them because I have to." This too was the beginning of the semester; however, I was not leaving this class. I often wondered if that college professor at HCC had any real idea of what he was talking about in regards to his favorite saying. I began working for the post office (PO) in December 1997; I went from welfare to work, and was able to purchase my first house by the age of twenty-five. For the most part, I enjoyed my co-workers at the PO and, due to it being December, I did not mind the physical labor of the job. It wasn't until I experienced my first sweltering summer months that I realized the Post Office was not for me. I recall often wanting to burst into tears and remaining oblivious as to why. One day, while at a bank of boxes, I felt myself once again wanting to bawl.

This time, I asked myself, "What is going on with me?" The answer came without a hitch: "I don't like my job." This revelation felt so good for me to acknowledge! As I was saying this to myself, I wanted to be as honest with myself as possible and saw no reason to sugarcoat it: "I HATE this goddamn job!" I wanted to dig deep down inside because it felt so good to vocalize this feeling, no longer ignoring it and coasting as if on autopilot, as I had done so many times before. It's 2004, I am still working at the PO; eight years in, experiencing major feelings of depression, and at home more than at work. I dreaded going to work, not to mention that I had graduated from not only feelings of depression, to actually verbalizing, "I hate my life," every morning when I opened my eyes. The Universe was listening to me loud and clear.

During the summer of 2004, I collapsed from suffering a pulmonary embolism (blood clots in my lungs). Prior to the actual collapse, I felt like I had a leg cramp that kept traveling upwards. It happened on a Saturday morning. I began to cook breakfast and felt my heart palpitating irregularly. I felt faint and decided to get back in bed. I phoned a friend, who suggested that I go to the emergency room, and I decided to take his advice. I said a prayer before putting the car in drive that my daughter and I would make it to the hospital safely. Once at the hospital, I recall walking through the automatic doors and noticing a strange feeling of my body trying to keep up with my spirit. I couldn't breathe as I rested at the nurses' station's window ledge. I experienced having a thought that encompassed many perspectives all at once. One would have to experience it to truly understand; however, I will do my best to describe what I experienced. Although my body was in distress, my mind was alert. I had a single thought that included, what would the gossipers say happened to me, should I die? At the same time, I thought, who cares? And at the exact same time, I thought, these people waiting their turn in the emergency room may witness me passing away. What about my children? The entire conversation all seemed to take place in one instance, in one thought. Not linear, as in first thought, followed by second thought, followed by third thought, and so on. The last thought, however, seemed to be separate from the others: I'm not ready yet! I awoke on the emergency room floor with the nurses shaking me, asking if I had hit my head. Someone came with a wheelchair and I was guided with the assistance of the nurses to sit and be wheeled to an oxygenated room. While being wheeled, I went out again, and this time I faded to black immediately. The next time I came to, I was in the oxygenated room and could see my daughter off to the side, crying. They eventually X-rayed my chest and found blood clots. I stayed in the hospital for about a little over a week.

During my hospital stay, I received a call from my son's elementary school principal informing me of a wake and funeral for one of the children who attended the school and who had recently passed. It was at this time that I realized there was no such thing as "outliving" someone. People of various ages die every second of the day. It was not my time. I got another chance to live and I would never say that I hated my life, ever again. I learned about the Law of Attraction in 2006. The writers of the book, *The Secret*, were on *The Oprah Winfrey Show*. My mind was blown! I could not help but think of the phrase from years ago that my college professor so loved to say. This was the law that I could stand by, trust, and believe in. I was so grateful to find out about these laws of the Universe that were so obedient and fair across the board. Man-made laws change, are not consistently applied, and definitely are not always based on fairness. Universal laws are always wonderfully dependable and unbiased. *The Secret* led to me manifesting *Ask and It Is Given,* by Esther and Jerry Hicks.

Because of my knowledge of both books, I immediately began to redirect the way in which I viewed situations in my life that I was not satisfied with. I applied the law of attraction's principles to my job at the post office. Instead of dreading going to work every day and walking through long stretches of yard, I began to focus on the beauty of the manicured lawns and started to be grateful for the exercise that the walking allowed me to acquire. I looked forward to interacting with the patrons that resided on my route. On my lunch breaks, I would park, read my books, and use my imagination to conjure up positive vibes of where I would like to see myself in the future. In the early hours of the morning before being walked off the clock at the PO, I remember being gently awakened by a loving embrace and me whispering, "thank you," as I dozed back off to sleep. The next day at work was similar to the days before, wherein I would be overloaded with mail, forcing me to bring the remainder back due to my doctor's orders of only working eight hours per day.

When I arrived back at the station this time, the supervisor was waiting. He said that upper management requested that I turn in my employee badge and go. As I walked to my car I felt a sense of relief, and was instantly reminded about the loving embrace that I'd received earlier that morning. I knew that the seeds I'd planted for my future away from the post office had come into fruition. I voiced a "thank you," and never had any worry or fear of what was to come.

Many of my desires have been realized since learning about the law of attraction, including being affiliated with one of the authors of *The Secret*. I am excited to share my journey with anyone that wants to lend an ear. The following poem was nudging me to write it as I was trying to meditate. The initial title was "For the Kids" and I changed it to add upon the well-known nursery rhyme "Row, Row, Row Your Boat". It was written to inspire children and others at an earlier age to understand how powerful and blessed they are.

**Life Is But a Dream** by Pearl Williams

1/ The first thing is that you ask, this should not be so hard to do.
2/ Do you realize that you are always asking and oftentimes don't have a clue?
3/ Everything is a thought before there is physical evidence of it.
4/ Is this not exciting, just thinking of it?
5/ Imagination is a powerful tool that one should utilize every day.
6/ For everything you have in your life comes to you in this way.
7/ You plant the seeds in your imagination and expect the seeds to grow.
8/ Doubt leads to drought... this you should know.
9/ Patience is a virtue and knowing that what you desire is your will.

You can tell what you are getting by how you currently feel.

1/ Live as if you already have the things you desire in mind.
2/ In time you will get what you planted, in kind.

## Pearl Williams

Pearl Williams was born and raised in Houston, Texas and currently resides in the suburb of Katy, Texas. She is a self-proclaimed student and teacher in the art of bringing oneself into vibrational alignment with one's desires.

Her employment journeys entail ten years as a letter carrier, eight and a half years as a parole officer, and her current position of three years as a therapist.

She has assisted many to believe in themselves and she has witnessed many transform their lives for the better. Pearl is fascinated by the laws of the universe and has an unwavering trust in the law of attraction to supply all of her wants and needs.

**Contact Pearl Williams:**

- www.tiktok.com/@pearlinewilliams7
- www.facebook.com/Pearlconsultant74
- @7672pearl

# Visiting Hours In Heaven

## By Renata Maria Wirtz

I was born clairvoyantly into a family of healers and doctors. So it happened that death was very much alive in my family at an early age. The fact that my father, as a family doctor and police doctor, was called to the dying was a natural part of my childhood. This family idyll was abruptly interrupted when my beloved father left the family and my parents divorced. After two near-death experiences of my own in my early twenties, I returned to this side of the veil with countless questions and a deep, unquenchable longing for the unconditional love in the Otherworld that I was privileged to experience.

Believing at that time that the answers to my questions could be found in the religions, I devoted a year of study to each great unification and philosophy. In search of answers, I visited the master teachers of the seventies and eighties. I went through reincarnation therapy, which introduced me to several of the most important parallel lives that were relevant to this, my present life. I immersed myself for many years in the Hawaiian Huna philosophy of the Kahunas. Here, among other things, I was introduced for the first time to what is called "clearing." This was a spiritual cleansing ritual, a purifying sacrifice in which a clear decision is made to forgive. Already, after the first experience of a "clearing," I was so familiar with this process that I could include it in my therapeutic work. I put experience and memory together in my brain.

A wave of the desire for forgiveness gripped the people I connected with this concept. With this module, they learned not only to forgive others, but above all to forgive themselves. From a meta-level, from an elevated body-mind consciousness, they were able to survey their lives on this side of the veil in deep compassion for themselves and their actions. However, I received the true answers to my continuing burning questions only in 1988 through the reading of a transmitted message, an ancient teacher personality, which had been prophesied to me some years earlier by an English medium.

I became a student of his school of ancient wisdom in the northwestern United States, and during this year-long study of the neurophysiology of the brain, I acquired a new expanded view of consciousness. The new knowledge I acquired was truly breathtaking. What was different from my previous knowledge? And what was now confirmed to me through this study? Here, I learned that we have an anatomical section in our brain that corresponds to the sonar in dolphins and whales. Through this section in our brain, we are receptive to the next, faster-vibrating level, which we also enter when spirit, soul, and consciousness leave the body in the process we call "dying." This frequency level is called "infrared." The phrase of Yeshua ben Yosef "In my Father's house are many mansions," came to mind. "Mansions" in this case was a metaphor for the states of consciousness with which we change these levels.

What I learned in the course of the study was that we do not have to die if we want to enter this plane. The soul remains in the body, while the spirit and consciousness can go to the infrared plane. And now comes the breathtaking thing: There, we can meet the still-earthbound soul beings who have already completed the full transition. We can contact them at any time. What was offered to me there surpassed all my imagination. A model was flung at me which threw all previous conceptions over the heap. Again, it was experiences and memories, which connected themselves with each other and became the certainty: Life is eternal, there is no death!

The world must know this!

Since then, in a process developed by me, I offer people the means to contact their beloved deceased directly again. There is no interposition of a medium in the communication. The meeting from here to there can take place directly and immediately at any time. I call this process "HolyClearing." Of course, I can claim the "HolyClearing" for myself as well. It was in the year when my mother passed away. She left to me my parents' house, with many debts that she had taken on for my brother. So, a buyer had to be found urgently for the house. Many weeks passed and there were many interested parties, but no buyer. This was completely incomprehensible considering the high-quality property in this particular location.

When I finally went to see my late mother on the other side, I found her sitting at a table in a library in the semi-darkness. She held her house pressed against her in miniature under a glass bell jar. In a gentle voice, I asked her to release her house, which had been her everything when she was alive. It took some persuasion on my part and the clarification of the financial situation of my brother on the other hand, about which she apparently had no information, to move her to the release of the house.

After quite some time, I was finally able to convince her of the necessity to release the house. Saddened and still doubtful, she pushed the house towards me and I was able to take possession of it. Three weeks later the house had found a buyer. Since my discovery of the therapeutically accompanied, direct communication with the deceased, which I call "HolyClearing," thousands of people have already taken this wonderful opportunity in my private practice to directly contact their deceased loved ones. The reasons for this can be manifold:

- Be it to find out quite pragmatically where the tax documents and the key to the safe are after the sudden death of the partner.
- Be it to say goodbye once again in person because the death was so unexpected.
- Or an unexpected death has plunged you into a deep depression. How do you find your way out of it?
- Be it to learn what or how a beloved family member died because the cause of death is unclear.
- Or to understand the true background of a stillbirth and be comforted by the prospect of a new pregnancy without complications.
- Or to understand the shocking motivation of a suicide.
- Be it to illuminate the true background of a sexual abuse and be relieved of it.
- Or even because your beloved animal has passed away and you miss him so much—you can also get in touch with him.

If you have always been looking for these answers, if this is what you have always been missing because you did not know that this direct connection was possible, then contact me.

This particular experience shows that death as people know it does not exist. These encounters usually include a labor of love for your loved ones who have changed levels, when they may not yet be able to find their way on the "other side."

Together, we (you and I) can offer them the best space in which to stay —according to their state of consciousness. Through this joint work, you too can lose the fear of death. You will experience that life does not end, that life does not pass away, that life is eternal.

"Until we meet again, eternity need not pass."

## Renata Maria Wirtz

As an advanced body and soul therapist, as an expert, I will guide you spiritually-metaphysically into the Otherworld in my sessions of "Therapeutic Accompanied After-Death Contact with your Deceased," the "HolyClearing." Here, the safe space is created for you, as well as the guidance being given, in order to be able to initiate direct contact with the deceased. It comes to the holy meeting with the living energy of the deceased partner, to the "HolyClearing."

I have been an expert in the field of direct communication with the deceased for three decades. I know both sides, the world on this side and the world beyond, from personal experience. If this extraordinary offer inspires or motivates you, please contact me and make an appointment with me for your "visiting hours in heaven." I am also the author of Author of the book: *Bewusstsein für die Liebe Deines Lebens.*

Book your own visiting time in heaven. Email at Larenata45@gmail.com

**Contact Renata Maria Wirtz:**

- www.linkedin.com/in/renata-maria-wirtz
- www.renatamariawirtz.de
- Larenata45@gmail.com

## Conclusion

It's my hope that reading through this book has left you with a reminder as to why you became an entrepreneur in the first place. I hope that you've managed to see a bit of yourself in these stories of trials and tribulations, courage, and, above all, unrelenting hope. May they keep you moving on your path and inspire you to manifest your goals and change the world with your products and services, one customer at a time.

I hope that this book has taught you the treasures that can await you when you learn to follow your intuition. When you honor that voice deep inside, the Universe will be waiting to reward you. After all, you've seen forty-nine stories of what can happen when a person is brave enough to follow their dreams and stick to the path, the one that leads straight towards Success and Abundance.

If you've found yourself moved by a particular author's story, I encourage you to check out the website of the co-author, to contact them on social media, and to enquire about their services or introductory sessions. If you're interested in being part of a future compilation book, please get in touch with us on publishing@mariediamond.com. The world is waiting for your contribution!

Finally, thank you again to each and every person who helped to bring this Amazing inspirational book to life.

All My Love,
Dame Marie Diamond
www.MarieDiamond.com

## *Dedication and Gratitude*

This book is dedicated to each and every entrepreneur across the world. Their unrelenting dedication to providing for their families, manifesting their dreams, and sharing their gifts with their communities through their products and services is something that will always continue to inspire me.

Firstly, I would like to thank the Universe/ God for giving me the inspiration for this book and helping me to manifest this project into existence. I would like to thank my friend and personal branding and marketing expert Lily Patrascu for joining me on this amazing journey, and also Lily's team, particularly Harry Sardinas and Shane, and the Marie Diamond Publishing team (Curtis Chase, Megan Fairbrace, Karin del Castillo, Bastian Gugger, Ace, and Eva) for all their help and hard work.

I would also like to thank my loving family for their unrelenting support and encouragement. They've stood by me throughout the highs and lows of my entrepreneurial journey and without them, I wouldn't be the Global Conscious Entrepreneur that I am today.

Lastly, I would like to thank each one of my incredible co-authors for putting their trust in me. It is an honor, and I am so proud of them for sharing their stories and wisdom so courageously. I have every faith that their stories will go on to inspire millions of up-and-coming entrepreneurs all over the world.

With Love,
Dame Marie Diamond
*www.MarieDiamond.com*

## About The Author

Marie Diamond is a globally renowned Transformational Leader and star of the worldwide movie phenomenon *The Secret*. She uses her extraordinary knowledge of quantum physics, the law of attraction, and Feng Shui to help people transform their lives. Her vision is to enlighten more than 500 million people during her lifetime.

Her clients include A-list celebrities in film and music (such as Steven Spielberg, Big Sean, Jason Bateman and Jodie Foster) and top-selling authors and speakers (such as Rhonda Byrne, Jack Canfield, John Gray, the late Bob Proctor, Marianne Williamson and Vishen Lakhiani). She has also advised leaders from Fortune 500 companies, sports athletes, governments, and royal families. Marie Diamond combines her intuitive gifts, the growing science of energy flow, ancient wisdom, and modern tools to enlighten homes, businesses, and people. She is known for her passion to help create enlightened leaders around the world.

She is a founding member of the Transformational Leadership Council, created by Jack Canfield, and President of the Association of Transformational Leaders in Europe.

She has more than one million online and in-person students in more than 190 countries. You can connect with her for personal mentoring, consultations, seminars, online courses, e-books, and home study courses at www.MarieDiamond.com. Her Spanish students can join her at www.MarieDiamondespanol.com.

Her teachings are published in online programs such as MindValley, Learning Strategies and YouUnity. For her charity work, she is a knighted Dame.

Currently, she lives between the south of France, London, and the USA with her family and her dogs.

## Recommended Products and Services

Marie Diamond is a global speaker who speaks on a range of topics, from the Law of Attraction and attracting Abundance and Success, to Global Conscious Leadership, branding your business, and manifesting your vision. Head here to view her upcoming events and speaking engagements:
www.mariediamond.com/news

You can also book her as a motivational speaker for your next event, or hire her for leadership training. Check here to enquire:
www.mariediamond.com/contact-us

Marie Diamond takes on a limited number of clients for personal or business mentoring. During these sessions, she can help you to clear mental and emotional blockages, restructure your goals, and set up an effective, long-term vision for success. Her clients include Jack Canfield, John Gray, Bob Proctor, Rhonda Byrne, Big Sean, Natasha Graziano, Vishen Lakhiani, Christy Whitman, Janette Atwood, Marci Shimoff, Mari Smith, and many CEOs and top management of Fortune 500 Companies.

If you'd like to know more, contact her at office@mariediamond.com and a member of her team will get back to you.

## Other Books Recommended By Marie Diamond Publishing:

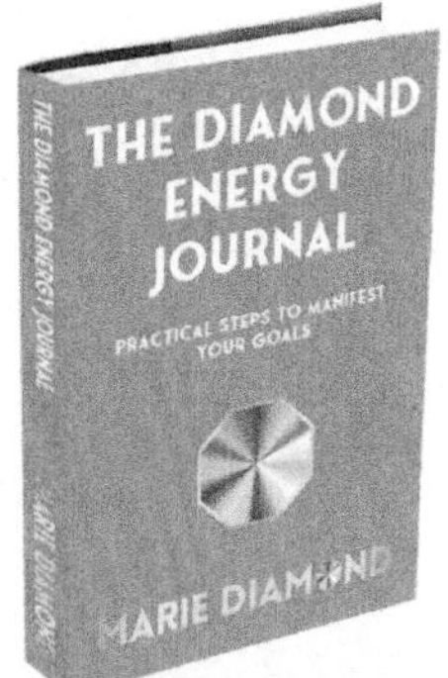


**The Diamond Energy Journal:**
Practical Steps To Manifest Your Goals

**Marie Diamond**

**The Diamond Energy Principles:**
The Secret Of Manifestation

**Marie Diamond**

**The Energy Number Book:**
Personal Feng Shui
For Your Home And Office

**Marie Diamond**

## ORDER YOUR BOOKS HERE:

www.mariediamond.com/booklaunch

Printed in Great Britain
by Amazon